# ALL THE PRESIDENTS' SPOKESMEN

New York Mayor John V. Lindsay, a candidate for president in 1972 in the nationwide Democratic primaries, swears in Woody Klein, his first press secretary, on January 1, 1966, at City Hall.

# ALL THE PRESIDENTS'
# SPOKESMEN

*Spinning the News—White House*

*Press Secretaries*

*From Franklin D. Roosevelt to George W. Bush*

WOODY KLEIN

*Forewords by Marlin Fitzwater and Dee Dee Myers*

port, Connecticut
London

Library of Congress Cataloging-in-Publication Data

Klein, Woody, 1929-
   All the presidents' spokesmen : spinning the news : White House press secretaries from Franklin D. Roosevelt to George W. Bush / Woody Klein ; forewords by Marlin Fitzwater and Dee Dee Myers.
      p.   cm.
   Includes bibliographical references and index.
   ISBN 978-0-275-99098-5 (alk. paper)
   1. Presidential press secretaries—United States—History—20th century—Anecdotes.   2. Presidential press secretaries—United States—History—21st century—Anecdotes.   3. Presidential press secretaries—United States—Biography—Anecdotes.   4. Government and the press—United States—History—20th century—Anecdotes.   5. Government and the press—United States—History—21st century—Anecdotes.   6. Public relations and politics—United States—History—20th century—Anecdotes.   7. Public relations and politics—United States—History—21st century—Anecdotes.   8. United States—Politics and government—1933–1945—Anecdotes.   9. United States—Politics and government—1945–1989—Anecdotes.   10. United States—Politics and government—1989– —Anecdotes.   I. Title.
   E176.47.K58 2008
   973.91092'2—dc22        2007043762

British Library Cataloguing in Publication Data is available.

Library of Congress Catalog Card Number: 2007043762
ISBN: 978-0-275-99098-5

First published in 2008

Praeger Publishers, 88 Post Road West, Westport, CT 06881
An imprint of Greenwood Publishing Group, Inc.
www.praeger.com

Printed in the United States of America

The paper used in this book complies with the Permanent Paper Standard issued by the National Information Standards Organization (Z39.48-1984).

10   9   8   7   6   5   4   3   2   1

*To John Vliet Lindsay (1921–2000)*
*Mayor of New York, 1965–1973*
*Democratic Candidate for President, 1972*
*Mentor and Friend*

# CONTENTS

Photo essay appears following page    158

# FOREWORD

*Press Secretaries Are Historical Figures*

## MARLIN FITZWATER

When the Cold War ended and the Berlin Wall fell, and when the United States liberated Kuwait, all on my watch as presidential press secretary, not one blogger could be found. But in less than twenty years, a technology-driven revolution in journalism has developed the Internet and blogger reporting, the satellite and live camera coverage of every world event, the rise of cable news coverage all day every day, and an insatiable demand for government information and presidential decisions. Presidents and their press secretaries became ever present in the American culture. This remarkable book chronicles the dialogue between presidential spokesmen and the American people, often in the press secretary's own words.

In the television era, people could bookmark the decades with pictures of Ron Ziegler explaining Watergate, Jim Brady being shot in the assassination attempt on President Reagan, myself announcing, "The Liberation of Kuwait has begun," Mike McCurry's steady presence during President Clinton's impeachment, or the announcement of Tony Snow in 2006 as the new spokesman for George W. Bush. Press secretaries have often become the faces of our time. After all, press secretaries are historical figures who have conducted themselves, and represented our government, with a set of principles unique to their own experience, but tied to the practices and traditions of American journalism. They are well aware that they have the power to influence minds and hearts. Woody Klein profiles the press secretaries with personality insights and historical perspective. He also lets the manner in which each press secretary works emerge as they cope with pointed questions from the White House press corps on a wide variety of national and international issues and controversies.

We are a small club, those of us who have faced the searching White House press corps every day, responsible for immediate answers and held accountable for every eventuality. What we say is often news in itself and, and although we diligently try to serve two masters at once—the press and the president—we are sometimes accused of "spinning" the news. I understand why that word is used by a somewhat adversarial media: Presidential press secretaries at times do try to put the best face on the news we release about our president's views; we choose our words carefully in answering questions from the press. Nonetheless, I like to think we stick to the facts.

Some secrets we must always keep for each other. I kept a three-by-five card on my desk for six years that said, "Remember, you don't have to explain what you don't say." Only the people in this book can fully appreciate that admonition. That's why I love every one of them, regardless of party or background. We have all been in the trenches. And it was the greatest of experiences.

—Marlin Fitzwater

Deale, MD, June 15, 2006

*Marlin Fitzwater, one of the longest-serving and most popular press secretaries in White House history, was press secretary to President Ronald Reagan from 1987–1989; after that, he served as press secretary to President George H.W. Bush from 1989–1993. Fitzwater, a former newspaper reporter, had a long career in government served at various federal agencies.*

# Foreword

*The First Woman Press Secretary*

## Dee Dee Myers

When I went to work for Arkansas Governor Bill Clinton in the fall of 1991, most people didn't give him much of a chance of being elected president the following year. He was young—forty-five. He came from a small, rural state with more than its share of problems. And he was running against a still-popular incumbent who had recently won a war. Before signing on as campaign press secretary, I'd only met the candidate a few times. But he impressed me; I thought he was talking about things that Democrats needed to talk about. At a minimum, I believed he'd be part of a robust debate. And maybe, just maybe, he could win the Democratic nomination. But let's just say I wasn't measuring windows in the West Wing of the White House for new drapes. It never really occurred to me that fifteen months later I'd be ordering business cards with "1600 Pennsylvania Avenue" as my new work address. Yet somehow it happened. On January 20, 1993, I became the first woman and one of the youngest people ever to serve as White House press secretary.

For the next two years, I traveled around the country and around the world with President Clinton. I met amazing people and participated in historical events, things I had only expected to read about in accounts of *other* people's lives. It was an extraordinary experience, and I will always be grateful to President Clinton for giving me the opportunity to serve him and to serve my country. My life will never be the same.

Ask any current or former presidential press secretary, and he (or I!) will tell you that it's a tough job. One of the toughest in the White House. But it's also a great job. It's tough because you're the spokesman for the leader of the free world, arguably the most powerful man on earth. It's tough because every day, you're responsible for a sweeping range of information, from the president's schedule to his state of mind, from health care to Hezbollah, from state dinners to the status of troops on the ground around the world. And it's tough because information moves fast, really fast—and if you make a mistake, you can hurt not just yourself but your president and his ability to get things done.

But it's great because you're in the center of the action every day. If something important is happening, you're part of the conversation. When the president travels, you're at his side. And day in and day out, you get to help shape the story, which becomes the first draft of history. It was never easy, but it was never dull. And I wouldn't trade a minute of it. Or at least not many minutes of it.

Every press secretary brings his or her own experience, personality, and unique moment in history to the job. So not surprisingly, each of us has done things a little differently. Still, we've all faced many of the same challenges, as described in this book by Woody Klein, in which he writes about press secretaries all the way back to Franklin Delano Roosevelt.

To begin with us, each of us has had to, in effect, serve two masters: the president and the press. Of course, the president's needs must come first. But to effectively serve the president, the press secretary must also be an effective advocate for the press. And that gets complicated.

I never would have become a press secretary if I didn't like reporters; I do. In fact, I eventually married a newspaperman (though not until after I left the White House, and I certainly didn't date him while I was working there). Reporters tend to be curious and well informed. Most of them are well read and interested in the world. And most of them care deeply about getting the story right. That said, they're as different as people in any profession, and I got along with some better than others; I trusted some more—and not because I thought they were ideologically in step with the president. Without exception, the reporters I most respected were the ones who worked hardest to get it right, who held the president and the administration accountable but also held their own news organizations accountable. They skewered me if I made a mistake, but they held themselves to the same high standard. They were pros.

Still even the pros could be a nuisance on some days. What's more, the relationship between the White House and the press corps *writ large* was—and is—by nature adversarial. They want to know stuff we don't want to tell them. They think we're too secretive, and we think they're too nosy. They think we hide the bad news; we think they only report the bad news. The tension is built in, and in many ways it's healthy.

Because if the press doesn't hold public institutions accountable, no one will. Without a free press, you can't have a free society.

When I first starting doing the daily briefings, I was stunned by just how nasty the questioning could get. On many days, reporters would ask me the same question six ways to Sunday, hoping to trip me into saying something I didn't want to say. Suddenly, I found I had great sympathy for substitute teachers. The kids in the class might not get along, but as soon as you walked in the door, they were allied against you. After a while, I learned not to take it personally, which made my life easier. But I wondered then—and I wonder now—if the daily briefing as a staple of the White House press operation has run its course. There was a time when reporters asked thoughtful questions, and press secretaries tried to provide candid answers. Now, with the television cameras running, too often the press tries to look tough for the folks at home, while the press secretary tries to avoid saying anything that could be construed—or misconstrued—as a mistake. It's more theater than meaningful dialogue.

In recent years, other external forces have had a profound effect on the relationship between the press and the president. First, speed. In the digital age, information moves around the world instantaneously. In a lot of ways, that's good. For example, if there's a disaster somewhere, people half a world away can mobilize resources immediately and save lives. But when it comes to the media, the results are mixed. In a world where the difference is measured in minutes or seconds rather than hours or days, news organizations' drive to be first means that sometimes accuracy gets sacrificed. What's more, the relentless pressure of the news cycle means that public leaders are under enormous strain to respond to any development immediately. And this means that all too often they have too little time to reflect on problems, consider their options, and make reasoned decisions.

And let's be honest: There's also been a lowering of standards. Things that simply would never have been printed in a family newspaper a generation ago now routinely find their way onto the front pages. There is virtually no zone of privacy left for public figures, including presidents. And that sense that anything a president has ever said or done could end up in the paper—too often out of context—has all but destroyed whatever modicum of trust that might have existed between presidents and reporters. And ironically, presidents and reporters have suffered, as the public has lost confidence in both.

New press secretaries will come and go, figuring out new ways to reach the public, to communicate the president's objectives, to minimize his flaws. And through it all, credibility will remain the coin of the realm. Without credibility, press secretaries are worthless. Much has been made in recent years about "spin." The public has come to believe that all public officials, especially press secretaries, spin. And that spin is tantamount to a lie. But that's wrong. Spin may be marshalling the facts in service of an argument, the way a skilled debater would. But a lie is still a lie. And once a press secretary gets caught—or even accused—of being less than truthful, the game is over.

The job will continue to change, along with culture, technology, and of course the personality of each subsequent president and administration. But one thing is sure to remain true: Being press secretary to the President of the United States is a great job and a great honor. And I'll be eternally grateful that I had the chance to do it.

———

*Dee Dee Myers, the first woman press secretary to a U.S. president, served with Bill Clinton from 1993–1994. She makes frequent appearances on TV as a guest political analyst and served as a consultant for the television show "The West Wing." She is author of* Why Women Should Rule the World: A Memoir.

# Preface

*The Life of a Press Secretary*

Woody Klein

My profound interest in the position of White House press secretary started more than forty years ago when I left my job as a political reporter for an afternoon daily newspaper in New York City in 1965 to become newly elected mayor John V. Lindsay's first press secretary, a position that enabled me to become involved with politics firsthand on the national level. I wanted to know what it would be like on "the other side" of the media and, at the same time, I had a strong interest in public service ever since John F. Kennedy had been elected president in 1960.

After being announced at a press conference by Lindsay, I immediately telephoned James C. (Jim) Hagerty, President Dwight D. Eisenhower's highly respected press secretary, who was then vice president of development for the America Broadcasting System, seeking his counsel on how to handle the press. His advice was terse and to the point: "Let them know who is in charge."

Another former White House press secretary with whom I talked during the course of Lindsay's contacts with President Lyndon B. Johnson was Bill Moyers, Johnson's longtime aide who was his press secretary at the time. I learned a great deal from him by the way he operated: He was candid, civil, and responded in a timely fashion.

When Lindsay first assumed office, he was ballyhooed in the national media as a possible future presidential candidate for 1968 because of his youth, his vigor, his idealistic outlook, his tall, athletic frame, and his handsome countenance. Because he had been a newsmaker as a congressman, he started out with a broader following than someone who had only been a local New York politician before running for mayor. Furthermore, not since John F. Kennedy—only a few short years before—had the nation seen a young political figure who represented so much hope for the future.

In fact, when I first took office officially in January 1966, I was overwhelmed with requests from the local and national press, as well as journalists from abroad—Great Britain, France, Ireland (Lindsay's heritage was from the Isle of Wight).

Indeed, during the course of my first six months, noted historian Theodore White (*The Making of the President, 1972*) called me in 1966 at City Hall and asked me to sit down with him over lunch for a long background conversation about Lindsay. White told me it was his practice to research thoroughly every potential candidate for president, Democrat and Republican. He said Lindsay was on his "short" list for 1968 as a result of the mayor's high profile as a fresh, young reformer who had beaten the entrenched Democratic establishment in New York City—something that had not been done since the days of Fiorello LaGuardia.

After lunching with White, I recall that far in the back in my mind I fantasized what it might be like to be press secretary to the president, if Lindsay ever did get to the White House. Later on, as the 1972 presidential election year approached, something of a groundswell—perhaps a continuation of the popularity that had propelled him into the mayor's office in 1965—catapulted Lindsay back into the national limelight.

On page 1 of *The New York Times* on Monday, September 21, 1970, the headline read: "Some Democrats Regard Lindsay as '72 Potential." The article reported the major findings of a forty-two-state survey of Republican and Democratic Party chairmen and other local party officials. The first paragraph read: "Leading Democratic politicians in all sections of the country except the Deep South regard John V. Lindsay as a potential Presidential candidate who could run well as a Democrat in 1972." In addition, two other well-known political observers, Jerry Bruno and Jeff Greenfield, believed Lindsay would have had a chance to beat Nixon in 1972. They wrote: "He's [Lindsay] got the ability to beat Nixon on the real issues that turn elections: trust, confidence, and humanity . . . he has the excitement and the glamour . . . And, more important: he has more of it than Nixon will have, even as an incumbent President in 1972."[1]

After he switched parties, Lindsay did, in fact, run for the Democratic presidential nomination in three primaries in 1972. He got in late and therefore skipped New Hampshire, finished no higher than fifth in the Florida primary,[2] but remained in the race through the Illinois and Wisconsin primaries, after which he dropped out—unable to rekindle the fire that had been ignited around him during his mayoral campaign of 1965.

In his book, Theodore White would later write of Lindsay's campaign: "Lindsay seemed the most formidable contender if he started early enough. . . . His responsibility for the world's greatest city had rubbed his nerve ends raw; he was running for President because the Federal government had alienated not only millions of the citizens in his city, but his conscience as Mayor, too . . . One should speak generously of John Lindsay . . . the big cities were to have only one spokesman in the campaign of 1972. Of all the Presidential candidates, only one, John Lindsay, seemed to grasp that American cities were ungovernable by old cultural values . . . Lindsay understood what the word 'alienation' meant. . . . Lindsay's cause was the case for the city in America." But as attractive a candidate as Lindsay was, White blamed his campaign handlers for Lindsay's overall poor showings in the primaries, which eventually caused him to drop out of the race.[3]

Curiously, however, Lindsay's name came up behind the scenes at the 1968 convention.[4] After Nixon had won the nomination on the first ballot, he asked then-congressman Gerald Ford during a midnight conference in his suite at the Republican Convention in 1968 in Miami Beach whether he [Ford] would like to be vice president. According to Gerald Ford's account of this meeting, Nixon asked: "I know that in the past, Jerry, you have thought about being Vice President. Would you take it this year?" Ford's account went on: "At the moment we had 187 Republicans in the House—and we had won forty-seven of those seats two years earlier. The Democrats were terribly divided by the Vietnam War and another big Republican win seemed a strong possibility. If we captured just thirty-one more seats, I'd be Speaker of the House. I thanked Nixon for his compliment but said I wasn't interested."

"Well, whom do you favor?" Nixon asked Ford.

> I replied that I'd found strong support in the House for New York City Mayor John V. Lindsay. As a Congressman, he'd been far to the left of most Republicans, but I wasn't concerned about that. He was an able attorney, a very articulate and attractive man. Lindsay, I told Nixon, would provide a nice balance to the ticket in 1968. California Representative Bob Wilson seconded my recommendation. Lindsay, he said, would be a superb nominee. But Nixon wasn't interested.

Ford recognized that there was some enmity between Nixon and Lindsay. Other names were bandied about and the meeting broke up without an apparent decision being made.

Ironically, however, Lindsay was selected by the Republican National Committee to nominate Spiro Agnew as Nixon's running mate for vice president at that same 1968 GOP Convention. I sometimes muse on the thought that if Nixon had taken Ford's advice, John Lindsay—instead of Gerald Ford—may have become president of the United States.

However, today—based on what I learned firsthand from the former presidential press secretaries interviewed for this book—I am certain, with the advantage of hindsight, that I did not possess either the political know-how or the even-handed temperament to be an effective presidential press secretary.

As a journalist, my fascination with White House politics and the news-making process has grown with the passing of time. Having worked as a political reporter for *The Washington Post*—where I occasionally covered White House events—and *The New York World-Telegram & Sun,* I try to be objective in this book. But if there is any bias, I guess it would be to empathize with the press secretaries because I had a taste of what they must endure. I have striven to reflect their wisdom as a guide throughout the following pages. I tried to emphasize their attributes and skills. I admire all of the presidential spokesmen for the extraordinary contribution they have made over the years toward making our country a well-informed, more perfect union.

This book is an attempt to pull open the curtain on how the role of White House press secretaries has broadened in stature and changed over time with the increasing importance of the high-tech, twenty-four/seven news cycle, how the development of news manipulation—or spin—has come into vogue to the point where the average consumer of news may be so cynical he or she does not know what to believe anymore. The news stories covered in this volume are necessarily selective, as I have chosen those crises and issues that have impacted major news stories on the national and international scenes.

One of the most revealing aspects of my research was reading the voluminous transcripts of the briefing to the White House correspondents given by the press secretaries all the way back to Franklin D. Roosevelt. I have excerpted numerous Q&As to give the reader a sense of being present at the briefings and reading word-for-word the exchanges—sometimes friendly, often not—between the press secretaries and the press.

My goal is to explain how spin is skillfully woven into the fabric of news announced and interpreted by the White House spin doctors on topics ranging from legislation to presidential scandals, to managing in wartime, to foreign policy, to responding to religious and environmental issues, to coping with natural disasters. I learned a great deal from the White House press secretaries, who cooperated in this journey to shed some light on the changing process of news dissemination from the White House to the news media and on to the public over the years.

For myself, it all started with John Lindsay, who died at the age of seventy-nine on December 20, 2000, after a long illness. I have dedicated this book in his memory because—for this writer during one brief moment in time—he represented genuine hope for our nation's future at a time when it was most needed.

## Notes

1. Bruno, Jerry, and Jeff Greenfield. *The Advance Man, An Offbeat Look at What Really Happens in Political Campaigns* (New York: William Morrow and Company, 1971) pp. 155, 162.

2. In the 1972 Florida primary, Lindsay won 6.5 percent of the vote, behind George Wallace (41.6 percent), Hubert Humphrey, (18.6 percent), Henry "Scoop" Jackson (13.5 percent), and Edmund Muskie (8.9 percent). However, it is noteworthy that he finished ahead of George McGovern (3.6 percent), Shirley Chisholm, Eugene McCarthy, and three other lesser candidates. "Presidential Elections, 1789–1992," *Congressional Quarterly* (1995): 182.

3. White, Theodore H. *The Making of the President, 1972* (New York: Atheneum, 1973), pp. 43, 89, 93–94.

4. Ford, Gerald R. *A Time to Heal* (New York: Harper & Row, 1979), pp. 85–86.

# ACKNOWLEDGMENTS

This book has been a big and most enjoyable journalistic adventure. I would not have been able to even contemplate it without the comforting support and the patience of my wife, Audrey, who not only assisted me in researching it but also was instrumental in editing and shaping the manuscript in its final stages.

I am enormously grateful to Nancy Kuhn-Clark, a top-notch professional "can-do" reference librarian at the Westport Public Library, for her painstaking and detailed research. For more than a year-and-a-half, she spent long hours looking for specific newspaper stories on microfiche, scanning the Internet, and discovering sources to find many of the documents, books, and publications needed to complete my manuscript. This book could not have been written without her dedicated assistance.

I wish to thank my acquisitions editors at Greenwood Publishing: Hilary Claggett, who helped me create the outline of the book, and Robert Hutchinson, who succeeded her and was of enormous help in reorganizing the manuscript, making constructive editing suggestions, and moving it along to the production process and into print. Additionally, my thanks to Greenwood's Brian J. Foster, editorial assistant who coordinated my project with my acquisition editors, and to Margaret Maybury, Kathleen Knakal, Megan Chalek, and Michael O'Connor.

I am also indebted to Kim Hoag, senior production coordinator of Bytheway Publishing Services, for designing the book and overseeing it in its final stage to press.

To Miggs Burroughs, an extraordinarily talented designer and my longtime colleague and friend, I offer my heartfelt thanks for his jacket design, as well as for his layout of the photo spread in the center of the book.

I also hasten to thank Betty Pessagno, my friend and freelance editor, for reviewing the manuscript and making constructive suggestions. And to Lucille Weener, my friend and researcher, for her assistance in obtaining the briefings of President Richard Nixon's press secretary, Ronald Ziegler, from the archives in Washington, D.C. My gratitude also to Edward W. Buckley, executive assistant to Tony Snow in the White House press office.

Other professional reference librarians at the Westport Public Library who assisted in this research project include Debbie Celia, Margie Freilich-Den, Janie Rhein, and Susan Madeo, and Marta Campbell, Head of Collection Management. My thanks also to Maxine Bleiweis, director of the Westport Public Library, for her continuing support of all of this writer's endeavors over the years.

The Presidential Library staffs should be recognized for their cooperation in providing transcripts of briefings by White House press secretaries, all in the public domain. Specifically, I wish to thank Mike Duggan, supervisory archivist at the Ronald Reagan Library; Laurie Spencer, archivist, George H.W. Bush Presidential Library; Herbert L. Pankratz, archivist, Dwight D. Eisenhower Presidential Library; and Virginia Lewick, archivist, Franklin D. Roosevelt Presidential Library. For accurate, firsthand background information on Franklin D. Roosevelt's press secretary, Stephen T. (Steve) Early, I am indebted to Professor Linda Lotridge Levin, author of *The Making of FDR: The Story of Stephen T. Early, the First Modern Press Secretary*. My thanks, too, to Prof. Steven E. Clayman, Sociology Department, UCLA, for sharing his valuable study, "Historical Trends in [the press] Questioning Presidents, 1953–2000."

In addition, I want to express my appreciation to all of the presidential press secretaries who made themselves available to me for interviews during the course of my research. I am especially grateful to Marlin Fitzwater, press secretary to Presidents George H.W. Bush and Ronald Reagan, who served as an informal consultant on this project and who wrote a Foreword; Dee Dee Myers, President Bill Clinton's first press secretary who wrote another Foreword; and to Tony Snow, former press secretary to President George W. Bush, for taking the time to be interviewed during his action-packed days while he was in the White House. In addition, I am indebted to President George W. Bush's press secretary, Dana Perino; and former press secretaries Scott McClellan, Ari Fleischer, Jake Siewert, Joe Lockhart, Mike McCurry,

Larry Speakes, Jody Powell, Ron Nessen, and Jerald terHorst, all of whom agreed to be interviewed for this book, and, therefore, added a great deal of authenticity to its contents.

I would also like to thank Albert Charles Lasher, my close friend stretching back to our experience together more than fifty years ago at the Columbia University Graduate School of Journalism, for his sound advice at the outset of this undertaking and for his valuable contributions to my research.

For his assistance in putting the final manuscript together, I thank Chris Zito, a computer expert who added to my knowledge of twenty-first century computer technology.

Finally, to my daughter, Wendy, I express my love for her enduring confidence in me as a professional journalist and author over these many years.

Woody Klein
Westport, Connecticut
August 15, 2007

## PRESIDENTIAL PRESS SECRETARIES

| | | | |
|---|---|---|---|
| 1933 | 1945 | Stephen T. Early | Franklin D. Roosevelt |
| 1945 | 1945 | J. Leonard Reinsch | Franklin D. Roosevelt |
| 1945 | 1945 | Jonathan W. Daniels | Franklin D. Roosevelt and Harry S. Truman |
| 1945 | 1950 | Charles G. Ross | Harry S. Truman |
| 1950 | 1950 | Stephen T. Early | Harry S. Truman |
| 1950 | 1952 | Joseph H. Short, Jr. | Harry S. Truman |
| 1952 | 1953 | Roger W. Tubby | Harry S. Truman |
| 1953 | 1961 | James C. Hagerty | Dwight D. Eisenhower |
| 1961 | 1964 | Pierre E. G. Salinger | John F. Kennedy and Lyndon B. Johnson |
| 1964 | 1965 | George E. Reedy | Lyndon B. Johnson |
| 1965 | 1966 | Bill D. Moyers | Lyndon B. Johnson |
| 1967 | 1969 | George E. Christian | Lyndon B. Johnson |
| 1969 | 1974 | Ronald L. Ziegler | Richard M. Nixon |
| 1974 | 1974 | Jerald F. terHorst | Gerald Ford |
| 1974 | 1977 | Ronald H. Nessen | Gerald Ford |
| 1977 | 1981 | Jody L. Powell | Jimmy Carter |
| 1981 | 1987 | James S. Brady | Ronald Reagan |
| 1981 | 1987 | Larry M. Speakes | Ronald Reagan |
| 1987 | 1993 | M. Marlin Fitzwater | Ronald Reagan and George H. W. Bush |
| 1993 | 1994 | M. J. (Dee Dee) Myers | Bill Clinton |
| 1994 | 1998 | Michael McCurry | Bill Clinton |
| 1998 | 2000 | Joseph Lockhart | Bill Clinton |
| 2000 | 2001 | Richard L. (Jake) Siewert | Bill Clinton |
| 2001 | 2003 | L. Ari Fleischer | George W. Bush |
| 2003 | 2006 | Scott McClellan | George W. Bush |
| 2006 | 2007 | R. A. (Tony) Snow | George W. Bush |
| 2007 | 2008 | Dana M. Perino | George W. Bush |

# INTRODUCTION

*The White House Press Secretary:*
*" 'After the Presidency Itself, The Toughest Job in the*
*White House' "*

In the world of American politics the word "spin" has become ubiqui-tous. It is an accepted term that describes the manner in which news is shaped by a spokesman for government officials—all the way up to the president of the United States. To some, the word has come to be seen as connoting a negative meaning. But in terms of the presidency, public relations practitioners interpret it as putting the best face on the news from the White House.

We hear a lot of rhetoric as the most intensely watched, longest, most expensive presidential race in American history unfolds. It is also the first time since 1952 where there is no incumbent president or vice president on the ballot. By the time it reaches its climax this fall, in ad-dition to the press secretary a bevy of spokesmen and spokeswomen for the presidential candidates from the political parties will have tra-versed America in search of money and, of course, votes. These senior campaign aides and outside political consultants or "spin doctors," as they are referred to by the media, are blanketing radio and television talk shows, the print media, the Internet, radio, and the blogosphere with messages—positive and negative—to gain attention in the twenty-four-hour, seven-day-a-week news cycle. The candidates' spin doctors are especially noticeable in the "spin rooms" after each of the debates, helping reporters with their interpretations of how their candidate "won."

When the election is over on Tuesday, November 4—assuming there is a clear winner—the nation will finally know who will be sworn in as the forty-fourth president of the United States on January 20, 2009. And when the new president is sworn in, they will immediately become familiar with the most high-profile White House staff aide—the press secretary to the president.

With the passage of time, the press secretary has come to have more and more influence because the press itself has forfeited its historic role as vigilant government-watcher—thereby giving the press secretary an opportunity to disseminate virtually any information he or she wants to. Helen Thomas, the sharp-tongued veteran Hearst Newspapers columnist and doyenne of the White House press corps, says the press has caved into the White House spokespeople. In her recent book, she wrote: "Something vital has been lost—or have American journalists forgotten that their role is to follow the truth, without fear or favor, wherever it leads them? The truth, rather than an agenda, should be the goal of a free press."[1] Thomas—who has the best perspective on White House press secretaries of any correspondent in the past four decades—writes: "It is natural for any administration to try to control all aspects of government information—and to hope that reporters take their press releases as gospel without question." She quickly adds: "The government can present its position, but then it is up to the reporter to find the *real* [italics hers] story." "Unfortunately, the events surrounding 9/11 and the war in Iraq subdued the natural skepticism of the press, due in part to its fear of being castigated as 'unpatriotic.'"[2]

What should a press secretary's role be in turns of balancing the interests of the president versus the press? Dana Perino, George W. Bush's press secretary, replied:

> I have been trained to get the media a correct answer as quickly as possible with as much detail as possible. There is no other way for us to work around here. It should come from the top down, however. My job is to give the president's views. The president wants to have good relationships with the press. That does not mean they are going to like him personally but they should respect the folks that work with him as long as we are making sure their calls are returned. When I am asked a question that I know the answer to but the president does not want the information released, I say, "That's not something I can get into right now."

What is it like to work for George W. Bush on a daily basis? Replied Perino:

> He is somebody who makes you work harder to be better every day. Whenever you are with him, he always asks you to zero in on 'the point' quickly,

better than anyone I have ever seen. He expects me to be a good adviser, to tell him both the good and bad, and that I continue to be professional in the press office. When I brief him before his press conferences, he wants to know what's on the press' minds and what he should be prepared for. He sometimes asks for advice on the answers to questions. Sometimes he jokes around when he tells me what he is going to say. And I dare him to say it. I enjoy him. He has a great sense of humor. I have been a supporter of his since 1998 when he was governor of Texas. I said then that he has to run for president. He would be the best leader for us at this time. I believe that in my heart. I am an unabashed fan. His focus is pretty amazing. I feel very comfortable around him. He lets personal criticism roll off of his back. He is a person who does not have a vindictive bone in his body. It's really impressive. I guess you have to be that way in his job.[3]

Tony Snow, Perino's immediate predecessor, described the press secretary's role this way: "The press secretary serves two masters—the press and the president—but not all masters are equal."[4] To be effective in the president's eyes, a press secretary's first loyalty has to be to the president. Should that not be the case, a president will begin to keep the press secretary at a distance, or "out of the loop," for fear of "leaks" to the media. And that can only compromise the credibility of a press secretary.

That being the case, if a presidential candidate believes a press secretary performs well during a presidential campaign, that spokesperson may turn out to be the same individual appointed to the post of press secretary after the candidate has been elected president. For example, that was the case with Jody Powell—a close aide to Georgia governor Jimmy Carter—who assisted him in his campaign of 1976 and was officially named press secretary after Carter took office. In the case of Marlin Fitzwater, arguably the best-known and most highly respected press secretary of the modern era, he served as Ronald Reagan's press secretary during Vice President George H.W. Bush's 1988 presidential campaign, and Bush named him his prospective White House press secretary immediately after the election in November of 1988. Fitzwater—who had already become a household name—remained with Reagan until inauguration day.

On January 20, 1989, Fitzwater was Reagan's press secretary in the morning and Bush's in the afternoon after the latter was sworn in. He is, in fact, the only press secretary in history to ride up to the Capitol in one presidential motorcade, and back down to the White House in another.

During Bill Clinton's 1992 campaign, Dee Dee Myers—who served as a press aide in the campaign—was officially named press secretary after Clinton was inaugurated. George Stephanopoulos, who had been Clinton's chief spokesman during his 1992 campaign, was named director of communications and served as de facto White House press secretary at the outset of the administration in 1993, even though Dee Dee Myers actually had the title of press secretary. President George W. Bush's first press secretary, Ari Fleischer, had served as Bush's campaign spokesman.

White House press secretaries, viewed through the lens of the media, arguably hold down the second most conspicuous position in the U.S. government. Their words carry the authority of the president of the United States. Their faces, at least in recent decades, are almost as familiar as that of the president himself. They are sometimes even viewed by the public as "celebrities"—men and women in the White House who, if they are known to be close to their boss, the commander-in-chief, really have the keys to the kingdom. They are the face and voice of the president to the press and to the public, worldwide.

Although former experience in newspaper and television or radio news reporting and familiarity with the needs of journalists is clearly an advantage, the real key to a press secretary's effectiveness, say those who have held the job, is not a resume or even if they have worked in the campaign, but whether the president trusts him or her completely and how much access he or she is given to the administration's thinking and secrets.

As Bill Safire, the former *New York Times* Pulitzer Prize–winning columnist and expert on the derivation and meaning of words, put it:

> An ordinary human being whose statements have been ignored all of his life will, upon taking a job in Washington, D.C., find his statements quoted and his picture appearing in newspapers across the country. The sensation that follows [appointment as presidential press secretary], often linked with the drinking of "heady wine," is euphoric; men who have always decried personal publicity find it necessary, after their appointments, to utilize the avenues of mass communications to get across their [president's] message.

Safire continued: "In 1988, the *Los Angeles Times* quoted a White House veteran on the sickness to which White House press secretaries are susceptible: 'We called it Potomac fever. Because people treat you like a star if you work in the White House, it's easy to start behaving like one. You're mentioned in talk shows and written about in books. Before long some start to feel as if they actually are a little President.'"[5]

Pierre Salinger, John F. Kennedy's press secretary, expressed the feeling of the prestige of his office this way: "I was press secretary to one of the two most powerful men in the world. It was heady stuff, and I reveled in it."[6] Even in the thousand days he spent with Kennedy, Salinger made some lasting innovations—putting the president's conferences on live TV, for example—he went about shifting the balance from the print media to television quite deliberately. He knew that the press corps had an "establishment" routine of calling on reporters from the written press first, which it guarded with pride. Salinger's suave, worldly touch gradually won them over by making the president accessible, responsive, and chummy with a few of the newspaper columnists and editors whom Kennedy trusted.

Bill Moyers, President Lyndon Johnson's loyal Texas friend and press secretary who has since become one of the nations most highly respected television commentators on Public Broadcasting System (PBS), is known as a more objective storyteller than most other press secretaries. In 1966, speaking at a National Newspaper Association meeting about his role with Johnson, he said: "Potomac Fever can produce a bloated sensation—particularly in the area of the ego—that causes press secretaries to take themselves much too seriously," he said. "There are many symptoms of this, including hyper vexation over the annoyances any reporter—especially the pathological troublemakers—can generate; myopia, which blurs their vision of things afar; and the tiger-in-the-tank syndrome manifested by supercharged reaction to criticisms, justified and unjustified."[7]

Moyers had—and still has—a reputation as a gentleman, soft-spoken, detailed-minded, and, above all, honest. His colleagues in the media have nothing but the highest praise for him. That does not mean, however, that he—like all other presidential spokesmen—was spared from the brickbats coming from the White House press corps during his brief tour as LBJ's press spokesman.

Perhaps the most single-minded and hard-hitting reporter in the White House press corps, the one who has given press secretaries and presidents more grief than anyone, is the irrepressible Helen Thomas, always hammering away for the public's right to know. She has been a shining example to her colleagues on how to persevere until she gets an acceptable answer to a question. She characterizes the Office of the Press Secretary this way:

> After the presidency itself, I believe that it is the toughest job in the White House. To be the bull's-eye every day is not easy. To reflect the views of the president is one thing, but to be an image-maker or public relations artist is

another. Certainly that podium is an honored place. And to speak for the White House is, in effect, to speak for the nation. That is why we believe in eternal vigilance. And we do feel that reporters are the watchdogs of what we like to think is the power center and the freedom tower.[8]

Dan Rather, the former CBS anchorman, expressed his thoughts about the White House press secretary and the media this way: "The greatest problem around the White House—it is very simple to say, but difficult to deal with—is to find out what the truth is."[9] And the venerable radio and television reporter and commentator Daniel Schorr said on National Public Radio, on a show titled *Spin Cycle out of Control*, "Washington these days feels a little like Moscow in Soviet times when the government routinely dispensed information to the public and the public routinely didn't believe it."[10] Indeed, many newspeople today believe the press secretary's main job is to keep the press from penetrating the veneer of the White House and finding out what's really going on. It also has become his or her responsibility to sell the president's policies by helping the press understand them better. There is where spin is both useful and practical.

Throughout the many dramatic changes over the past eight decades in the sensitive relationships among the president of the United States, the White House press secretary, the press, and the public one thing has remained constant: The president's spokesman has always tried to put the best face on news distributed to the press or in answering questions from the press. The style and manner in which news has been given out changes with every press secretary, but one thing they all have in common is the responsibility of serving and protecting their boss, the president, in the most effective way possible.

Spin has become daily routine to the point where virtually anyone who reads a newspaper, listens to radio, or watches television carrying news from President George W. Bush's White House spokesmen questions its veracity. Safire defines "spin" as "deliberate shading of news perception; attempted control of political reaction." He defines "sound bite" as "a snappy snippet of taped comment or news."[11]

Safire dilates:

> The first thing to remember is that the presidential press secretary is not the press's press secretary or journalism's punching bag, but is the president's press secretary. The increased hostility and suspicion of the press corps since Watergate (actually, since the Vietnam War) has made the job of presenting the administrations' views positively more difficult, but—as Tony Snow

demonstrated—a certain deftness, knowledgeability, stage presence, and sense of humor helps the policy medicine go down. The relationship between press and White House in our system of checks and balances should, in most matters, be adversarial without being hostile. The tension that exists when a press secretary cannot tell the whole truth while the press tries to elicit the whole truth is a healthy tension.[12]

It is instructive to look at the definitions that many of the press secretaries during the period covered in this book give of the use of "spin"—although it has not always been called by the name. Starting with the present and working backward to 1969, they are:

- *Dana Perino* (George W. Bush, 2007–2008): "In my opinion, if we tell the truth and we can explain what the president's decision is, we are providing the information from our point of view. And other people have other points of view. Spin has become a verb with a negative connotation that basically describes what my job is. I do not necessarily think it is a negative word. My job is to make sure there is the best possible coverage of the president."[13]

- *Tony Snow* (George W. Bush, 2006–2007): "I like being at close quarters with everybody and I think, fortunately, I missed spin school and I paid a price for that from time to time."[14]

- *Scott McClellan* (George W. Bush, 2003–2006): "People like to say government officials 'spin' things a certain way. People also say the media 'slants' coverage a certain way. There is some truth to both."[15]

- *Ari Fleischer* (George W. Bush, 2001–2003): "The relationship between the press secretary and the press corps is designed to be a relationship that has some levels of tension built into it. It is the press's job to ask anything about everything. I always do my best to give the fullest answers from the President that I possibly can."[16]

- *Jake Siewert* (Bill Clinton, 2000–2001): "If you start with the assumption you are there to provide accurate information and you are living in an era of increased transparency, the best you can do for the president is provide context for his decisions. The press accuses people in the White House of spinning the tale largely because their role as deciders of what was new is usurped in many ways by the president."[17]

- *Joe Lockhart* (Bill Clinton, 1998–2000): "I don't take much notice of what pundits say about spin. My job is standing up there and the journalist's job is to poke at the information to test the validity of it. Hopefully, at the end of the day, what they write about what the President says is accurate."[18]

- *Mike McCurry* (Bill Clinton, 1994–1998): "I personally believe people are becoming so distrustful of spin and political propaganda and being artful in the way information is dispensed that they want factual information. They would prefer if most people got away from political argumentation. And I plead guilty for having overpoliticized the podium."[19]

- *Dee Dee Myers* (Bill Clinton, 1993–1994): "The public has come to believe that all public officials, especially press secretaries, spin. And that spin is tantamount to a lie. But that's wrong. Spin may be marshalling the facts in service of an argument, the way a skilled debater would."[20]

- *Marlin Fitzwater* (Ronald Reagan and George H.W. Bush, 1987–1993): "Spin is always difficult to define and to talk about because, for the most part, 95 percent of spin is putting the best face on things. And the press gives you that."[21]

- *Larry Speakes* (Ronald Reagan, 1981–1987): "Spinning aims to minimize the damage by surrounding bad facts with context and good facts. And, if possible, with a credible interpretation of the facts. You really want to put your good foot forward for the guy you work for."[22]

- *Jody Powell* (Jimmy Carter, 1977–1981): "a press secretary does have a responsibility to make the best arguments he or she can for the administration. I don't shy away from that at all."[23]

- *Ron Nessen* (Gerald R. Ford, 1974–1977): "I think most people will tell you that spin is kind of a defensive activity, that reporters always put the most negative interpretation on the story and that the press secretaries are just trying to get a fair shake by spinning it to emphasize the good parts of it."[24]

- *Jerald terHorst* (Gerald R. Ford, 1974): "Nowadays, press secretaries are taking it upon themselves—or being required—the task of defending presidential decisions. They are much more involved in defending the president's policies than they were earlier. They have to either neutralize bad news or make it look positive."[25]

- *Ron Ziegler* (Richard Nixon, 1969–1974): "Press secretaries do find themselves in a situation where they do in fact lie because of the information that one of their colleagues gave them, which they felt to be true ends up not to be true. So that is a dilemma that a press secretary faces."[26]

One of journalism's giants, Benjamin C. Bradlee, former executive editor of *The Washington Post* and the man who made history by supervising the Watergate expose, says that spin comes with the press secretary's job. "I would define spin as the shaping of events to make you look better than anybody else. I think it is, you know, an art form now and it gets in the way of the truth," he says.[27] Bradlee is known as an advocate of "creative tension" between the press and the White House.

David Gergen, commentator, author, editor, professor of public service at the Kennedy School of Government, and advisor to Presidents Nixon, Ford, Reagan, and Clinton on communications, says this about spin:

> As someone who started a "spin patrol" back in the Reagan years, I was aghast at how it has been corrupted. How could we have taught a younger generation of public officials the wrong lessons about governance? Where had we gone wrong? While officials since the beginning of the Republic have been cajoling the press, one of my deepest regrets in public life is a feeling that I have contributed to this deterioration. Spin has spun out of control and we need to put it back in its box.[28]

Scholars Brooks Jackson and Kathleen Hall Jamison wrote in their book, *UnSpun,*

> We live in a world of spin. It flies at us in the form of misleading commercials for products and political candidates and about public policy matters. It comes from businesses, political leaders, lobbying groups, and political parties. . . . Spin is a polite word for deception. Spinners mislead by means that range from subtle omission to outright lies. Spin paints a false picture of reality, by bending facts, mischaracterizing the words of others, ignoring or denying evidence, or just "spinning a yarn"—by making things up. Some degree of spin can be considered harmless, as when a person puts his best foot forward in hopes that we won't notice that the other shoe may be a bit scuffed.[29]

There is no record of exactly who originated the word "spin." It may well have started with Edward L. Bernays, a practitioner in the art of public relations who can be traced back to the 1920s. A biography of Bernays is titled "The Father of Spin."[30] Bernays is portrayed in that book as the man who, perhaps more than any other individual, defined public relations as a full-fledged profession, which today is the basis of much of the nation's political discourse.

Another giant in the world of public relations, Harold Burson of Burson-Marsteller (one of the world's largest public relations firms), emphasizes what may be the single most important aspect of making news: time contraints. All the spin in the world can fall on deaf ears unless it is timed correctly. He writes: "Today's 24-hour news cycle works at the speed of light, recognizing no national boundaries, no oceans, and non-discriminating on the receiving end. This creates a 'time frame compression' that demands immediate response."[31]

A radio series exploring the origins of American cultural icons, an examination of spin called "Present at the Creation," by NPR's Linda Wertheimer on Bob Edwards's "Morning Edition" program on November 4, 2002, declared: "I actually was present at the creation of spin, as we now use the term. Let me take you back in time." She referred to the 1984 presidential debates between then-president Ronald Reagan and former vice president Walter Mondale. Werthheimer explained:

> It's [spin] been around since—well, maybe since the beginning of man. But it's only had a name for about 20 years. It's not quite lying. It's not quite the truth. It's spin. In today's media-saturated political climate, the distinction between politics and spin might seem superfluous. But during the presidential election of 1984, thanks to a growing news media coupled with creative and quick-witted campaign officials, it was a certified phenomenon.

She added:

> Elizabeth Bumiller [now of *The New York Times*] witnessed the Reagan-Mondale debates firsthand. In a story for *The Washington Post*, she described the pandemonium that ensued after each candidate had abandoned his podium. "It was very intense. I just remember these clumps, masses of reporters around each clump," she said. "All the candidates' spokespeople, staff, campaign managers, would start saying 'He won, let me tell you why he won and all the great points he made.'" I remember [political consultant] Lee Atwater gesturing, making his arguments like a court case. It looked important. Atwater, who served on many campaigns, including Reagan's trek to the 1984 election, is generally remembered as the superstar of spin, the inevitable man at the center of that great clump of reporters with outstretched microphones.

Atwater was a perfect example of what *The New York Times* described, in an editorial that ran October 21, 1984, the day of the final debate, as a "spin doctor." The editorial by Jack Rosenthal read, in part:

> Tonight at about 9:30, seconds after the Reagan-Mondale debate ends, a bazaar will suddenly materialize in the pressroom. . . . A dozen men in good suits and women in silk dresses will circulate smoothly among the reporters, spouting confident opinions. They won't be just press agents trying to impart a favorable spin to a routine release. They'll be Spin Doctors, senior advisors to the candidates.[32]

The use of spin can at times turn into a free-for-all, with one reporter shouting questions over another's voice trying to goad a press secretary into agreeing to a negative phrase offered by a reporter, starting the question with something like "Would you say that . . .?" when, in fact, there is no clear "yes" or "no" answer. It starts with the press secretary's talk at the morning "gaggle" followed a few hours later by a "press briefing." The gaggle may be defined as an informal, "on-the-record" session with the press secretary, without video recording, though transcripts are usually made available. The "briefing" is a more formal live televised event, now normally carried on C-Span every day, in which the press secretary is the star and the reporters are the supporting cast. However, at times, one wonders if the reporters are trying to steal the limelight with some very hard-hitting—and often repetitive—questions. Speaking of "on the record," information can be dispensed to reporters in any number of ways.

Marlin Fitzwater, press secretary to Presidents Reagan and Bush, explained the terminology rarely understood by the public. Fitzwater defined the language as follows:[33]

- *On the record*. Anything a source says may be used and attributed to the source by name, title, and organization.
- *Off the record*. Anything said will not be published or broadcast, nor will it be repeated to others for any reason. Nonetheless, it is intended to help shape the news. This definition is the most misused and misunderstood. Sooner or later, reporters almost always talk, or sources tell their secrets to someone else. "Off the record" information, if confirmed by a second source, often winds up being made public.
- *Background briefing*. Information provided to a reporter can be used—but not by the name of the source—and can be used as quotes. An example would be "according to a high administration official," or "a senior administration official."

- *Deep background.* Means information may be used for publication or broadcast, but with no source identification, and not in quotes.
- *Press briefing.* Any time an official gathers reporters to tell them something. For example, the White House press secretary usually holds a daily briefing, though not always in the White House itself. It could take place, for example, on Air Force One if the president is traveling.
- *Not for attribution.* Sources often use this term to emphasize that the source cannot be identified in any way but can be quoted.
- *Anonymous sources.* Individuals who may be quoted, but not by name.
- *Administration official.* Means anybody who works for the government with relevant information. A reporter could literally use this term to identify the president or a washroom attendant.
- *Embargoed.* The information may be published or broadcast after a certain time and date.
- *Leak.* Information provided to the press that is not authorized.

Adds Fitzwater:

> Just giving these definitions brings back great stories of how these terms have been used. Henry Kissinger was one of the first great 'deep backgrounders.' James A. Baker III virtually used 'not for attribution' as a management tool. 'Backgrounders' are now standard practice for almost all White House briefings on foreign policy. 'Embargoed' is almost obsolete now because of the Internet. Max Frankel, former executive editor of *The New York Times*, once banned 'anonymous sources' from the paper, only to be beaten on so many stories that he lifted the ban after a few weeks.

White House press briefings have alternately been called "a political chess game in which both sides view everything the other side is doing as a tactic," "rhetorical combat," "a war zone," "a wrestling match," and "a duel or a face-off." In military terms, a press secretary is "under fire" from a "hostile media," desperately scrambling and bailing to keep a torrent of scandals from sinking a battered ship of state. And White House press secretaries are often maligned in the vernacular as "spinmeisters," "flaks," "PR men," "publicists," "pugilist," "propagandist," "smear artist," and "propaganda pushers" by a few hostile media people who, generally, do not fully trust them, believe them, or—for that matter—respect them. "Press secretaries are, at times, bullied, challenged, shouted at, and publicly kicked around by confrontational members of the White House press corps. Yet, they remain in the public eye as the last hope for the citizenry to shine some light on Foggy Bottom."[34]

Presidential press secretaries as a group do their best to bring Americans the news, as they believe their bosses wish the American people to see them. And because they are the authorized sources of information about what the president of the United States is thinking about on almost any subject, the public continues to listen carefully to them as they parse their words. For most West Wing watchers, other than the president himself, press secretaries are the people to whom reporters look for information. Nonetheless, looking at the dark side of the use of "spin" by the White House, Bill Moyers, press secretary for President Johnson and now one of the most respected television and print journalists in America—said more than a decade ago, "A nation can die from too many [government] lies."[35]

When did the White House press secretary emerge as a major player speaking for the White House? For the most part, a majority of the White House press secretaries have been former journalists. Interestingly, the first thirty U.S. presidents saw no apparent need for an official spokesman. A survey of the press and the presidents from the early Republic through the end of the nineteenth century reveals that William McKinley (1897–1901) had occasional cordial contact with reporters, but it was not until 1901, when Theodore Roosevelt entered the White House, that the president even talked with a group of reporters, although it was infrequent and unscheduled. T.R. was the first president to set up a room for the press. Political folklore has it that Teddy Roosevelt spouted off whenever he felt like it, even when his barber shaved him. Hoping to turn his press meetings into part of what he called "the bully pulpit," T.R. used the news media to serve his own purposes. He brought the media into the White House literally as well as figuratively. T.R., who had served as police commissioner of New York, was the first president known to befriend a reporter, crusading journalist Jacob Riis,[36] and he collaborated with the reporter on measures to clean up the tenements of New York of his era—all for the public good. Riis, a Danish immigrant, had come to the United States in the 1870s and befriended Roosevelt, thus making Roosevelt a valuable source who gave him stories in his newspaper. There would be many more relationships like this to follow in subsequent administrations. Presidents comfortable with the press often give exclusive interviews to correspondents they believe are sympathetic to their political views.

Not until Franklin Delano Roosevelt became president was the job of press secretary officially created.[37] Stephen T. Early, a member of his small cadre of secretaries and a close friend of FDR for forty years, was designated by the president to be the first press "official" secretary. Indeed, FDR's administration is called "the first public relations presidency" by some longtime observers of the Washington political scene. Early made certain that FDR met with journalists two or three times a week for thirteen years, usually with a hearty exchange.

At the close of FDR's first official press conference, starting at 10:10 A.M. on March 8, 1933, the reporters actually broke into applause—a phenomenon that, according to modern-day historians and reporters, has never happened since. On that day, some 125 White House correspondents swarmed into the president's private office. They found him seated at a desk covered with letters and communications.

Early had gained the president's assurance beforehand that FDR would allow him to set all press policies. FDR could be charming and entertaining, but it was clear to the members of the press corps that the president was in charge. He called the shots and they wrote down what he said, although the rule laid down by Press Secretary Early from the outset was that the president could not be directly quoted.

Early was seen as an "authentic public figure—almost an assistant to the President."[38] FDR met with reporters in an informal setting in the Oval Office with Early at his side at the ready. The White House press nicknamed him "Steady Steve" because of his easy manner and dependability. In some situations, the president would turn to Early for details on a given topic and Early seemed to have all the answers. It was not unusual for the two of them to quietly exchange words with one another during a press conference. In an effort to "educate" the reporters so they would be fully aware of how government works, Roosevelt held off-the-record background discussions with the press that were more like seminars on economics and government. He wanted all of them to fully understand the complexities of government and, therefore, the difficult job he had to do.

Early was admired for instituting FDR's now-famous "Fireside Chats" on radio, to which the American people listened intently in their living rooms. Early knew that his boss had a superb radio voice and spoke in such a clear, Harvard-educated intonation that FDR's command of the English language came across, at once, as both sophisticated for the rich to identify with and yet in such plain, humorous language that the workingman understood only too well.

Many of the reporters referred to FDR as "the greatest managing editor" in the news business. Especially during his first "100 days" and throughout his first term, FDR was making so many announcements of actions to help the nation recover from the Depression that a White

House reporter could almost count on getting a front-page story every day. Indeed, for the first time in the history of the give-and-take relationship between the president and the press, reporters actually could not wait to get to the White House every day for big news—an unusual happening in Washington, D.C., which would not occur again until John F. Kennedy was elected president in 1960. Perhaps the most obvious—and most practical—advice that Roosevelt followed from Early was to treat all members of the press impartially—not to play favorites, as has often been the case since. Roosevelt's breathtaking actions in the form of bills he sent to Congress dominated the news and won him plaudits from most newspapers—that is, until he introduced the Social Security Act of 1935 and drew sharp criticism from corporate heads and affluent publishers who saw it as a form of socialism. But FDR applied his own "spin" by taking to the airwaves and going over the heads of the media to drum up support among the working men and women of America with his regular radio chats. With Early's guiding hand, FDR spoke in plain language everyone could understand.

It was obvious to all the reporters who covered the president that Early's presence meant a great deal to him personally. FDR would exhibit his affection for Early as often and in as many ways as he could. On August 27, 1940, for example, with Europe in great danger and the United States involvement in a war looming on the horizon, Roosevelt wheeled himself out to chat with the press at 4:20 in the afternoon just as they were wrapping up their day. There was an unwritten code or understanding between White House officials and reporters during the Roosevelt years that nobody would write about FDR's disability from infantile paralysis. Reporters obediently agreed to the White House's request that FDR not be photographed sitting in his wheelchair.

The president was smiling with his famous cigarette holder jutting out from his clenched teeth. He announced to the wide-eyed assemblage, who had not been given the usual advance notice by Early: "I think the only news of interest I have is that today is a red letter day in American history. I very nearly issued a national Proclamation on the subject. It is Steve's birthday." The reporters turned toward Early and, in a chorus, sang the traditional Happy Birthday song. At that point, the president turned to resume his work, saying; "So I leave him in your tender care. Maybe you will get a free drink out of it, I don't know." Said one reporter: "Maybe." And another: "How about getting a piece of news out of him?" Roosevelt quipped, as he departed: "A piece of news out of him—that's an idea. I do not think I have anything else." One could feel the warmth and affection that the president felt for his spokesman to the world. It can be safely said that Early, who dominated the communications coming from the White House, set the stage for what was to come in the future in terms of press secretaries attempting to keep reporters' attention focused on a specific topic each day.[39]

One of the most effective ways in which the majority of presidential press secretaries since Early have tried to control the news is to put out what is known in politics as "the line of the day"—meaning one specific topic agreed upon ahead of time by the press secretary and other White House advisors to the president. It is intended to help an administration speak with one voice—to stay focused on the message. In addition, during the Reagan years in the 1980s members of the president's staff led by David Gergen, the manipulative "spinmeister"— referred to as the creator of "spin patrol" who has since said it has spun out of control—took the initiative with reporters when they wanted to make certain a piece of news is interpreted correctly.

Following Roosevelt's death on April 12, 1945, Harry S.. Truman— who up to that point the press had viewed as a marginalized and ineffectual vice president—stepped up to the challenge. Holding press conferences twice a week instead of three, Truman took command and required reporters to identify themselves and the newspapers or radio stations they worked for—as a forerunner for today's process of reporters being selected by the president to ask questions—singling them out to be personally responsible for the questions they were asking. In another major change from FDR's policy of not being quoted, Truman made it a point to let the media know that he would gladly be quoted. He also permitted radio to tape his comments for delayed broadcasting, exercising more caution that the previous live radio addresses by Calvin Coolidge and FDR. At the end of his term in 1952, however, Truman set a precedent that would continue to this day by allowing newsreel cameras to record his last press conference.

Early helped Truman in the transition immediately after FDR's death, but soon gave way to a succession of men, including J. Leonard Reinsch, who had served as an advisor to Roosevelt and was one of the most famous names in radio broadcasting; Jonathan Daniels, a former newspaper editor who had worked for FDR on various projects; and Charles G. Ross, the *St. Louis Post-Dispatch* Washington bureau chief who had won a Pulitzer Prize. Ross became Harry Truman's press secretary in 1945. Charming, intelligent, and highly respected as he was as a Washington newspaper correspondent, Ross was not especially innovative as a press secretary. He did not play the usual role of trying to improve the president's image. By the time he reluctantly agreed to join his friend Harry Truman, Ross did not appear to have the energy or imagination to play the usual role of building up his boss's image. In fact, it appeared at the time that the pressure was too much for him. He died suddenly in the White House in December 1950 after giving a press conference, causing Truman to recall Steve Early until he hired Joseph H. Short, who had been a correspondent for *The Baltimore Sun*. Short died in September 1952, two months before the election of Dwight D. Eisenhower. Short was followed briefly by Roger Tubby, a former newspaper reporter and editor who had been Short's assistant.

Throughout the eight years of Dwight D. Eisenhower's presidency (1953–1961), James C. Hagerty—Gov. Thomas E. Dewey's former press secretary—served as the White House press secretary.

Together with Stephen Early, Hagerty was the longest serving White House press secretary of all time and, according to a majority of contemporary reporters, Hagerty is still remembered best as a genius in political image-making. He was knowledgeable about everything that was going on in the White House, with Eisenhower insisting that he attend Cabinet meetings, at which Hagerty freely gave his advice to the various Cabinet officials which they usually followed. Hagerty is remembered for his no-holds-barred rules to protect "Ike" from the press and the public.

One example was his playing down Eisenhower's heart attack on September 24, 1955, while he was vacationing in Colorado. Word from the press secretary's office was that Ike had suffered a "digestive upset," but then Hagerty shrewdly let it be known that he had, indeed, suffered a "mild" heart attack although he was completely in charge and attending to his presidential duties. In fact, Hagerty gave out so many details of the president's daily physical improvement that one reporter remarked only doctors could understand what Hagerty was saying. In short order, Hagerty created the image of a vigorous, sixty-five-year-old man who was moving toward recovery and assuming his normal duties with a reelection campaign coming up.

Hagerty wanted to get Eisenhower back on track in terms of the perception of his physical condition. He announced almost daily that Ike was having visitors. As a result of his constant availability, Hagerty gained a great deal of goodwill which he would need again when the president once again underwent an operation on June 9, 1956, for ileitis. The Republican National Convention was only two months away.

Hagerty minimized the seriousness of the president's condition and, even though some reporters remained skeptical, he had earned so much credibility with the press that he could well afford to manipulate or "spin" the news in favor of Ike. Hagerty did come under some fire for refusing to allow the press to talk to the president's medical team, but he successfully achieved his goal: Eisenhower was renominated by acclamation and subsequently rolled over his widely admired opponent, former Illinois governor Adlai Stevenson, in a landslide. No mean accomplishment for a presidential press secretary.

John Tebbel and Sarah Miles Watts wrote about the selection of Hagerty: "Eisenhower made the best choice possible."[40] Hagerty is generally regarded today as one of the most effective, well-respected press secretaries in history. He stood at the president's elbow and steered him safely through hundreds of potentially damaging encounters. Hagerty is noted for setting up the first presidential press conference at which full picture coverage was permitted on January 19, 1955. He permitted photographers to set up their equipment in the back of the room as reporters awaited the arrival of the president.

Hagerty handled both the president and the press with compassion and understanding—he knew what each wanted and tried to balance the needs of both. Over the years, a touch of old-school sentimentality has been attached to Hagerty who, like a character in playwright Ben Hecht's *Front Page* drama, was a chain-smoking, hard-drinking reporter-turned–press secretary who talked tough but was as smooth and sophisticated as anyone who worked in a Madison Avenue advertising agency. Though he appeared stern-faced and humorless—he was always firmly in control.

Eisenhower was followed by the handsome, charming John F. Kennedy, whose youth stood in sharp contrast with his grandfatherly predecessor. JFK represented a new generation of Americans who were filled with lofty ideals and a dream of what the future might hold, willing to serve their vibrant new leader. His press secretary Pierre Salinger, a native of San Francisco, spent the early years of his career as a reporter with the *San Francisco Chronicle* and as a contributing editor for *Collier's* magazine. His research in 1956 for articles on labor leader Jimmy Hoffa led him to a close association with Robert F. Kennedy, who hired Salinger when Bobby Kennedy was legal counsel for the Senate Select Committee investigating organized crime. Bobby recommended him to his older brother, Jack, who hired him as his press secretary when he was still a Democratic senator running for president in 1960. Salinger was appointed White House press secretary after the election. Salinger set a White House precedent with President Kennedy by launching the first live telecast of a presidential press conference on January 25, 1961.

Salinger was seen by the press as having a great deal of power because he had total access to the president, almost around the clock. His unusual persona also attracted attention. A cigar-smoking descendant of French lineage, he was only thirty-four when he joined Kennedy. Historian Arthur M. Schlesinger Jr. described him as man "who entertained the press with jocular daily briefings."[41]

JFK's extraordinary personal charm and Salinger's candid, sometimes blunt style may well have explained why the White House press corps maintained a hands-off policy when it came to Kennedy's extramarital affairs. They were an open secret to many, if not most, of the reporters who covered him, but the public was kept in the dark. Those were the unwritten rules in those days and Salinger was able to persuade the press not to break them. Had it been otherwise, a major scandal would have undoubtedly erupted in the White House.

Not only was Kennedy's private life protected by his press secretary, but his legacy was carefully honed by his widow Jacqueline, who—with the knowledge and assistance of Salinger—worked closely with the prestigious historian Theodore H. White, an admirer and friend of JFK's and a close friend of Salinger's. One could argue that there was no better example of how an entire presidency could be encapsulated and spun—in this case by a writer, with the help of a press secretary. According to a number of accounts, shortly after the assassination on November 22, 1963, Jacqueline Kennedy spent four hours talking to White. She told him that her husband often listened to the song "Camelot" from the musical Broadway play of the same name. His favorite lines, Jacqueline Kennedy said, were: "Don't let it be forgot, that once there was a spot, for one brief shining moment, that was known as Camelot." On December 6, 1961, *Life* magazine published White's romanticized essay, "For President Kennedy: An Epilogue." The article became the foundation of the mythology of Kennedy's Camelot—his 1036 days in the White House. Chalk up one historic spin story for Jacqueline Kennedy, with the capable assistance of Pierre Salinger; and inspired, no doubt, by their grief for the loss of a man they both loved and whose legacy was uppermost in their minds.

Immediately after the shocking assassination of Kennedy, Vice President Lyndon B. Johnson was sworn in on Air Force One on his way back to Washington from Dallas. Everything seemed frozen in time, and in the immediate aftermath of the tragedy, Johnson asked Salinger to stay on—no easy assignment for one of JFK's closest advisers. When Salinger eventually resigned in August 1964 to join the prestigious public relations firm of Burson-Marsteller, Johnson handpicked George Reedy to succeed him. Reedy had been a reporter for United Press International in Washington, D.C., before joining Johnson's Senate staff in 1951. He worked as an aide to Johnson during his presidential campaign in 1960 and remained with him when he became vice president.

Reedy might best be remembered among political scholars as the one man in the White House who tried to bring Lyndon Johnson and the Rev. Doctor Martin Luther King Jr. together. Shortly after the president and King posed for a photograph on July 2, 1964, at the signing of the historic Civil Rights Act, Johnson chewed Reedy out for having told reporters at one of his briefings that "the President has been in continuous touch with [King]." Two days later, Johnson called Reedy by phone and said: "I haven't been in touch with him at all. . . . You know his record." Johnson was referring to the pile of reports he had been receiving from FBI director J. Edgar Hoover, who was trying to discredit King.[42] Truly, "no good deed goes unpunished." Reedy would be the first of Johnson's three White House press secretaries. He was known as a taskmaster and a workaholic who drove his staff as hard as he drove himself.

Ever mindful of his place in history, Johnson turned to an old friend of his from Texas, young Bill Moyers, who had been deputy director of the Peace Corps under Kennedy. He had been a top aide to President Kennedy and reluctantly accepted the job as Johnson's White House press secretary from July 1965 to December 15, 1966. Moyers clearly saw the paradox of the press secretary's job. "The job of a journalist is precisely opposite that of a press secretary . . . The job of trying to tell the truth about people, whose job it is to hide the truth is almost as complicated and difficult as trying to hide it in the first place."[43]

Moyers was succeeded by George Christian, another old steady-as-you-go Texas pal of Johnson's. A native of Austin, he had spent seven years as a reporter covering Texas state government for the International News Service prior to serving as press secretary first for Texas governor Price Daniel and then for Governor John Connally. He moved to Washington, D.C., to join the staff of President Lyndon B. Johnson to deal with the press during the turbulent Vietnam War period.

Richard Nixon's press secretary Ron Ziegler was a bird of a different feather, having originally come from an advertising background rather than the media. He worked as a press aide on Nixon's unsuccessful

California gubernatorial campaign in 1962. In 1969, when he was just twenty-nine, Ziegler became the youngest White House press secretary in history.

Ziegler's experience in manipulating information was a necessity in the Nixon White House, but it hardly endeared him to the press. He also lacked some credibility because he did not report directly to the president; instead, his boss was H. R. Haldeman, Nixon's chief of staff—in what was seen as a conscious move to subordinate the role of press secretary while enhancing the chief of staff's powers. Herb Klein, Nixon's director of communications, also outranked Ziegler, leaving the press secretary even less clout with the press.

Ziegler was the White House press secretary for the Nixon administration during the Watergate scandal. Ziegler's first response to the report of the break-in at Democratic headquarters on June 17, 1972, was to dismiss it as a "third rate burglary." He would live to regret his offhand remark. Within two years after that statement, Nixon would resign under threat of impeachment. Ziegler remained with Nixon for a period of time after the president's historic resignation to handle continuing inquiries from the media. Furthermore, unlike his predecessors, Nixon had shut the media out, neither holding off-the-record dinners with columnists or highly favored reporters nor sharing any personal anecdotes as Truman did during his time in office.

Nixon, instead, favored speeches on television because he could control the content of his words and not answer any questions, even though that emerging medium was not kind to him. With a tense expression on his face, sometimes appearing slightly unshaven, he would remain emblazoned in the public mind more for his phrase, "I am not a crook," than for almost anything else. In the end, Nixon's perception—that everyone was out to get him—proved to be his greatest flaw and it did him and his press secretary a disservice.

In terms of spin, Ziegler was releasing information that had already been pre-spun, that is, he was given information that was incorrect on the face of it and that had been manipulated by others in the administration before he released it.

When Vice President Gerald R. Ford was sworn in as president on August 9, 1974, he too picked someone who had served him before and with whom he felt comfortable, namely, Jerald terHorst, Washington bureau chief for *The Detroit News*.

TerHorst accepted the post with the understanding with Ford that he would be up front and totally honest with reporters. TerHorst served for only one month (August 9–September 8, 1974) before resigning in the wake of President Ford's unexpected announcement that he would pardon former president Richard Nixon for any possible crimes connected with the Watergate scandal.

TerHorst said in his resignation letter to Ford, dated September 8, 1974, that he found he could not "in good conscience support your decision to pardon former President Nixon even before he had been charged with the commission of any crime,"[44] especially in light of the president's refusal to pardon those who evaded the draft during the Vietnam War. Furthermore, terHorst had not been informed of the pardon beforehand, thus badly compromising his credibility with the press. Before being appointed press secretary, terHorst had been a newspaper reporter from Michigan who had covered Ford's career since 1948. TerHorst's colleagues in the press saw him as a man of integrity.

His successor was Ron Nessen, Washington correspondent for NBC News, who served until the end of the Ford Administration in 1976. Nessen served five tours as an NBC war correspondent in Vietnam and later served as NBC News White House correspondent during the Johnson administration. He was corporate vice president for news at Westwood One, Inc., where he managed the news departments of the Mutual Broadcasting System and NBC Radio Network and executive vice president and managing director of the Washington Office for Marston and Rothenberg Public Affairs.

Along came Jimmy Carter, former governor of Georgia, who—like previous presidents—turned to a trusted aide, Jody Powell, for his press secretary. Powell had worked on Carter's presidential campaign in 1976 and became a member of the so-called Georgia Mafia, a group of close aides from Georgia who moved to high positions in Carter's administration. Powell served during Carter's entire term from 1977–1981.

The election of California Governor Ronald Reagan in November 1980 would bring a major change in how the media covered the White House. The former actor needed no on-the-job training for TV cameras. Accordingly, he brought in James Brady, an experienced hand at government media relations who had worked in Housing and Urban Development, for the Director of the Office of Management and Budget, and in the Department of Defense. Reagan appointed Brady as his first press secretary on January 20, 1981.

Just two months after his appointment, Brady was among the victims of John Hinckley Jr.'s attempted assassination of Reagan in Washington, D.C., on March 30, 1981. Brady suffered a life-threatening head wound, which left him partially paralyzed and confined to a wheelchair. Brady retained the title of Press Secretary to the President for the duration of Reagan's two terms in office (1981–1989), although he never returned to work at the White House after the shooting. The White House press briefing room, which was refurbished in 2007, is named in his honor.[45]

Brady's deputy, Larry Speakes, a veteran White House staffer who had served under Nixon, took over after the shooting incident. He remained the chief press spokesman and dealt easily with the media until January 1987. Speakes was a former Mississippi newspaperman who earlier served as press secretary to Senator James Eastland of Mississippi and as assistant press secretary to President Ford.

Speakes was succeeded by Marlin Fitzwater, who had been on the White House staff since 1983, serving as special assistant to President Reagan and deputy press secretary for domestic affairs. He got along extremely well with the reporters and was adept at getting the White House out of difficult situations because of the good will he had built up. Undoubtedly Fitzwater helped Reagan become "The Great Communicator." With Fitzwater nearby, the majority of reporters deferred to Reagan's easy manner, but ABC television correspondent Sam Donaldson was critical: "They [Reagan White House] are very good at directing the news by making available something on a story that they want out and withholding from sight—remember television—something they aren't prepared to discuss."[46]

Fitzwater continued on as press secretary to President Bush from 1989 to 1993. During the first Gulf War, Fitzwater famously announced in 1991 that, "The liberation of Kuwait has begun," and was the voice of NATO and the White House. Veteran members of the media often viewed Fitzwater as a modern-day Steve Early or Jim Hagerty and ranked him with the best of press secretaries. The White House environment for the media changed markedly after the Reagan-George H.W. Bush years—the most notable changes being the introduction of the cable news networks—especially the twenty-four/seven CNN news—talk radio, the Internet, and in recent times the "bloggers," who may or may not be trained journalists, more often not. There are also the news/entertainment shows—most notably *The Daily Show* with Jon Stewart, *The Colbert Report* with Steve Colbert, and *Real Time* with Bill Maher.

When Bush lost to Clinton in 1992, the new president set a precedent by naming the first woman, Dee Dee Myers, as press secretary. She served two years, from January 20, 1993, to December 22, 1994. In a somewhat unorthodox arrangement, Clinton advisor George Stephanopoulos, who had been Clinton's director of communications during the 1992 campaign, conducted the daily press briefings instead of Myers. However, Stephanopoulos did not prove as adept at the feed and caring of the White House press corps as he had been on the campaign trail. Stephanopoulos, with whom the technique was closely identified, once defined spin as "a hope dressed up as an observation."

Early in the Clinton administration, Stephanopoulos was replaced with the veteran newsman and White House communications adviser David Gergen in an obvious move to reverse the negative news coverage of the White House. Gergen was given the impressive title of Counselor to the President and Communications Director; he was sympathetic to reporters' requests for greater access to Clinton. In addition, he was effective as a source of background information by telephoning newsmen and newswomen after a press conference and spinning the news to favor the president.

These informal briefings offered more insight into the administration's programs than the daily briefings did, thus earning Gergen the informal recognition by the Washington press corps of the "chief spinmeister" of the Clinton White House, but he did not eclipse the press secretary. Said Gergen: "My view is that the press secretary must have unquestioned access to any meeting he wants to come to, so that he knows the nuances and disagreements and where the lines are drawn—so he knows better what to say and how to say it."[47]

In an effort to bolster Dee Dee Myers's credibility, Gergen restored Myers to the traditional role of the press secretary—replacing Stephanopoulos as the president's chief spokesman. Once she took hold, she was accepted by the male-dominated Clinton inner circle and did a highly professional job. In addition to being the first woman (See Foreword, p. xi), she was the second youngest press secretary ever, at the age of thirty-five.

Myers was succeeded by three more press secretaries under Clinton, starting with Mike McCurry (1994–1998). McCurry had been an authoritative spokesman under Secretary of State Warren Christopher and knew the ropes in Washington politics. From 1988 to 1990, McCurry had served as director of communications for the Democratic National Committee, and also as press secretary for the presidential campaigns of John Glenn (1984), Bruce Babbitt (1988), and Bob Kerrey (1992), as well as the 1988 vice presidential campaign for Lloyd Bentsen. McCurry was respected by the White House press corps for his dry humor, competency, and personal warmth.

McCurry had the bad luck of being in the job of press secretary during the Monica Lewinsky scandal. He made a point of not asking

Clinton about the truth of the matter, but preferred to remain at arm's length. From the time the story broke on January 21, 1998—a year and a day after Clinton's second inauguration—the press relentlessly demanded that McCurry explain what the president was thinking and what he intended to do—even up to the impeachment hearings. McCurry literally stonewalled the questions—quietly and with a smile—saying he would not respond to any questions about the scandal but would leave that to Lanny Davis, special counsel to the president from 1996 to 1998 and Clinton's spokesman for personal legal issues.

Few if any members of the White House press corps, however, blamed McCurry for taking himself out of the spotlight when it came to the sex scandal. Davis—an outspoken supporter of the president's—was a valuable asset in terms of talking about Clinton's accomplishments with talk-show hosts. "It is certainly possible," Davis wrote in his book, "to view the Lewinsky episode as unique and not comparable to the prior abuses of the scandal machinery seen in the previous two decades. One conclusion cannot be overlooked, however. When all was said and done, there was no criminal sanctions for his conduct in the Lewinsky matter and the rest of the so-called Clinton scandals were mostly smoke and little fire."[48]

While Salinger was the first spokesman to permit "live" press conferences by John Kennedy, McCurry is perhaps best remembered as the first press secretary who allowed "live television" to broadcast the press secretary's own daily briefings. This had its advantages and disadvantages. For some newsmen, it was an opportunity to show off their toughness on television. One such correspondent was ABC newsman Sam Donaldson. His first stint in the press room spanned 1977 to 1987, the second from 1998 to 1999, when the briefings first went live. Donaldson—one of the most flamboyant and aggressive questioners ever seen in a White House press conference—commented on the introduction of TV on NPR's "On the Media" program on September 29, 2000: "I think it was a great impact on the briefing process, and, I think, negatively, and I've thought that for years. And I noticed the other day that [Press Secretary] Mike McCurry, the man who had instituted that process, said he thought it was one of his mistakes, and I agree."

Indeed, when McCurry started allowing TV media to carry his daily press briefings live, he profoundly changed the daily ritual. Donaldson added: "In the White House briefing room, the press secretary for whichever administration—it doesn't matter—comes out to say only what the President wants him to say and no more. And, of course, reporters want to know more and want to talk about maybe the bad news, not just the good news. So it can get very tense at times, and you go back and forth. And when people see this on television, they say, well, what are these nasty, vicious dogs of the press doing assailing that fine, upstanding individual [the press secretary]."

When McCurry stepped down in 1998, he was succeeded by Joe Lockhart, a tough-talking, hardworking spokesman with a glint in his eye—and even a smile—who handled the press during the frustrating and toughest times from October 5, 1998, to September 29, 2000, during the Clinton impeachment trials. He had shuttled back and forth from ABC and CNN jobs to press secretary positions with Senate and presidential candidates, including Walter Mondale and Michael Dukakis, before joining Clinton. Lockhart was followed, briefly, by Jake Siewert, press secretary from September 30, 2000, to January 20, 2001. He closed out the Clinton presidency and was faced with numerous questions about the president's pardons as well as trivia such as what the Clintons took from the White House on their way out.

George W. Bush entered the White House with great expectations, even though he had won a controversial victory. He selected a staff around him, including his press secretary, that he knew would be loyal to him.[49] He picked Ari Fleischer as spokesman; he had worked as deputy communications director for Bush's father's 1992 reelection campaign and had prior experience as a spokesman for several congressmen. Fleischer was bright, tight-lipped, distant, but occasionally showed a dry sense of humor that could only help the Bush administration's image. He took the initial fire from the press at the outset of the Iraq war and during the ensuing controversies about the war. He remained in his post for two years, replaced by Deputy Press Secretary Scott McClellan on July 15, 2003.

McClellan, another Texan, was Governor Bush's traveling press secretary during the 2000 presidential election and became White House deputy press secretary. McClellan was cautious—even reticent at times—in his dealings with the press and was known to repeat the same answer over and over again in response to the same question that one or two reporters would continue to ask, hoping he would give a different answer. McClellan was a business-like press secretary who often replied with short answers and was sometimes evasive when he did not know the answer. In point of fact, however, McClellan made it a point to check with his sources before every press conference to make certain he knew the facts.

[*Author's Note*: That made it all the more surprising when, more than a year-and-a-half after he had left office with a warm exchange of words between the president and himself at a White House press conference, the Associated Press carried a story picked up by a number of other news sources that McClellan had written a book, *WHAT HAP-PENED, Inside the Bush White House and What's Wrong With Washington.* In it, he reportedly revealed that he had unknowingly lied to the press as a result of receiving false information about a scandal involving the "outing" of a CIA operative by high-ranking White House officials, including the president, the vice president, and several top-ranking aides.][50]

On April 26, 2006, Bush showered praise on McClellan and replaced him with Tony Snow. Snow previously worked for President George H. W. Bush as chief speechwriter and deputy assistant of media affairs. His selection as press secretary was initially cast in a negative light by several critics due to some of his past negative comments about Bush. In his new position, Snow required as a condition for joining the Bush team that he be given "a seat at the table" during the administration's internal policy debates.

Snow is a genial person who prides himself on getting along with the media through a mixture of humor and straight talk. Previously, he had served as the first host of FOX Sunday News, a morning interview and roundtable program produced by Fox News. Snow is an erudite, well-mannered, good-looking spokesman who has even won over many former Bush-bashers.

Nobody embodies the image of the modern press secretary better than Tony Snow. Perhaps he symbolized a new kind of spokesman— the "celebrity press secretary," who travels the political landscape himself making speeches to drum up support for his boss's domestic and international policies. In this way, he brought a new and refreshing approach to his job by doubling as a spokesman for the administration's programs on the pro bono speech circuit as well as in the White House.

The experimental combination of roles raised some eyebrows but few complaints. He was, indeed, the chief spokesman for President Bush and both he and the public knew it. He earned high marks for being thorough and as helpful as he could be to the media. And he proved to be the model of what a press secretary should be: well-informed, comfortable with the press, good-humored, and—above all—he had the trust of the president and, again, everyone knew it. He was a master at getting across his viewpoint in a way that sounds sincere and believable.

In an interview Snow described his role as "the person who expresses the President's views on whatever the issues of the day are. When the press wants to figure out the president's position, I'm there to do it for them." Suppose he does not agree with some of the president's major policies?

> This is a question I get a lot of. Fortunately I have never been forced into that kind of dilemma. If it got to the point where I thought it would cost me my credibility, I would have no choice but to walk away. Fortunately, I have never been placed in that position mainly because I agree with the President on all the big stuff.

Snow says he is present at what is called "policy time" in the White House every morning where all the senior staff sits down with the president and you hash through things.[51] Asked how he feels about the word "spin," Snow responded:

> Spin is really a pejorative term that people try to use to say that they are getting something less than the truth, the whole truth, and nothing but the truth. One of the things I try to do is to take the spin out of questions because a lot of times there would be presumption embedded in the questions that are themselves questionable. Either they rely on a false reading of facts or a false analysis of the situation. So I think that probably more than most press secretaries, I will start by trying to de-spin the question so that we have a greater opportunity to give a straight answer.

Snow, upbeat and soft-spoken, describes his experience:

> I love the job. I love the fact that for one, you are the in the White House and part of the senior staff and play an active part of a presidency that is not only historic in terms of the problems we are forced to confront but also the way we are doing it. I love working with the president. I love the personal relationship with him. I really like working for the press and the constant intellectual stimulation of dealing with changing issues and for somebody who has been in politics and in policy as long as I have, it just doesn't get any better.

What are the ideal background credentials for someone to become a presidential press secretary? "Certainly you need to understand national politics and you have to be loyal to your principal for whom you are working and, at the same time you have to understand the needs of the press. And realize that reporters are doing their best to tell the story and figure out what the facts are and it's your job to accommodate them the best you can," Snow says.

Snow was succeeded by Dana Perino, who was the acting White House press secretary while Tony Snow underwent treatment for a recurrence of colon cancer. On September 14, 2007, Snow resigned, saying that he wanted to earn more money to support his family. At the time his government salary was $160,000 a year—modest in comparison with the hefty stipends he had received from his previous television jobs as news commentator and host.

President Bush announced Perino as his replacement. She is the second woman to serve as a presidential press secretary. Her background is in television public affairs reporting and she had also worked for two different Colorado congressmen, as a staff assistant for one and then as press secretary to another. She also has served as spokesperson for Attorney General John Ashcroft at the Department of Justice in the Bush administration and as director of communications for the White House Council on Environmental Quality. In 2006, she was named by Bush as deputy assistant press secretary to the president.

Press secretaries generally do not like the word "spin." But they do, in fact, use it by another name: public relations, or putting the best face on the president. Indeed, the one veteran White House press corps correspondent who has seen more press secretaries come and go than anyone else is Helen Thomas. Her opinion about spin? "I don't believe there has been any administration that has not tried to manage, control, censor, or 'spin' the news from the White House. It goes with the turf and reflects the efforts of image-makers to always try to put the president's best foot forward. How the press reacts to that manipulation is another story. . . . The government can present its position, but then it is up to the reporters to find the *real* [Italics in original] story."[52]

Even some scholars have analyzed the process of spin. One dissertation, "Caretaker of the Presidential Image," states that White House press spokesmen are

> the individuals whose charge is to assist the President in presenting himself and his policies—[and present] the Presidential image . . . in the best possible light, in whatever fashion and through whatever medium the President chose. In addition to possessing generalized skills in public relations, advertising, the media, and other related fields, they also must become marketing experts in the art of merchandizing the President.[53]

Yet another academic study, "Historical Trends in Questioning Presidents, 1953–2000," has concluded that the compressed time period for getting the news out has brought additional pressures on White House press secretaries from reporters ever anxious to get straight answers to their questions. The UCLA study provides clear evidence of this phenomenon. The study measured reporters' attitudes toward presidents over time; it found that, indeed, the press has grown more hostile with the arrival of each new presidency, thus raising the stakes on the vital importance of the quality and integrity of press secretaries' briefings to the press. The study reported that "all trends thus point in the same general direction, indicating a long-term decline in journalistic deference to the president and a rise in more aggressive forms of questioning . . . The White House press corps thus remains a force to be reckoned with."[54]

Summing up, here is how one of the greatest newspapermen in history, Merriman Smith of the United Press International—who covered Roosevelt and Truman as a White House correspondent and who was famous for initiating the "Thank you, Mr. President," at the close of each press conference, explained the role of the press in a sentence: "The most direct channel of communication, the most frequently used line between the President of the United States and the public is the White House correspondent."[55]

The renowned presidential historian Doris Kearns Goodwin once wrote that her goal in writing about historic figures is "to bring empathy to our subjects so that the past can truly come alive, even if just for a few moments."[56] In this spirit, I have tried to emphasize the attributes and skills of presidential press secretaries, all of whom have played a critical role in American history. They have worked long and hard to keep our democracy—with all of its warts—alive and well in good times and in bad. I admire all of the presidential spokesmen and women for the extraordinary contributions they have made collectively to this nation and toward making it a more perfect union.

## NOTES

1. Thomas, Helen, *Watchdog of Democracy? The Waning Washington Press Corps and How it Has Failed the Public* (New York: Scribner, 2006), p. xiii.
2. Thomas, *Democracy*, pp. 57–58.
3. Author's interview with Dana Perino, September 12, 2007.
4. Author's interview with Tony Snow, June 14, 2007.

5. Safire, William. *Safire's New Political Dictionary: The Definitive Guide to the New Language of Politics.* (New York: Random House, 1993), p. 598–599.

6. Salinger, Pierre. *P.S.: A Memoir* (New York: St. Martin's Griffin, 1995), p. 119.

7. Safire, *Dictionary*, pp. 598–599. Moyers speaking to the National Newspaper Association in 1966 about his role as Lyndon Johnson's press secretary.

8. Thomas, Helen. Panel discussion on "The Presidency and the Press," Lyndon B. Johnson School of Public Affairs, 1976.

9. Rather, Dan. Panel discussion on "The Presidency and The Press," Lyndon B. Johnson School of Public Affairs, 1976.

10. National Public Radio broadcast, January 21, 2005.

11. Safire, *Dictionary*, pp. 733, 740–741. Safire states "As a verb meaning 'to whirl,' *spin* dates back to Old English; by the 1950s, the verb also meant 'to deceive,' perhaps based on 'to spin a yarn.' Functional shift occurred in the nineteenth century, turning the verb into a noun *spin*, used for the curve or twist put upon a ball in cricket (in billiards, that spin is known as *English*), just as [baseball] pitchers nowadays 'put spin' on baseballs. As a current noun, *spin* means 'twist' or 'interpretation,' from the combined senses of twisting fiber and telling tales. . . . *Spin doctor* may be based on the slang sense of the verb *doctor*, as in illegally "doctoring" records; the noun phrase was perhaps built on the analogy of *play doctor*, a writer who fixes an ailing script. An earlier German term that may have led to the political *spin doctor* is *Kopfverdreher*, which literally means 'head turner' and figuratively suggests 'mind bender.' *Spin* terms have several derivatives, from *spin control* by *spin doctors* or *spinmeisters* who have formed a *spin patrol* operating in an area called *spin valley*."

12. Author's interview with William Safire, December 14, 2006.

13. Author's interview with Dana Perino, September 12, 2007.

14. Author's interview with Tony Snow, June 14, 2007.

15. Author's interview with Scott McClellan, October 27, 2006.

16. Author's interview with Ari Fleischer, May 16, 2006.

17. Author's interview with Jake Siewert, November 17, 2005.

18. Author's interview with Joe Lockhart, December 13, 2005.

19. Author's interview with Mike McCurry, December 6, 2005

20. Author's interview with Dee Dee Myers, December 5, 2005.

21. Author's interview with Marlin Fitzwater, June 15, 2006.

22. Author's interview with Larry Speakes, July 17, 2006

23. Author's interview with Jody Powell, December 7, 2005.

24. Author's interview with Ron Nessen, May 1, 2006.

25. Author's interview with Jerald terHorst, June 15, 2006.

26. Pamphlet, "The Presidency and The Press," edited by Hoyt Purvis, from transcript of seminar at the Lyndon B. Johnson School of Public Affairs, 1976.

27. Author's interview with Ben Bradlee, October 23, 2006.

28. Gergen, David. *Eyewitness to Power: The Essence of Leadership, Nixon to Clinton* (New York: Simon & Schuster, 2000), p. 336. Safire, *Dictionary*, p 158.

29. Jackson, Brooks, and Kathleen Hall Jamison. *unSpun* (New York: Random House, 2007), p. vii.

30. Bernays was hailed for his pioneering work in public relations in Larry Tye, *The Father of Spin* (New York: Crown Publishers, 1998).

31. Harold Burson's Blog at Burson-Marsteller, June 14, 2007.

32. *The New York Times*, October 21, 1984.

33. Author's interview with Marlin Fitzwater, March 16, 2007.

34. Partington, Alan. *The Linguistics of Political Argument: The Spin-Doctor and the Wolf-Pack at the White House* (London: Routledge, 2003, ), pp. vi–vii.

35. Published in Cairo by AL-AHRAM, April 27, 2004, Issue No. 6684.

36. *History of Jacob Riis*. Available online at www.google.com.

37. Before FDR, George Akerson served as informal press secretary to President Herbert Hoover from 1929 until 1930. From 1930–1933, Theodore Goldsmith Joslin served in the same capacity for Hoover. They were followed by what historians refer to as the first "modern day" press secretary, Stephen T. Early, who spoke for Franklin D. Roosevelt. Early greatly expanded the role of press secretary. Today, the position still reflects his ideas and influence. Source: John T. Woolley and Gerhard Peters, *The American Presidency Project* [online]. Santa Barbara, CA: University of California (hosted), Gerhard Peters (database).

38. Levin, Linda Lotridge. *The Making of FDR: The Story of Stephen T. Early, the First Modern Press Secretary* (New York: Prometheus Books, 2007).

39. Transcript of FDR's press conference, August 27, 1940, FDR Library, Hyde Park, NY.

40. Tebbel, John, and Sarah Miles Watts. *The Press and the Presidency From George Washington to Ronald Reagan* New York: Oxford University Press, 1985), pp. 466–467.

41. Schlesinger Jr., Arthur M. *A Thousand Days: John F. Kennedy in the White House* (Boston: Houghton Mifflin, 1965), p. 207.

42. Kotz, Nick.*Judgment Days, Lyndon Baines Johnson, Martin Luther King, Jr., and the Laws That Changed America* (Boston: Mariner Books, 2006), p. 179.

43. Moyers, Bill. *Moyers on America: A Journalist and His Time* (New York: New Press, 2004), pp. 99–100. Moyers writes:

> When I look back at the twists and turns in my life I still puzzle at the unexpected and unwanted detour I took through the Office of the White House press Secretary. The first time the president asked me to be his spokesman I declined. [Moyers was serving at the time as deputy director of the Peace Corps under President John F. Kennedy]. He asked me again, and again I declined. The third time he didn't ask. My arm still hurts. That night, I told my wife that "this is the beginning of the end." "Why?" she asked. "Because no man can serve two masters," I answered. Less than two years later I was gone.

44. Stated in a letter of resignation by Jerald terHorst to Ford dated September 8, 1974.

45. Brady's wife, Sarah, persevered in Congress until she successfully got a new gun law passed. It included restrictions on purchases and background checks on all buyers of handguns, passed in her husband's name. The "Brady Bill," as it became known, passed both Houses, and President Bill Clinton signed it into law on November 30, 1993.

46. Hertsgaard, Mark. *On Bended Knee: The Press and the Reagan Presidency* (New York: Farrar Straus Group, 1988), p. 27.

47. Dickinson, Mollie.*Thumbs Up: The Life and Courageous Comeback of White House Press Secretary Jim Brady* New York: William Morrow and Company, 1987), p. 445.

48. Davis Lanny, *Scandal: How 'Gotcha' Politics is Destroying America* (New York: Palgrave Macmillan, 2006), p. 174.

49. Weisberg, Jacob. "Beyond Spin. The Propaganda Presidency of George W Bush" *Slate*, December 7, 2005.

50. According to an Associated Press report on November 20, 2007, in a forthcoming book McClellan recounted the 2003 news conference in which he told reporters that White House aides Karl Rove and I. Lewis "Scooter" Libby [a Cheney aide] were "not involved" in the leak involving CIA operative Valerie Plame. "There was one problem. It was not true," McClellan wrote, according to a brief excerpt released by the publisher, Public Affairs Books. "I had unknowingly passed along false information. And five of the highest-ranking officials in the administration were involved in my doing so: Rove, Libby, the vice president, the president's chief of staff, and the president himself."

The excerpt, posted on the Web site of publisher Public Affairs, raised new questions about what went on in the West Wing and how much Bush and Cheney knew about the leak. For years it was McClellan's job to field—and often duck—those types of questions. Plame maintained the White House quietly outed her to reporters. Plame and her husband, former Ambassador Joseph Wilson, said the leak was retribution for his public criticism of the Iraq war. The accusation dogged the administration and made Plame a cause celebre among many Democrats, the AP story said.

McClellan's book, *WHAT HAPPENED: Inside the Bush White House and What's Wrong With Washington,* was not due out until the spring of 2008, and the excerpt released was merely a teaser. It doesn't get into detail about how Bush and Cheney were involved or reveal what happened behind the scenes, the AP reported.

In the fall of 2003, after authorities began investigating the leak, McClellan had told reporters that he'd personally spoken to Rove, who was Bush's top political adviser, and Libby, who was Cheney's chief of staff. "They're good individuals, they're important members of our White House team, and that's why I spoke with them, so that I could come back to you and say that they were not involved," McClellan said at the time.

Both men, according to McClellan, however, were involved. Rove was one of the original sources for the newspaper column that identified Plame. Libby also spoke to reporters about the CIA officer and was convicted of lying about those discussions. He is the only person to be charged in the case. Since the 2003 news conference, the official White House stance has shifted and it has been difficult to get a clear picture of what happened behind closed doors around the time of the leak. McClellan's flat denials gave way to a steady drumbeat of 'no comment.' And Bush's original pledge to fire anyone involved in the leak became a promise to fire anyone who "committed a crime." Bush addressed the issue in July 2007 after commuting Libby's 30-month prison term. He acknowledged that some in the White House were involved in the leak. Then, after repeatedly declining to discuss the ongoing investigation, he said the case was closed and it was time to move on, according to the AP.

51. Author interview with Tony Snow, June 14, 2007.

52. Thomas, Helen, *Watchdog of Democracy*? p. 57.

53. Burkholder, Donald R. "Caretaker of the Presidential Image," A Dissertation, submitted to the Office of Graduate Studies, Graduate Division of Wayne State University, Detroit, MI, in partial fulfillment of the requirements for the degree of Doctor of Philosophy, November 16, 1973, pp. 1–3, 142.

54. "Historical Trends in [the press] Questioning Presidents, 1953–2000," study by Clayman, Steven E., Sociology Department, UCLA; Marc N. Elliott, RAND; John Heritage, Sociology Department, UCLA; Laurie McDonald, RAND.

55. Smith, Merriman. *Thank You, Mr. President* (New York: Harper & Brother, 1946), p. 1.

56. Goodwin, Doris Kearns. *Power and the Presidency* (New York: BBS Public Affairs, 1999), p. 43.

# CHAPTER 1

## HOT WAR

*"A Date Which Will Live in Infamy"*: 1941
Franklin Delano Roosevelt
STEPHEN EARLY

Three days before the Japanese attacked Pearl Harbor on December 7, 1941, a story was published in the *Chicago Tribune* reporting that the president had sent confidential letters to the secretary of the Navy and the secretary of War asking them to draw up plans to be ready for a possible attack by Japan on the United States. Shortly after 9 A.M. on December 4,[1] reporters hurriedly converged on the office of Stephen (Steve) T. Early, the president's longtime close friend and highly respected White House press secretary, clamoring for confirmation of this startling news which, it appeared, had been leaked by a government source.

"What about the *Chicago Tribune* story?" a reporter asked Early, who had been Roosevelt's spokesman for nearly a decade and had Roosevelt's agreement to liberalize the press policy. Taking his time answering, the tall, slim, 170-pound, fifty-two-year-old Early wanted to calm down the anxious group of journalists and make it appear as if there was nothing unusual afoot. In other words, he wanted to spin the story as not very important. The press knew that Early was extraordinarily knowledgeable, so much so that he could give a reporter an instantaneous backgrounder on something as erudite as the gold standard and something as mundane as when the next briefing would take place. Early knew that he had credibility with the press and he intended to put it to good use.

When he responded to the question, Early said he hoped that the reporters would "accommodate" Roosevelt as they had for most of his presidency. Here are a few excerpts of his briefing on December 4, 1941, which clearly show Early's desire to enlist the assistance of the press up front, lay down the ground rules for reporting, and prevent as much damage to the White House as possible by issuing a warning. In other words, it was an exercise in spin.

EARLY: You are going to be as helpful as you can, aren't you? I think all that can be said is that I have not talked to the President about this story. I am not in a position to confirm or deny it. I will say that there are two branches—one in the War Department and one in the Navy Department—both known as War Plans. It is their duty, even in peace-time, to study and to devise plans for all possible emergencies. Even the most improbable situations are studied and planned. An unlimited national emergency has been declared. If they lacked plans to meet this emergency or any phase of it they would be guilty of inefficiency. And, if the President of the United States permitted them to face an emer-gency without a plan, he, too would be guilty of negligence. I think that statement will cover it.

*Q: One thing I would like to ask. What is the—(interruption).*
EARLY: Well, I just want you to know that I have not seen the plan, nor has anyone else around the White House and the President himself has not seen the letter published. The President did his job. He has not seen the plan nor has anyone around the White House seen it.

*Q: What has been the rule around here about publishing presidential letters that have not been released?*
EARLY: The rule is not to publish unless permission is given. Those who have gotten copies of the president's letters they desire to pub-lish and have asked for permission, usually have received it. In this instance no request was received at the White House for permission to publish it.

*Q: Steve, do you know if the President has seen the story?*
EARLY: No, I don't. I haven't spoken to the President about the story.

*Q: Here is a very important story out. May we request you to ask the Presi-dent whether it is true or not?*
EARLY: I will talk to the president at the first opportunity.

*Q: Steve, I don't know whether you want to answer this question—but here is a very difficult problem that our editors are up against. Are we free now to print extracts from this, other than saying that the Tribune printed it, and if they did say the Tribune printed it, would they also be guilty of any violation of the so-called voluntary censorship? [FDR had asked the media to voluntarily censor itself and check with Early before publishing any news of reports that the United States was preparing for war.]*

EARLY: I don't think anyone would be correct in printing it unless they got it from the government source with permission to use it.

*Q: Will any investigation be made?*
EARLY: Undoubtedly, it will be investigated by the government.

*Q: Will this investigation be ordered by the Commander-in-Chief?*
EARLY: Suppose you received a letter from the President of the United States and you were in his Cabinet as Secretary of War or Secretary of the Navy. You were told to proceed with these conferences. Then you awoke some morning to see it printed in the papers—a very confidential document. What would you do?

*Q: I would investigate.*
EARLY: I think he will, too. Promptly.

*Q: Off the record—this is probably one of the unfortunate episodes of a new paper being started in Chicago [The Chicago Tribune]?*
EARLY: That's as far as I can go now, fellows.

The reporters held off on the story for a day. This is but one example of how Early, attempting to avoid what today is called a "feeding frenzy," skillfully eased the concerns of the White House press corps by saying he could not confirm the truth of the published story and that he would come back to them after he had spoken to the president. It was a calculated effort to take the heat off of the White House.

Two days later, on Saturday, December 6, Early was in a lighthearted mood, informing the press:[2] "I can't see any news for pads and pencils or even minds this morning. I think the President decided you fellows have been so busy lately and Christmas is coming so close that he would give you a day off to do some shopping." Despite the fact that Early made light of the news, one reporter asked, "I suppose he [Roosevelt] is over at the house writing a declaration of war, isn't he?" Early answered with humor: "He is over at the house. He is not writing. At the present time, he is shaving." Pressing Early, another reporter asked: "I hope it isn't one of those nervous-lid days—on again—off again."

Early responded: "No, I can only give you the lid right now. The only appointment he has is with the budget director at 11:15 to sign some papers—routine. No appointments for today and none for tomorrow, and I don't assume there will be."

On December 7, the first Sunday in December, Roosevelt was working in his study with Harry Hopkins, his close friend and aide, when the phone rang at about 1:30 P.M. "Mr. President," said Secretary of the Navy Henry Knox, "it looks like the Japanese have attacked Pearl Harbor." Hopkins told the president he thought someone had made a mistake. However, the president told him it might well be something the Japanese would do in the middle of discussing peace in the Pacific with the United States. Minutes later, Admiral Harold Stark called the president with the same news. Roosevelt sat for a moment to keep his composure. His wife Eleanor later described him as "completely calm. His reaction to any event was always to be calm. If it was something that was bad, he just became almost like an iceberg, and there was never the slightest emotion that he allowed to show."[3] Roosevelt then wrote something that would become an historic note. He picked up the phone and called the White House switchboard to reach Steve Early.

Early was relaxing in his study in his home on Morningside Drive in the northeast section of Washington, D.C. As was his custom, he was scan-reading the morning papers to bring himself up to speed on any news that might be developing. He normally did not conduct any business with reporters from his home. Suddenly, however, the telephone connecting his home with the White House rang, disrupting the calm quiet of the afternoon. FDR was on the line. The president said in a deadly serious voice: "I have a very important statement. It ought to go out verbatim."

Moving with a sense of urgency he had long developed as a former reporter who well understood a newsman's thirst for big news, Early arranged through the White House operator for an immediate hookup with the three wire services—the Associated Press, the United Press, and the International News Service. At 2:22 P.M. Eastern Standard Time, Early released a statement to the press at the White House from his home, dated December 7, 1941. It read:

> Following is the first message telephoned Mr. Early by the President and which Mr. Early telephoned simultaneously from his home to the A.P., U.P., and I.N.S., and had the White House switchboard repeat to the entire newspaper list: "The Japanese have attacked Pearl Harbor from the air and all

naval and military activities on the island of Oahu, the principal American base in the Hawaiian Islands."[4]

He asked the White House operator to send the same message to radio networks, the British Press Service, and all New York and Washington daily newspapers, the *Chicago Tribune*, *The Baltimore Sun*, and the *Philadelphia Record*. Early telephoned a second statement about five minutes later: "A second air attack is reported. This one has been made on Army and Navy bases in Manila." Early then left his home for the White House about 2:35 P.M.

At 3:10 P.M. Early issued another statement from the White House, which read:

> I can give you just a little additional information to what I flashed to your offices a while ago: So far as known now the attacks on Hawaii and Manila were made wholly without warning—when both nations were at peace—and were delivered within an hour or so of the time the Japanese ambassador and special envoy had gone to the State Department and handed to the Secretary of State Japan's reply to the Secretary's memorandum of November 26, 1941.

As soon as the information of the attacks on Manila and Hawaii was received by the War and Navy Departments, it was flashed immediately to the president at the White House. The president directed the Army and the Navy to execute all previously prepared orders looking to the defense of the United States. The president was with the secretary of War and the secretary of the Navy. Steps were being taken to advise the congressional leaders.

Five minutes later, at 3:15 P.M. Early made another announcement to the press:

> So far as the President's information goes and so far as we know at the moment, the attacks are still in progress. We don't know, in other words, that the Japanese have bombed and left. In other words, both of the attacks are still in progress as far as we know.

Yet another announcement was released at 3:20 P.M.

> The President has just received a dispatch from the War Department reporting the torpedoing of an Army Transport—1300 miles west of San Francisco. Fortunately, the Transport was carrying a cargo of lumber rather than personnel of the Army.

At 4 P.M., eager to do all he could to keep the press informed, Early held a press conference in the White House, during which he told reporters that the president had just decided to call a cabinet meeting for 8:30 that evening and then to have congressional leaders from both parties join with them in a joint meeting at 9 P.M. He said the president was assembling all of the facts as rapidly as possible and that, in all probability, he would as quickly as possible make a full informative report to the Congress. That report probably would be in the form of a Message from the president to Congress. One half hour later, Early informed the press that "he is employing his time at the moment in dictation to [his secretary] Miss Grace Tully of a first draft of a Message for the Congress." At the same time, the press secretary brought the reporters up to date with the latest report from Hawaii. This report, he said, indicated there has been heavy damage in a dawn attack on Hawaii and that there has been heavy loss of life. Early continued to issue bulletins at 6:10 P.M. and 6:22 P.M. saying the president had been advised that Guam was also under attack. At 7:40 P.M. William (Bill) Hassett, an assistant to the president and deputy press secretary, stepped in for Early to tell reporters that preliminary reports from the War Department "showed that the losses in the Army only on the Island of Guam and Oahu were about 104 dead and over 300 wounded."

And on it went, with the media covering what turned out to be the beginning of, arguably, the most important story of the twentieth century.

Putting Pearl Harbor in historical perspective, Roosevelt had signed a bill calling for compulsory military service [the draft] on September 16, 1940. In 1941 a number of actions were taken by President Roosevelt, who everyone anticipated—and many Republicans feared—would get America involved in the war against Germany. Alarmed by the prospect of the United States entering the war, reporters queried Early about what actions the president was taking to avoid war. In what could be labeled a soft spin, Early tried to tamp down such fears and ease public panic by making it a point to explain to the White House reporters that FDR was not talking about ordering U.S. convoys into action. He had also told reporters in the spring of 1941 that he had not discussed with the president what powers might be exercised under a proclamation of a full national emergency. Nor did he know if any executive orders from the president would-be forthcoming.[5]

Nonetheless, the press was afraid of a pending war based on recent events. On September 4, after the U.S. destroyer *Greer* was attacked by a German U-boat while on convoy escort, Roosevelt issued a stern order to "shoot on sight" any Axis war ships within the American

Defense Zone; on November 26, Secretary of State Cordell Hull delivered an ultimatum to Japan to withdraw its troops from China and Indochina; on December 1, the Japanese government rejected the terms offered to Emperor Hirohito to use his influence to avoid war; and, finally, on December 6, fearing the worst, Roosevelt appealed to Emperor Hirohito to avoid war in the Pacific.

The next day, December 7, even as Japan's ambassadors had finished conferring with their American counterparts in Washington, a wave of 189 Japanese planes attacked the U.S. Pacific fleet at anchor in Pearl Harbor, sinking twenty-nine ships, destroying 347 planes, and killing 2,403 U.S. personnel. Furthermore, Steve Early revealed at a press briefing that the Japanese also attacked American bases in the Philippines, Guam, and Midway, as well as British bases in Malaya and Hong Kong, but he tried to offer a tidbit of "good" news by adding that, "a number of U.S. bombers arrived from San Francisco" to join in the fighting. [As it turned out, the full impact of the December 4 story leaked to the *Chicago Tribune* about the president's top-secret plan to prepare for an attack by Japan set off a lengthy investigation by a congressional board of inquiry, which issued its detailed findings in a report made public four years later—on December 11, 1945.][6]

The next day, Monday, December 8, following a message delivered personally by Roosevelt to the a joint session of the Senate and the House of Representatives that took just six minutes and thirty seconds, the United States formally declared war on Japan. Congress swiftly approved a resolution in only thirty-three minutes. At exactly 4:10 P.M. the president signed the resolution. The vote had been 82 to 0 in the Senate and 388 to 1 in the House. Early immediately released a statement from Roosevelt that put the blame on Germany for "pushing Japan into the war." Although he asked not to be quoted, Early laid the groundwork for future presidential actions by offering his own interpretation—or spin—of the president's message to reporters at the White House. He explained that in wartime the government has the power to take whatever steps it needs to meet the emergency.[7]

At the same time, after consultation with Early, the War Department issued wartime bans on making public information deemed of possible value to the enemy. In a memorandum to the media, the department specifically described such: "movement of transports within or without territorial waters, information about the number of troops, designation of units, and disposition of forces overseas." In addition, all outgoing cables and cables from Hawaii and the Philippines would be censored at the source. The officials also asked the press to refrain from publishing, without clearance from the government, from crews, or members of their families.

The next day, Tuesday, December 9, Early called a brief press conference to spin the White House story that during this crisis, America was being well defended. He told the press that the newspapers had printed essentially all the details received by the government from the war zone. One reporter asked: "How was it, if the reports from San Francisco are true, that Japanese planes could get so near our West Coast?" Early responded: "You can be sure that the Army and Navy, on the President's instructions, are on the alert for defense." Early added that the rumors about aircraft off the West Coast were only one phase of the entire war, stating that "the picture is much larger." In a further effort to reassure relatives of Americans who happened to be in Japan, Early reported that the State Department in Tokyo, the Embassy in Peking, the Consulate General in Shanghai, the Consulate General at Hong Kong, and the Consulate at Manila were safe and well.

He was obviously looking for crumbs of good news amid all the chaos—clearly an attempt to do what he could to keep the public as calm as possible. Early also felt that the president should reinforce the gravity of the tragedy so that all Americans clearly understood the situation. His point was that the president could only call upon people to sacrifice if they knew the enormity of the setback to the nation. Working with a team of White House officials, Early strongly advised the president to put into motion one of the oldest axioms of public relations: If you have bad news, get it out before you are asked about it. Ironically, that gives you credibility. FDR did just that in a nationwide radio address in which he bluntly told the American people that "so far all the news has been bad. . . . Our enemies have performed a brilliant feat of deception," he said, "perfectly timed and executed with great skill."

At the same time, Roosevelt informed Americans that adverse news would continue to be made public in detail, but only if it would not "prove valuable to the enemy directly or indirectly." The fine hand of Steve Early could be seen when the president made a plea for restraint by the media in the national interest:

> To all newspapers and radio stations—all those who reach the eyes and ears of the American people—I say this: You have a responsibility in the nation now and for the duration of this year. If you feel that your government is not disclosing enough of the truth, you have every right to say so. But—in the absence of all the facts, as revealed by official sources—you have no right in the ethics of patriotism to deal out unconfirmed reports in such a way as to make people believe that they are gospel truth.[8]

The next day, December 11, Roosevelt—after conferring with several top aides—including Early—gave a speech to Congress asking it to unanimously recognize that "a state of war exists between the United States, Germany and Italy."[9] The battle was joined. From a logistics point of view, Early knew right away that the press would be hungry for news—any kind of news. So he prepared some notes for a press briefing he held on Wednesday, December 17. At the outset a reporter asked whether a censorship [by government agencies] had begun. The press secretary was prepared. He would tell it like it was, but spinning his reply with a rationale for the censorship. He answered the question by emphasizing why it was in the best interests of everyone to set up a pre-clearance system within the government agencies headed by Byron Price, a former leading journalist at Associated Press. A couple of days after the bombing of Pearl Harbor, President Roosevelt had asked Price if he would become head of a new organization that he intended set-ting up to control civilian censorship.[10] Early explained the reason for such action was that a good many people in the government informa-tion centers had never functioned before in a time of war, and they needed to be brought up to speed quickly on what they could and could not release. Early assured reporters, at the same time, that infor-mational sources in the departments would remain open to them and would remain decentralized. If anyone had an "exception"—such as an "exclusive" story—they could immediately appeal to Price's office.[11]

Early was a one-man band when it came to effective public relations for FDR, who trusted him implicitly. As two scholars of White House press secretary history wrote:

> The whole administration was a public relations effort, and Early was right in the middle of it. Early took charge and ran publicity for the government. Roosevelt always kept Early informed. He always had access to the president. Early played a major role in Roosevelt's decision to hold frequent press con-ferences, to allow newsreel cameras to film re-creations of his radio addresses, and to provide services for the special needs of the larger White House press corps that covered Washington when the New Deal took office.[12]

One professor, Linda Lotridge Levin, the best-informed expert on Early, spent twelve years researching and writing a book on him. She comments:

> There were several reasons why Steve Early was so effective as the press secretary to a sometimes demanding and mercurial President Franklin D. Roosevelt. The two men were friends, beginning with Early's assignment as

an Associated Press reporter to cover the Navy Department when Roosevelt was undersecretary of the Navy. Their relationship continued, both professionally and personally, until Roosevelt was elected President. By then Early had spent nearly two decades as a journalist, for the Associated Press and for Paramount Newsreel in Washington, and the result was that he was well known in the journalism community. Finally, in the first week of the Presidency, Early, with FDR's blessing, told reporters he would have an open door policy and would hold his own daily press conference, both of which he continued throughout the Depression and the war. He also made sure that Roosevelt met weekly when possible with reporters. The convergence of their friendship, Early's successful journalism career, and the opening of the White House to the press on a regular basis led to one of the most effective relationships between the press and the White House in American history.[13]

It should be noted that to meet the demands of an increasingly large pool of radio reporters, Roosevelt brought in yet another press advisor, J. Leonard Reinsch, a well-known name in radio broadcasting, who assisted with the press and also served as a key advisor to the president. Reinsch, from Illinois, majored in advertising at Northwestern University while working at Radio Station WLS. He started in radio in 1924. He was instrumental in getting an association with Governor Cox in Dayton, Ohio, in 1934 and was sent to Atlanta in 1939 when the governor purchased *The Atlanta Journal* and the *Georgian* and the radio stations. In 1942 he was put in charge of the three radio stations.

Reinsch and other presidential advisors felt that Roosevelt was at his best manipulating of public opinion in his "Fireside Chats" by radio and that was by far his best medium of communication to the public—because its content could be completely controlled.

*The Death of a President: 1945*
Franklin Delano Roosevelt
STEVE EARLY/JONATHAN DANIELS

On April 12, 1945, with the end of World War II in sight, Franklin Roosevelt quite unexpectedly suffered a cerebral hemorrhage and collapsed while relaxing at one of his favorite places—Warm Springs, GA. Bill Hassett, the deputy press secretary who had been so helpful to Early when the Japanese attacked Pearl Harbor in 1941, had accompanied the presidential party at Warm Springs. He immediately contacted Early and Jonathan Daniels in Washington. Early accompanied Eleanor Roosevelt to Warm Springs, and at 6 P.M., shortly after arriving, Early called a press conference with himself and Admiral Ross McIntire, the Navy Surgeon General. McIntrye reported that the cerebral hemorrhage "came out of the clear sky." Early used that information in an official statement he put out stating that "the President was given a thorough examination by seven or eight physicians, including some of the most eminent in the country. He was pronounced organically sound in every way." We now know that was not the full story and that Early had, in effect, covered up the extent of Roosevelt's illnesses from the first day he went to work for him.[14]

Early moved swiftly to make certain the press was fully informed. He held a press conference later in the afternoon and told reporters of Mrs. Roosevelt's reaction: "I am more sorry for the people of this country and the world than I am for us." Early said Truman had asked Mrs. Roosevelt, "What can I do?" and the First Lady had replied by asking the question in return to Truman—"Tell us what we can do. Is there any way we can help you?" That same day, Daniels remarked to a reporter: "He [FDR] seemed *all things to all men* [italics added]," thus coining a phrase that was to last to the present day.[15]

Daniels also wrote in his diary that the moment he heard the news from Steve Early, he went to the vice president, Harry S. Truman, and told Truman the press were asking for a quotation from Truman. Daniels suggested something to the effect that he [Truman] intended to vigorously prosecute the war against both our enemies. Truman nodded his head in agreement, adding: "We will prosecute the war with all the vigor we have, to a successful conclusion on both fronts, the east and the west."[16]

At 6:30 P.M., anxious to show the world that there was a smooth transition and, therefore, to allay any fears the public might have, Early called a makeshift press briefing in the lobby of the White House to announce that the vice president was in the Cabinet Room meeting with members of the Cabinet. "He has asked me to say, for the time being, that he prefers not to hold a press conference—[he] merely wants to say that it will be his effort to carry on as he believes the President would have done." With the clock under Woodrow Wilson's portrait registering 7:09 P.M., in a somber ceremony, Truman was sworn in with all the members of Roosevelt's Cabinet present by Chief Justice Harlan F. Stone exactly two hours and thirty-four minutes after Roosevelt's sudden death at Warm Springs. Looking very sober and slightly apprehensive, Truman became the thirty-second president of the United States in a ceremony lasting not more than a minute in the Cabinet Room.

At about 7:30 P.M. Jonathan Daniels emerged in the pressroom and held a short briefing with the reporters to announce that President Truman would be at his White House desk at 9:00 the following morning. He was asked about what Truman had said up to that time and this gave him an opening to frame the news in the best possible context: Daniels told the press that the president would carry out the policies of FDR, and then read Truman's statement. "The world may be sure that we will prosecute the war on both fronts, East and West, with all the vigor we possess, to a successful conclusion."

Finally, at 1 A.M. on April 13, Early held one more briefing at which he read a telegram from Winston Churchill to Mrs. Roosevelt. It read:

> I send my most profound sympathy in your grievous loss. It is also a loss of the British nation and of the cause of freedom in every land. I feel so deeply for you all. As for myself, I have lost a dear and cherished friend, which was forged in the fire of war. I trust you may find some consolation in the glory of his name and the magnitude of his work.

Early held another briefing at 4 P.M.on April 13 to lay out the logistics for the hordes of newspaper reporters and photographers who wanted to cover the funeral. In addition, he handed out a press release, which was a digest of opinion from selected radio commentators, by name, who had talked about Roosevelt on April 12 on the air. It was Early's last tribute to his boss in the form of flattering words about the president. It was, in effect, the final spin of a press secretary who loved his president and wanted to make certain that the commentaries of some leading journalistic names in America would be part of the legacy that Early had contributed to Roosevelt's memory.

Early had frequently taken the initiative to make certain Roosevelt would comment on topics he wanted to address. One observer said: "Early was the first person to plant ideas in the minds of reporters in an offhanded way about what questions to ask. This would bring results in most cases. In preparing for press conferences, Early started out by having a chat with FDR on current hot topics. In some cases, newsmen submitted their questions in advance so they knew that FDR would have ready answers. In those days, if Early was out of town he used telegraphic communications with the president."[17]

As for the special relationship between Early and Roosevelt, rarely have two men in American politics had a lasting and close friendship that benefited both men and the nation as well. Early, a reporter for the Associated Press, met Roosevelt while Early was covering the 1912 Democratic Convention, which nominated Woodrow Wilson. After serving in World War I with an infantry regiment and with the U.S. Army newspaper, *Stars and Stripes*, Early returned to the United States and was asked by Roosevelt to be the advance man for FDR's 1920 vice presidential campaign. After the election, Early returned to the Associated Press, and in 1927 became the Washington representative of Paramount News. After the election of 1932, Roosevelt asked him to serve as one of the White House secretaries and be responsible for press relations. He was an obvious choice as Roosevelt's first press secretary because he was perceived as one of FDR's closest cronies, along with Louis Howe and Harry Hopkins, but few could have predicted that he would remain at FDR's side as long as he did—essentially because of their personal friendship and Early's personal dedication to helping a friend in some of the toughest times this country has ever known.

One of the key reasons why Early was so successful is that when he was appointed, he asked for and received Roosevelt's assurance that the president would cooperate in making himself more accessible to the press than many of his predecessors had in the Oval Office. As two scholars of Roosevelt wrote: "What is most remarkable about Roosevelt's press relations is their consistency. Until the end, he controlled and used the correspondents along the lines he had laid down at his first press conference, and, although he may have alienated some reporters in the process, they were in the minority."[18]

Deferring to Steve Early's advice, at his first meeting with the press on March 8, 1933, FDR laid down a new set of rules.

> We're not going to have any more written questions and of course while I cannot answer seventy-five or a hundred questions, because I simply haven't got the physical time, I see no reason why I should not talk to you ladies and gentlemen off the record just the way I have been doing in Albany and the way I used to do it in the Navy Department down here. In regard to news announcements, Steve and I thought that it was best that street news for use out of here should be always without direct quotations. In other words, I don't want to be directly quoted, with the exception that direct questions will be given out by Steve in writing.

FDR also said "background information" would be material that could be used by reporters but must not be attributed to the White House; and "off the record" would mean confidential information which would be given only to those who attend the conferences. FDR further asked the reporters not to repeat off-the-record confidential information either to their own editors or associates. In other words, this would be only for those present at the time. FDR then told reporters he had just signed an application to be a member of the Press Club—much to their delight.[19]

At presidential press conferences in the president's oval-shaped office, Early and two of FDR's other close aides—son James Roosevelt and Marvin McIntrye—sat next to the president, who was in his swivel chair behind his office desk. The press conferences—always held on Tuesdays at 4 P.M. and on Fridays at 10:30 A.M.—were considered by the press as some of the most exclusive gatherings in Washington. Only bona fide members of the White House Press Association were permitted to attend. The press conferences ended when questioning began to peter out and Early would then bring it to a close with a resounding, "Thank you, Mr. President," a tradition that has endured ever since, although members of the press corps themselves take on the task.

Early died on August 11, 1951, at the age of 61, from a heart attack. He was highly praised by Harry Truman: "Through that long and eventful period [1933–1945] whether the crisis was due to domestic depression, national preparedness or the prosecution of the most devastating war in human annals, he was always at the side of President Roosevelt as secretary, friend and sagacious adviser."[20]

---

## The End of World War II: 1945
### Harry S. Truman
### CHARLES ROSS/JONATHAN DANIELS

---

Harry Truman took hold almost immediately. Early stayed on at Truman's request. On April 16, 1945, Early returned from Hyde Park and Roosevelt's funeral to help Truman. Daniels, William Hassett, and Roosevelt's longtime friend Sam Rosenman were still at the White House. Truman held what he called his first "radio and press conference" on April 17, 1945. He would later share in his memoirs his insights into how vital the press was as an avenue to successfully get his views across to the public. "It is often helpful," he wrote,

> for a president to judge, from the questions put to him by the reporters, what is going on in the minds of the people. Good reporters are always in close touch with developments and with what the people want to know. They try

to do an honest job of reporting the facts. But many of their bosses—the editors and publishers—have their own special interests, and the news is often slanted to serve those interests, which unfortunately are not always for the benefit of the public as a whole.

But every so often Truman was known to exhibit public outbursts at reporters, some of whom he castigated for not being entirely accurate—at least in his eyes.[21]

Five days later, on April 21, 1945, Early was sworn in as a special assistant to Truman to help with the transition. However, by mid-May Early had accepted a job with Pullman-Standard Car Manufacturing Company, and by June 1, 1945, he had left the White House—with Daniels and Charles G. (Charlie) Ross, a native of Independence, MO, and a lifelong friend of Truman's, assuming his press secretary duties. Ross, who had been appointed by Truman on May 15, 1945, was a Pulitzer Prize–winning journalist. Ross would remain quiet if Truman made mistakes, unlike Early, who would interrupt Roosevelt if he could add some important information to Roosevelt's reply to a question. Still, Truman and Ross were intimate friends and confidants. Early's shoes were hard to fill because he had his own special relationship with FDR and with the press. In response to a request from the press for transcripts of all presidential press conferences, Early happily obliged.

Ross was popular as an individual among reporters because they knew very well that Truman trusted Ross. They also knew that Ross was one of few Roosevelt aides who could bluntly tell Truman behind the scenes when he thought the president was making a mistake and that Truman would listen to him. In addition, Truman counted on Ross, among others, to gauge what the man in the street was thinking better than any so-called political expert or newspaper story could divine. Ross was credited with introducing the practice of briefing the president just prior to a press conference with a shorthand version of any complicated new initiatives that any government agency was about to undertake.

At 1:55 P.M. on Tuesday, May 7, 1945, Daniels rounded up the White House reporters and handed out a statement quoting Truman saying that he had agreed with the London and Moscow governments that he would make no announcement with reference to surrender of the enemy forces in Europe or elsewhere until a simultaneous statement could be made by the three governments. Daniels announced at 6:20 P.M. that day that Truman was gearing up for a major speech broadcast to the nation on the next day, which, Daniels noted, happened to be Truman's sixty-fifth birthday. There had been speculation—labeled an "open secret" in the press—about a pending announcement of victory in Europe. Obviously upbeat about what was about to be announced, Daniels declined to comment on whether it would be V-E Day, saying only that the statement "speaks for itself."

Nonetheless, there was a build-up of speculation and extraordinary interest in the White House press office. It was a pressure-packed day on the news front. Observers—particularly those who were going to have to do something about managing the official recognition of V-E Day—were left fairly exhausted, especially because *The New York Times* headline on May 8, 1945, read: "THE WAR IN EUROPE IS ENDED. SURRENDER UNCONDITIONAL. V-E WILL BE PROCLAIMED TODAY. OUR TROOPS ON OKINAWA GAIN." Many felt that after a false armistice [report] on April 28 and that day's [May 7] apparently premature break, the formal news, when it came, would be anticlimactic. Nonetheless, the streets in Washington, D.C., were thronged with people, including a large crowd outside the White House. When Truman decided to cancel previously announced plans to leave the White House for luncheon at 1 P.M. and decided instead to have lunch at his desk, the tension got worse. Raising hopes even more, Elmer Davis, director of the Office of War Information, was seen entering the White House to see Daniels to get some documents. But reporters could not find out what it was about. And the press corps, which was described in the newspaper as "the size of a small mob," hung out at the White House awaiting word. Truman's radio broadcast, announcing the unconditional surrender of Germany marking the end of the war, which he described as "a solemn but a glorious hour," was officially announced on May 8. At the suggestion of his press secretary, at the very outset of his broadcast, the president said: "I only wish that Franklin D. Roosevelt had lived to witness this day."

Shortly afterward came what could be—in retrospect—the most momentous news in American war history: the dropping of an atomic bomb nicknamed "Little Boy" on August 6, 1945, on the city of Hiroshima, the site of what American officials said was a major military supply depot and port of embarkation for the Japanese. The bomb was reported to have killed 160,000 people of the city's population of 318,000, according to one newspaper account. The announcement made by a sober President Truman made it plain that is was one of the scientific landmarks of the century and ushered in what Truman called "the age of atomic energy." The news of Hiroshima was announced to the world at 11 A.M. on August 6, 1945, by Assistant Press Secretary Eben Ayers, who distributed the news release that stunned the world.

At this point, it should be noted that Russia declared war on Japan on August 8, an action that Ross was asked for comment on during his August 9 press briefing. He said the word came directly to the president and Secretary Byrnes in a message from Foreign Minister Molotov. It came about 2:30; the president made the announcement at 3:00, at the same time the announcement was made in Moscow. He waited long enough to make sure the times were synchronized. In a radio report to the nation, Truman threatened Japan with obliteration by an atomic bomb unless it surrendered unconditionally, noting that bombs would have to be dropped on war industries and civilian lives would be lost. "We have used it," he said, "against those who attacked us without warning at Pearl Harbor, against those who have starved and beaten and executed American prisoners of war, against those who have abandoned all pretense of obeying international laws of warfare. We have used it to shorten the agony of the war, in order to save the lives of thousands and thousands of young Americans."[22]

When the Japanese failed to surrender immediately, a second bomb nicknamed "Fat Man" was dropped on the city of Nagasaki on August 9, killing about 10,000. American forces were readied for an occupation. Meanwhile, at the White House on Tuesday, August 14, Charlie Ross told the press: "It looks as if our long vigil is coming to an end soon. That is the present outlook. The Japanese reply to our message last Saturday is now in the hands of the Swiss. It was received at Berne, where it had to be decoded and then encoded for transmission to America, to the Swiss Legation here. That takes some time, several hours." He then explained that the surrender would be made simultaneously to the four Allied governments.

On August 15, 1945, Ross announced that the president would hold a press conference the next morning. The Japanese surrendered on August 15, with its government broadcasting a statement indicating it was prepared to "issue such orders as may be required by the Supreme Commander of the Allied Forces" and that the Four Powers had outlined in the Potsdam Declaration of July 26, 1945. Truman announced that the Japanese had surrendered and it marked the end of the war— some three years and 250 days since the bombing of Pearl Harbor. *The New York Times* headline on Wednesday, August 15 read: "JAPAN SURRENDERS, END OF WAR! EMPEROR ACCEPTS ALLIED RULE; M'ARTHUR SUPREME COMMANDER; OUR MANPOWER CURBS VOIDED."

At his first briefing at the White House at 10:30 on Saturday, September 1, Ross announced that he had just received word that the Japanese surrender ceremony on the battleship Missouri in Tokyo Bay would go on the air at 10:30 A.M. "on the split second," adding that would be September 2 in Tokyo.[23] The formal surrender documents were signed by General Douglas A. MacArthur and by Aamoru Shigemitsu on behalf of Emperor Hirohito on the U.S.S. Missouri in Tokyo on September 2, 1945—in a formal ceremony attended by some 315 correspondents and cameramen—thus closing a chapter in American history that no press secretary to the president of the United States could have imagined possible. At the White House, Daniels and Ross conveyed to the reporters at the White House, who had worked with them for so long during the prolonged crisis, a mood of somberness rather than jubilation. They had all been through too much to be anything but.

At the regular morning briefing on Friday, September 7, Ross showed both imagination and good judgment when he notified the assembled press corps that in fifteen minutes—at 10:45 A.M.—that he had an especially newsworthy item up his sleeve. "I shall and try to make this brief," he said, with a smile, "because I think you will want to attend the very interesting ceremony to beheld in the President's Office at 10:45 when the Japanese surrender papers which arrived last night [by carrier] will be presented to the president. The plan, as I get it," Ross explained, "is for the carrier to hand them to the Secretary of War, who will then present them to the President. But you can see that for yourselves." That was one last spin by Ross to make his new boss look good.

---

### The Korean War: 1950–1953
Harry S. Truman
CHARLES ROSS/JOSEPH SHORT/ROGER TUBBY

---

The Korean War began suddenly on Sunday, June 25, 1950, when the North Korean army struck in the pre-dawn hours, crossing the thirty-eighth parallel. The invasion of South Korea came as a surprise to the United States and the other Western powers; in the preceding week Dean Acheson of the State Department had told Congress on June 20, 1950, that no such war was likely. The South Korean Army had 65,000 soldiers present for duty, and was deficient in armor and artillery. There were no large foreign, including American, combat units in the country when the invasion began, but there were large American forces stationed in nearby Japan.

That same night, Truman called a meeting of his key advisers—including Secretary of State Dean Acheson and Secretary of Defense Louis Johnson—at Blair House. The attendees avoided reporters' questions on the way in and, thanks to the skillful logistical planning by Assistant Press Secretary Eben Ayers, left by the rear door without being seen. Ayers told the press they did so because "their cars were parked in the back." Ayers also said he could not reveal anything that had been said at the meeting. The next morning, June 26, 1950, about 10:00 A.M., the president met with Press Secretary Charles Ross and a few other advisers in his office to discuss the contents of a press release on the Korean invasion. He handed each a draft release that had been sent over by Secretary of State Dean Acheson, and that the president had revised. Ross made several suggestions for editorial reasons, all of which were accepted by the president, then left to brief the press. Ross, grim-faced and all business, then made copies of the release and handed them out to reporters at the start of his news briefing at 11:45 A.M. The president's statement noted that the U.S. government, in accordance with the resolution of the Security Council, would vigorously support the effort of the council to determine this serious breach of the peace because American military personnel in Korea would be directly affected.

On Tuesday, June 27, Truman, acting independently, announced that he had ordered U.S. air and Navy units into combat in North Korea because the United States was a member of the United Nations, to enforce a "cease fire" order given by the U.S. Security Council two days before. North Korea labeled the council's order "illegal," and on June 28 Russia also called the UN police action "illegal." It would not be until Thursday, June 29, however, that Truman tried to clarify the murky situation by responding to a reporter's question: "Mr. President, everybody is asking in this country, are we or are we not at war?" The president replied, "We are not at war." Truman characterized the U.S. combat operations in Korea as a "police action" for the United Nations against an "unlawful bandit attack" on South Korea.[24] Nonetheless, a full-scale ground war was under way. Truman ordered U.S. naval and air forces to stem the North Korean advance, but they were not allowed to attack north of the thirty-eighth parallel, and especially not into Chinese or Russian territory.

The initial units sent in came from the U.S. occupation forces in Japan under the command of popular General Douglas A. MacArthur. Truman ordered MacArthur to transfer munitions to the South Korean army and to use air cover to protect the evacuation of American citizens.

Truman also ordered the Seventh Fleet to protect the island of Taiwan. And so the war unfolded as the public watched and listened and learned about the struggle between the UN forces and the considerable might of the North Korean Army ground troops backed by the Chinese communists.

The administration released some encouraging news but it was also followed by some setbacks. Inside the White House, the press operation underwent a sudden, unexpected change when, shortly after a press briefing on December 5, 1950, Charlie Ross died at his desk in his White House office of a heart attack. Truman turned to Steve Early to step in and he did until a successor, Joseph H. Short Jr. of *The Baltimore Sun*, took over. Short immediately got the help of Roger Tubby, who stayed with Truman until his term was up. Tubby had worked in Bennington, VT, for the *Bennington Banner* as a reporter and editor. During the war, he was part of the Board of Economic Warfare, and when that became the Foreign Economic Administration he became the assistant to the administrator. Subsequently, he went to the Department of Commerce as director of information of the Office of International Trade; and after that to the Department of State in 1946. In 1950, he went to the White House as the assistant White House press secretary under Joseph Short. In 1953, John Foster Dulles asked him to come back to the State Department and be his press secretary.

By April of 1951, with the U.S. military forces locked in what seemed to be a stalemate, Joe Short had become fully acquainted with his job and with the reporters covering Truman. Short, a former reporter for the Associated Press, *Chicago Sun*, and *Baltimore Sun*, knew very well how the press operated and felt quite at home with his former colleagues.

Thus, it was Short who was faced with the delicate task of explaining to the press why President Truman had fired General Douglas A. MacArthur, the supreme commander for the Allied forces. Even before Truman gave a national radio speech explaining why he was relieving MacArthur, the topic became controversial at the White House. On April 11, 1951, Short handed out a packet of previously classified documents that served as concrete proof of the general's refusal to follow Truman's orders when he talked openly—without clearance from the White House—of carrying the fight in Korea northward to the Chinese communists. Short, in effect, was justifying Truman's powers as commander-in-chief and laying the groundwork for what would soon follow. Many historians see this confrontation as the classic example of civilian authority over the military in U.S. history.

Short told the reporters:

> Several instances have occurred recently which indicate that it is questionable whether General MacArthur is in full sympathy with this Government's policy. The first one of these background documents is a Presidential directive regarding the clearance of statements and speeches on foreign policies and military subjects. As is indicated by the documents that directive went to General MacArthur December 10, 1950. I also call your attention to an exchange of telegrams between the Joint Chiefs of Staff and General MacArthur. This exchange makes clear that General MacArthur in substance recommended against the arming of additional South Koreans.

Asked about the president's announcement relieving MacArthur of his command, Short replied: "The President was authorized by the United Nations to select the military commander in Korea, and it is under that authorization that he relieved MacArthur and appointed General [Matthew A.] Ridgeway." Short then announced that the president would address the nation that night at 10:30 "on our policy in the Far East." It was that night that Truman issued his explanation to the American people in a twenty-one-minute speech that he was "trying to prevent a third World War." He added: "A number of events have made it evident that General MacArthur did not agree with that policy. I have therefore considered it essential to relieve General MacArthur so that there would be no doubt or confusion as to the real purpose and aim of our policy."

Short then made certain the White House reporters fully understood and appreciated the reasons for the action the president had taken regarding an extremely popular war hero who had a major following back home. He summed up three reasons why the general was relieved: He failed to clear statements as required by the president's orders; he had challenged the president as the spokesman for American foreign policy; and he had openly disagreed with the president's clear policy of trying to limit the war to Korea. He reminded the press of the generations-old tradition in American government that the military is subordinate to the civilian leaders. But MacArthur, he said, ignored the chain of command and wrote letters about what the United States should do in Korea—which amounted to an escalation possibly involving the Chinese. The Korean War ended with the armistice agreement singed on June 26, 1953, between the commander-in-chief [President Truman], United Nations Command, and the supreme commander of the Korean People's Army and the commander of the Chinese people's volunteers.

After Short died in September 1952, Truman had Tubby as his last—and arguably most helpful—press secretary. One journalist, Edward T. Folliard, the distinguished White House correspondent for *The Washington Post*, said of Roger Tubby: "I thought that Roger Tubby was very good as a press secretary. He was a very calm fellow, and we got along very well with him."[25] Tubby, in an interview long after he left office, said he enjoyed working for Truman because,

> Truman felt the important thing was to set forth clearly whatever the policy was [and] I believed strongly in Mr. Truman's positions . . . I think that the press were very fond of Mr. Truman and liked him, not only for the kind of human being he was and is, but liked him for his candor. I think they were fond of him and I think they had a respect for him. So, having this kind of an ambiance between the working press . . . and the President, made it a lot easier for the rest of us.[26]

Indeed, Truman valued the friendships he made with the press; he often played poker with reporters as a form of relaxation at the White House. His casual conviviality often put reporters at ease, but they also knew how distant and combustible he could be at press conferences. Once in a rare while, when he felt a question was inappropriate, he would bluntly tell a reporter: "It's none of your business."

*The Vietnam War: 1964–1975*
Lyndon B. Johnson–Richard M. Nixon
GEORGE REEDY/BILL MOYERS/GEORGE CHRISTIAN

The justification for the Vietnam War, historians say, stemmed from a North Vietnamese attack on two U.S. destroyers in the Gulf of Tonkin thirty miles off of the shores of Vietnam on August 2 and August 4, 1965. On August 3, Johnson, who had replaced the departing Pierre Salinger with Press Secretary George Reedy,[27] invited the White House reporters to the Oval Office and the president read a brief statement to the effect that he had ordered the U.S. Navy to fire back at any ships that attacked U.S. vessels.

The next day, in a television address to the nation the president said he had ordered the navy to send planes to destroy North Vietnam's gunboat capability. Reedy, responding to questions from reporters that same day was asked about details of Johnson's retaliatory actions. He ducked the military questions by referring them to the Department of Defense. At that point, Helen Thomas—always the reporter who went straight to the heart of the matter—asked:

Q: *Was there any contact with [Soviet Premier Nikita] Khrushchev via the hotline or anything?*
REEDY: I never discuss the hotline, Helen.

Q: *Any communication with the Soviet Union?*
REEDY: I know of no direct communications. Obviously—I know of no communications. I wouldn't comment on them if I did.

On August 7, 1964, determined to back the president in this time of crisis, Congress passed a resolution, requested by Johnson, giving prior approval of "all necessary measures" that the president may take "to repel any armed attack" against the United States "to prevent further aggression."[28] Critics would later say that, in effect, Congress had given the president a green light to prosecute a war in any way he wanted. The president, however, had a strategy. He would first attempt a peaceful solution. The following April 7, having been elected in his own right to the presidency in a landslide over Senator Barry M. Goldwater of Missouri, Johnson strengthened his hand with a memorable speech at Johns Hopkins University, in which he stated that the United States would be willing to engage Hanoi, without any prior conditions at all, in diplomatic discussions to try and end the steadily escalating, bloody war in Vietnam. The speech was widely interpreted by the media as an attempt by the president to take the high road, but nonetheless the war would continue with ever-increasing use of force. Large numbers of American combat troops began to arrive in 1965.

As the president stepped up the war in 1965, Reedy was force-fed information from the military that, in essence, he questioned himself, but he played the role of a good soldier and handed it out. For example, in one briefing during this crisis, a reporter asked him a question that would seemingly involve the president's judgment about how the war was going in Vietnam: The reporter asked: "On Vietnam, is it the President's view that the situation in Vietnam will have to improve?" Reedy replied, simply, with what is known in the press as a non-answer. He said: "When that situation does change obviously we would reassess it." At the risk of being unresponsive, Reedy was not about to be trapped into speaking for the president's views on how the war was proceeding, how many troops were being killed, or any other strategic information. In fact, one reason for Reedy's reluctance to speak for LBJ is that he was not comfortable spinning the news as a public relations man.

Reedy had been a reporter for United Press International in Washington, D.C., before joining Johnson's Senate staff in 1951. He continued to work for Johnson during LBJ's presidential campaign in 1960, and when Johnson became vice president. When Pierre Salinger resigned as press secretary in August 1964, Reedy replaced him. During the escalation of the American involvement in Vietnam beginning in March 1965, press questions over the veracity of the Johnson administration's public assessments of the war led to charges of a so-called credibility gap. In 1965 Reedy took a leave of absence over his disagreement with Johnson's Vietnam policies. In 1968 he returned to the White House to work as a special assistant shortly before Johnson's surprise announcement that he would not seek reelection.

After that, Reedy let the world know how he felt about the questionable figures he was releasing when his book *The Twilight of the Presidency* was published. From the outset, wrote Reedy, Johnson exaggerated the good news from Vietnam and either played down or underestimated the casualty figures. As Reedy explained: "How valid were any of the figures out of Vietnam? I never had—and do not now have—suspicions that they were fictitious. But they were all based on 'assumptions,' and assumptions control the answers that one gets from a computer." Reedy was seen by Johnson and others as a scholarly, highly intelligent, somewhat overweight person with a huge mop of unkempt hair, which Johnson often made fun of.[29]

Reedy offered a philosophical overview of Lyndon Johnson's presidency and the Vietnam War: "In talking to friends about the presidency," he said,

> I have found the hardest point to explain is that setbacks often impel presidents to redouble their efforts without changing their policies. This seems to be perversity because very few of us have the opportunity to make decisions of colossal consequences. When our projects go wrong, it is not too difficult for most of us to shrug our shoulders, cut our losses, and take off on a new tack. Our egos may be bruised. But we can live with that. It is a different thing altogether when we can give orders that can lead to large-scale death and destruction or even to economic devastation. Such a situation brings into play psychological factors that are virtually unconquerable. Suppose,

for example, that a president gives the military an order that leads to the deaths of several soldiers in combat. Can any human being who did such a thing say to himself: "Those men died because I was a goddamned fool! Their blood is on my hands." The more likely thought is: "Those men died in a noble cause and we must see to it that their sacrifice was not in vain." This, of course, could well be the "right" answer. But even if it is the wrong answer, it is virtually certain to be the one that will be accepted. Therefore, more men are sent—and then more. Every death makes a pullout more unacceptable. Furthermore, when a large amount of blood has been spilled, a point can be reached where popular opposition to a policy will actually spur a president to redoubled effort in its behalf. This is due to the aura of history that envelops every occupant of the Oval Office. He lives in a museum, a structure dedicated to preserving the greatness of the American past.[30]

A one-time reporter for the United Press, Reedy left his post because of a serious foot problem and took a leave of absence.[31]

What was Reedy's legacy working side-by-side with a dominant figure like Lyndon Johnson? Two journalism scholars, in a book about the presidency and the press, quoted Reedy's criticism of Johnson during the Vietnam War: "Gradually, a credibility gap began to develop as Johnson made statements that turned out to be wrong and denied rumors that proved to be true. . . . The credibility gap was beginning to open wider. Johnson made statements that turned out to be wrong and denied rumors that proved to be true." The authors continued:

> Reedy did his best to repair the damage, but it was a losing struggle. His conception, as he said later, was that the president had political problems, not press problems, but in fact they were inextricably mingled. Reedy was further handicapped by the fact that the correspondents were soon aware he did not have the full confidence of his boss—not that anyone else could have merited it. At the beginning they had supposed him to be close to the president as the result of their long association, but then it turned out that the president had a loudspeaker connection with the room where Reedy held his own meetings with the press and listened to the proceedings. When something disturbed him, he rushed out of his office and into Reedy's, bearing corrections and his own comments. Reedy said this only happened on one occasion.[32]

Reedy, reportedly under pressure from Lady Bird Johnson, resigned early in July 1965, at odds with the president over his Vietnam decisions. Both Johnsons [Lyndon and Lady Bird] wanted Bill Moyers as

Reedy's successor. After succumbing to LBJ's persuasive manner, Moyers agreed to add the press secretary's job to his other responsibilities on Johnson's staff. Moyers, another Texan, who had worked for LBJ's radio and television stations in Austin and later on his Senate staff, was also an ordained minister. At the time of Kennedy's assassination, he was deputy director of the Peace Corps. Arriving in the hornet's nest of the Press Office at the age of twenty-nine, Moyers was a far more intellectual and thoughtful man than most of his predecessors. Although he did not like the job he did his best for eighteen months.

Moyers was a man of principle and, he has since admitted publicly, he reluctantly took on the press secretary post because he was far more interested in remaining with Johnson as an adviser on substantive domestic and foreign issues. Said Moyers:

> I still puzzle at the unexpected and unwanted detours I took through the Office of White House Press Secretary. The first time the president asked me to be his spokesman, I declined. I said that I wanted to return to my post as deputy director of the Peace Corps, from which I had taken leave when the assassination of John F. Kennedy thrust LBJ into the presidency, or to keep working on domestic policy and legislation from my corner office in the White House. He asked me again, and again I declined. The third time he didn't ask. My arm still hurts.[33]

Moyers, nonetheless, did his best to adhere to Johnson's spin. At the outset of 1966, for example, Moyers faced a barrage of questions at a morning press briefing about Johnson's failure to keep the Congress fully informed about the war. From the outset, there were rumblings from various members of Congress that Johnson was too deeply involved in the military strategy of the war and had not kept the Congress fully informed. Following, excerpts from Moyers's January 25, 1966, briefing and Q&A with the press, as an example of spin:

*Q: Bill, do you think the President might consult with the Senate Foreign Relations Committee on the future course of the Vietnam War as suggested by Senator [William] Fulbright?*

MOYERS: I think this last year every member of Congress received a full briefing at the White House as well as constant briefings on the Hill in which they were given access to our thinking on Vietnam and the facts we had on Vietnam. That process, I believe, will continue this year. [He] is very anxious to have everyone's views on Vietnam, whatever opinion they hold, whatever the viewpoint they wish to express.

He thinks it is important that he has this information and these views and will continue to solicit it. Just precisely how that will be done is moseying. I don't know at this time.

*Q: Bill, to put it another way, does the President feel there is any obligation to consult with the Foreign Relations Committee or any other committee in Congress before making decisions with respect to the conduct of the war?*
MOYERS: The Constitution gives the President, as Commander-in-chief, the responsibility for decisions, but President Johnson has always felt and still feels that consultation with the Congress on every aspect of foreign policy is desirable and I think the record since he has been in office clearly underscores and underlines that very basic feeling.

At this point, the press asked a series of questions that suggested Johnson had not met enough personally with Fulbright and that there was a difference in opinion as to whether his consultations had been frequent enough. Moyers was asked specifically how often the president had met with Fulbright, an opponent of the war.

MOYERS: I don't know the specific times, but I do know that he has been meeting with Fulbright.

*Q: Bill, are you suggesting this difference does not exist in reality but it is something the press invented?*
MOYERS: There are differences of opinion on policy between the Executive Branch and the Congressional Branch dating back to the beginning of the system, and that is important to the system that everyone expresses an opinion. I am saying the personal disenchantment that I read about so constantly in the press is not, in my opinion, justified by any fact or incident of which I am aware.

At a briefing on February 7, 1966, after the president had met in a plenary session at Camp Smith, Hawaii, with Nguyen Ngoc Linh, official spokesman for the Republic of South Vietnam, and a number of other top-ranking Vietnamese officials and generals, as well as top-ranking American officials and military men, Moyers summed up for the reporters what Johnson had said at the meeting:[34] "The President first stressed the importance of the Republic of South Vietnam continuing to exercise the leadership and stay in the lead in the efforts of South Vietnam both militarily and socially and economically. He said, 'Unless you do, all that America does will be of no consequence.'" Moyers then read out another quote from the president addressed to the South Vietnamese leaders:

> Gentlemen, let me make clear our resolve and our determination to see this thing through. We, South Vietnam and the United States, are brothers in arms. We will not tire; we intend to work with you. We intend to help you. We intend to fight with you in defeating the Communist aggressor. While we are waging this effort, we will wage the other great effort in the South to make the dream of a better life a reality.

Moyers added his own spin to his briefing on what the president had said, when he emphasized Johnson's conclusions for the reporters: "The President concluded that, number one, aggression must be defeated; two, social misery must be ameliorated; three, a just society must be built. I think that summarizes it."

At an evening briefing that same day, Moyers departed from his practice of not giving his own opinion when he was asked how he thought the meetings between American and Vietnamese officials went. "The only observation I have is that talks are going along on substantive matters with a minimum of irrelevances, as long as they are going that well, in my opinion, he [President Johnson] will want to keep that momentum. Tonight's session was a very good session and I don't usually, as you know, attempt to characterize meetings."

Even Bill Moyers, the quintessential objective press secretary, could not resist an opportunity to give his boss a boost by spinning the outcome of the meetings.

Moyers had his own problems with Johnson's attitude, despite their long friendship stemming from their days in Texas. "President Johnson had ambivalent feelings about the press," he later said. "One day he would tell me to let them all in—'I want to see them.' The next day he'd say, 'I don't want to see the S.O.B.'s.'" Moyers added:

> There are two ways to be the press secretary. One is simply to report what the President wants reported. The other is to try to be analytical—to say what he wants said, but to tell what it all means. I tried to be the latter, but it didn't work. The mistake he [Johnson] made and the mistake I made was in my attending the National Security Council meetings. I learned there what was going on in Vietnam. And because I had at one time been one his chief advisers on domestic affairs, I tried to make some points at those meetings. It got so when I entered the room, the President would say, "Here comes Ban-the-Bomb Bill."

By 1967, it was clear to the world that the war in Vietnam was not going well. Nonetheless, Moyers, who had resigned on February 15, 1967—about two years after he became press secretary—became the publisher of the daily newspaper *Newsday* in Long Island, NY. Despite his unhappy experience as press secretary, he was still loyal to his old boss—predicting that Johnson's chance for reelection on April 15, 1968, were better than the polls indicated—in a speech to the 22nd Annual Citizenship Education Conference at Syracuse, NY. However, Moyers attached a condition to his prediction, saying that in 1968 LBJ would win if "he has convinced Americans that Vietnam is not a one-way street leading to a hopeless blind alley."[35] As it turned out, of course, Moyers read the future correctly—the war became an albatross around Johnson's neck precisely because Johnson could not convince the electorate the war was going better.

Meanwhile, Johnson had replaced Moyers with George E. Christian, who had the right political pedigree, having worked in Texas politics for a decade as former governor John B. Connally's press secretary. One of Christian's first tasks was to polish up the president's image. The president's attention was on major demonstrations against the war in Vietnam, a report from J. Edgar Hoover on "antiwar activity," and another report from Ambassador Henry Cabot Lodge on progress in the war. It was Christian himself, in a calculated risk, who—in response to questions—disclosed to the press a series of reports that were awaiting Johnson at his ranch in Texas.

The press secretary was asked if the antiwar activity referred to the report from Hoover, the FBI director, which dealt with mass protests by antiwar demonstrators in New York City outside the United Nations building and in San Francisco. Christian answered in the affirmative. One reporter asked Christian if it was unusual for the press secretary to disclose such information. "No," he replied, "it has been done before." He admitted that Hoover submitted such reports to the president whenever he had anything of interest. Christian added that the White House had not made most of the reports public. Christian said he would not comment on the protests themselves. As for the report from Lodge, Christian once again offered a little spin when he characterized it as containing evidence of "unmistakable progress" in cargo movement and management at the Port of Saigon, the capital of South Vietnam.

A few days later, on April 17, 1968, however, Christian was not as talkative. He declined to comment on a statement by former vice president Richard Nixon—gearing up for his second try for the presidency in 1968—while he was visiting Saigon. Nixon had told reporters: "It can be said now that the defeat of the Communist forces in South Vietnam is inevitable. The only question is, how soon?" Ironically, in a prelude to what he himself would do a year later, Nixon urged Johnson to order a sharp increase in the war effort. Political leaders who opposed the war, Nixon said, were giving aid and comfort to the enemy by contributing to the "monstrous delusion" that they represented more than a small minority—put by Nixon at 15 or 20 percent of the population—that wanted negotiations.

Christian's role in the fateful year of 1968—which turned out to be Johnson's last year in office—was described by two experts as follows:

> Viewers of American television got another bloody firsthand look at the realities of the war, and it marked a turning point in the public's view of both the war and Lyndon Johnson. Through it all, and through succeeding crises, George Christian exhibited the same unwavering loyalty and integrity that had appealed to the president and impressed the reporters, even though the credibility of Johnson and his military leaders was slipping rapidly. The celebrated "credibility gap" was probably the most explosive and significant element in the history of Johnson's press relations.[36]

Christian had a full plate in 1968. After the Vietnamese launched the Tet Offensive—which the American forces turned back—came a call for more troops from American generals in Vietnam, the announcement in March by President Johnson that he would not run for reelection, and the start of peace talks between North Vietnamese and American negotiators in Paris, with Ambassador W. Averell Harriman representing the United States.

Finally, on October 31, 1968, Johnson announced a complete halt to all American air, naval, and artillery bombardment. "I have reached this decision," he said, "on the basis of the developments in the Paris talks, and I have reached it in the belief that this action can lead to progress toward a peaceful settlement of the Vietnamese war." The announcement came just five days before the November elections—something which many veteran political observers believed the shrewd old politician scheduled to help the Democrats, specifically his vice president, Hubert Humphrey, who was the Democratic standard-bearer. It was a case of too little, too late.

Richard M. Nixon was elected in 1968 promising that he had a plan to end the war in Vietnam, but there were few outward signs that the newly elected president was following through, except for his appoint-ment on January 1, 1969, of Henry Cabot Lodge, former American am-bassador to South Vietnam, as senior U.S. negotiator at the Paris peace talks. On April 30, 1969, U.S. troop levels peaked at 543,000, with 33,641 Americans killed by then—a total greater than the Korean War. This raised some serious questions among the press. At a briefing on May 9, 1969, Nixon's press secretary Ron Ziegler was put on the spot. He was evasive and, because of the information he was given by Nixon aides, unknowingly spun his answers. For example:

*Q: Ron, it has been said in the past that President Nixon does, as you say, have a plan and a course of action set out to bring peace to Vietnam. It has been said recently, within the last couple of weeks, that that plan is proceeding according to its schedule or as has been expected. In light of all the questions that have come about, can we still say and refer back to the statement that Mr. Nixon's plan is going according to schedule?*

ZIEGLER: I think you can accurately say that the President is follow-ing a course of action and you can indicate what he has said publicly on this matter.

On June 8, 1969, in a public attempt to keep his promise, Nixon met with Republic of Vietnam President Nguyen Van Thieu on Midway Island and announced a troop reduction in Vietnam, which drew a mixed reaction at home. Ziegler hailed the announcement as a "break-through" for the president. In a further effort to bolster an image of peacemaker just before he took off for Bangkok, Thailand, Nixon met with reporters on Guam Island on July 25, with Ziegler laying down a rule that the press could report what Nixon would say but not for di-rect quotation—more as "background." When asked specifically what he meant, Ziegler replied: "Without quotation marks, to be more pre-cise, 'The President said,' (without quoting him directly) or 'The Presi-dent feels' or 'The President's objectives of the trip are.' " It was a bit of a letdown, however, when Nixon finally did meet with reporters and all he said was that he had no plans to go to Vietnam on this trip, but he would be meeting in Manila on July 27, 1969, with Asian leaders. The president assured them that he had not lost interest in their coun-tries because, as he put it, "Asia's where the action is."

At the same time, however, he made it clear that Asian problems would ultimately require Asian solutions. Ziegler traveled with Nixon on this trip and, as was usually the case, offered his advice. Nixon relied heavily on Ziegler, a quiet sort of man who was comfortable out of the spotlight in the shadow of a president whom he admired. On July 30, 1969, however, Nixon changed his mind and—despite the strenuous objections of the Secret Service—made a quick, dangerous trip to the war zone in South Vietnam, which combined public displays of loyalty to that country with intense private deliberations over future troop withdrawals and possible changes in military tactics. He mixed with the American troops, called the difficult war "one of America's finest hours," and said the war had been fought to allow the South Vietnamese "to choose their own way" and to "reduce the chances of more wars in the future." Nixon added, as he mingled with the troops, "What happens in Vietnam, how this war is ended, may well determine what happens to peace and freedom in the world."[37]

Unlike many of his predecessors, Ziegler—up to that time the youngest person ever to become press secretary at age twenty-nine—did not have a newspaper background. The White House press corps was delighted, hoping to take advantage of this lack of hard news experience. His background was in advertising. In 1962, he took his first political job as a press aide to Nixon adviser Herbert G. Klein in Nixon's unsuccessful campaign for governor of California in 1962. After Nixon lost that race, Ziegler joined H.R. Haldeman at the J. Walter Thompson advertising firm. Haldeman would later become Nixon's White House chief of staff. Ziegler had become a major figure in the 1968 election team and would continue to be Nixon's face to the public.

In 1973, in a newspaper interview, Ziegler described his role this way: "My job is mainly as a spokesman for the President, to communicate as directly as possible, to answer as closely as possible the way the President would answer. Despite what they say, I do have some friends among the press. [And] The President doesn't even mind." [Author's note: For more on Ziegler's controversial dealings with the press during the Watergate controversy, see Chapter 3, "Presidential Scandals."] In 1976, long after Ziegler had left Nixon, he was asked in an interview whether or not he was ever asked to evade the truth. Ziegler replied:

> Now, there are times when a press secretary is faced with a President of the United States—is faced with a situation where you cannot speak or cannot go into an issue and should not get into an issue—and that happens often. However, press secretaries do find themselves in a situation where *they do in fact lie* [italics added] because of the information that one of their colleagues gave them, which they felt to be true, and that ends up not to be true. So that is a dilemma that a press secretary faces.[38]

Nixon announced on December 30, 1972—without any warning—that he had ordered a halt to the bombing in North Vietnam and told Kissinger to return to Paris for peace talks. Deputy White House Press Secretary Gerald L. Warren put a rosy spin on this piece of news during a briefing for White House newsmen by stating, "as soon as it was clear that serious negotiations could be resumed at both the technical level and between the principals, the president ordered that all bombing be discontinued."

This was followed quickly on January 3, 1973, by the convening of the 93rd Congress, during which the Senate Democratic leader, Mike Mansfield, told his Democratic followers that he wanted to find out "whether there is legislative route to the end of this bloody [Vietnam] travesty." In the House of Representatives Speaker Carl Albert sought an "immediate" cutoff of appropriations to support the war. Meanwhile, administration officials made it clear that although negotiations were resuming in Paris, they cautioned against any undue optimism.

Ziegler offered no details about the talks but cautioned against a "growing antiwar mood on Capitol Hill, which he said could jeopardize the negotiations." He spun his statement this way: "Members of Congress should ask themselves if they want to take the responsibility of raising doubts in the minds of the enemy about the United States position and thereby prolong the negotiations. Our objective is to bring an end to the conflict in Vietnam through a negotiated settlement, but at such negotiations there can be only one negotiator." In an obvious attempt to build support for the president, Ziegler warned that Hanoi might be encouraged to "hold out" until Congress took some action. He also set the table for any failure in Paris by telling reporters that he hoped North Vietnam did not revert to the delaying tactics that they pursued in the past month that caused the talks to break down.

A short time later, on January 23, 1973, Nixon announced there was a cease-fire agreement that, he said, "brings peace with honor in Vietnam and Southeast Asia," signed in Paris. Ziegler reminded the press that the "peace with honor" phraseology had been Nixon's original public goal when he first took office in 1968. The agreement was signed in Paris on January 27, 1973. He then followed by announcing that the military draft had ended. But it had been America's costliest war with 529,000 Americans having fought in Vietnam, of which more than 50,000 died. There was no celebration in D.C. Deputy Press Secretary Gerald L. Warren told reporters: "Everyone was too busy or too tired."

Withdrawal of U.S. forces from Vietnam took time. By March 26, in response to a question asking for the number of military personnel left in Vietnam, Ziegler replied: "There are 825 military personnel connected with the 4-party Joint Military Commission. They, of course, will complete their work when the work of the Commission is completed."

*Q: Does this end the American military presence in Vietnam, and does the Commission go out of business on Thursday [March? 29]?*

ZIEGLER: To answer your first question, this does and will end the U.S. military presence in Vietnam, and it also means that all of our prisoners will be back on Thursday. Secondly, in terms of the Commission, I am not prepared this morning to state when they will complete their work.

Ziegler's flat statement about prisoners of war, of course, later proved to be untrue, but at the time he shared all of the information he had and it made a nice, clean end to the war, leaving the impression that the war was—finally—all over. It should be noted that the war continued in the spring of 1974 on an unofficial basis. The North Vietnamese initiated a concerted effort to liberate Saigon. The South Vietnamese agreed to an unconditional surrender to the communists in the early hours of April 30, 1974, with the fall of the South Vietnamese capital of Saigon to North Vietnamese forces. As the few remaining Americans evacuated Saigon, the last two U.S. servicemen to die in Vietnam were killed when their helicopter crashed.

On March 29, 1975, the last American troops withdrew as Nixon declared, "The day we have all worked and prayed for has finally come," marking the end of the war. On April 30, 1975, at 8:30 A.M. the last Americans, ten Marines from the embassy, were evacuated from the U.S. embassy in Saigon by helicopter—a photograph of which was published in virtually every major newspaper in America and burned in the collective memory of Americans—concluding the U.S. presence in Vietnam, and by 11 A.M. the red and blue Viet Cong flag flew from the presidential palace. North Vietnamese troops poured into Saigon and encountered little resistance. President Minh broadcasted a message of unconditional surrender. The war was over.

---

## *"Mission Accomplished": 2003–2007*
### George W. Bush
#### ARI FLEISCHER/SCOTT MCCLELLAN

---

The Iraq War, which was officially launched by President George W. Bush on March 19, 2003, provides some of the best examples of how an administration spins a war until it runs out of ways to do it and the facts belie what the press secretary is saying. Even now, the spokesmen for President Bush continue—until this writing—to deny, dissemble, and manipulate the facts in such a way that Bush continues the war in the face of outspoken resistance by Congress and by the American people themselves. Polls show that in mid-2007 more than 60 percent of the American voters opposed the war and favored some kind of withdrawal.

For purposes of demonstrating how spin has been fully utilized by the White House Press Office in this war, following is an example of a much-ballyhooed milestone in which the press secretaries purposely—and skillfully—practiced the fine art of spin. First, a summary of the news story, then the press secretaries' subsequent explanations.

*The Event*: The "Mission Accomplished" banner and President Bush's unqualified declaration of May 1, 2003, that, "In the battle of Iraq, the United States and our Allies have prevailed."

*The News*:

> May 1, 2003 (CNN)—President George W. Bush declared combat operations over in a televised speech from atop an aircraft carrier off the coast of California. The exterior of the four-seat Navy S-3B Viking was marked with "Navy 1" in the back and "George W. Bush Commander-in-Chief" just below the cockpit window. On the plane's tail was the insignia of the squadron, the "Blue Wolves." Moments after the landing, the president, wearing a green flight suit and holding a white helmet, got off the plane, saluted those on the flight deck and shook hands with them. Above him, the tower was adorned with a big sign that read: "Mission Accomplished."

The landing came just hours before Bush told the nation that *"major combat operations in Iraq have ended"* (italics added). The speech was delivered from the carrier's flight deck at 9 P.M. EDT. The picture-perfect landing, covered live on television, marked a carefully staged effort by the White House to showcase Bush as commander-in-chief, flight uniform and all.

From Ari Fleischer's point of view, the initial staging of the event was shortsighted. After the fact, in a later press briefing, Fleischer, accepting the outcome, philosophized:

> In politics and government, no good event can last forever and I should have known then and there that the press's euphoric coverage would somehow reverse itself, given their self-appointed role as a leveler in our society.

The pictures were too beneficial to the President's image, and the press didn't think it was their job to show the President, any president, in a favorable light for any length of time. It didn't take long for the landing's success to turn into the landing's controversy. In the cycle of journalism, good news can't stay good for very long.[39]

Later in 2003, Bush defended his speech on the aircraft carrier and the "Mission Accomplished" banner as the right thing to do. "We had just come off a very successful military operation," he said in a *New York Times* interview, "I was there to thank the troops. My statement was a clear statement basically recognizing that this phase of the war for Iraq was over and there was a lot of dangerous work [remaining]. And it's proved to be right. It is dangerous in Iraq." When asked if his comments had not been premature when he stood under the banner, Bush responded testily that the "Mission Accomplished" banner had not been put up by the White House advance staff.[40]

Here is the administration's spinning of the "Mission Accomplished" statement over a period of four years, showing subsequent spins about the term "Mission Accomplished" since 2003: There can be no doubt that the "Mission Accomplished" slogan has become an albatross around the president's head and, no doubt, will continue each year to be pointed out by the press as long as the war continues.

Press Secretary McClellan's Press Briefing: April 30, 2004:

*Q: You said [in 2003] the President onboard the U.S.S. Lincoln thanked the troops. And then he looked the American people in the eye and said major combat operations are over. He was wrong. Major combat operations are still going on.*

McCLELLAN: Let me talk to you this way: There are still certain areas in Iraq where there are pockets of resistance. And certainly we have troops in harm's way that are fighting to defeat those remnants of the former regime, and those foreign fighters who have come into Iraq, and those thugs.

McClellan's Press Briefing: May 1, 2005:

*Q: On May 1, 2003, President Bush stood in front of a "Mission Accomplished" banner, and announced that major combat operations in Iraq had been completed. Is that still the case, or are we in a new phase in Iraq?*

McCLELLAN: Well, let's keep in perspective differences there. I think one was talking about an initial major bombing operation, so I think you need to look at it in the context of what this is.

McClellan's Press Briefing: May 1, 2006:

*Q: Scott, three years ago today, the President said that major combat was over. At this point, how far does the administration think they are, or how close do they think they are to victory, what you would call victory in Iraq?*

McCLELLAN: Well, we're making real progress on our plan for victory. We've seen real progress made over the last two years, and even three years, from where we were to where we are today.

Tony Snow's press briefing on April 30, 2007:

*Q: Tony, can we look ahead to tomorrow's "Mission Accomplished" appearance at Central Command? I'm assuming that this was scheduled with the anniversary in mind?*

SNOW: No, it wasn't. No.

*Q: Really?*

SNOW: I don't think so. I did not see anything in the briefing notes that would indicate—

*Q: What is the—is there a particular message behind this visit?*

SNOW: Yes, it's an annual conference at Central Command [CENTCOM].

*Q: Tony, are we winning the war?*

SNOW: Are we winning the war?

*Q: Welcome back. (Laughter.)*

SNOW: Yes, exactly, welcome back. (Laughter.) You know, we're fighting the war, and it's an important thing to understand that the only way to lose the war is to walk away from it, and that this country not only has made a commitment to the people of Iraq, but the people of Iraq have made a commitment in blood and treasure, as well. And we are working to create a situation where that government, in fact, is going to be able to provide for its citizens, not only economically, but most importantly, a democracy that will respect the rights of all, that will protect those rights, and that will be able to stand tall among the community of nations.

*Q: How long should we fight the war before we just turn tail—*

SNOW: The notion that somehow the United States walks away and there are no consequences I think is the sort of thing that—it doesn't make any sense. Think of it this way: The United States walks away, who stands to benefit? Answer, terrorists, al Qaeda, the people who are fighting democracy. Let me put it this way: Our allies do not want us simply to leave on a timetable. The Iraqis do not want us to leave. People within the region do not want us to leave, because it does create the possibility of chaos and bloodshed on a horrific scale. So the idea—again, if we turn tail, to use your formulation, what it means is that we weaken ourselves, and we weaken ourselves not only over there, but on our own soil, as well.

At a second briefing on May 1, 2007:
Deputy Press Secretary Dana Perino was somewhat at a loss as to the furor that had been made over previous May 1 anniversaries of Bush's "Mission Accomplished" banner on the aircraft carrier in 2003—was asked at the daily briefing:

*Q: Does the President regret the "mission accomplished" speech?*
PERINO: Look, I've never heard him describe it that way, absolutely not. Let me just remind everybody, in case you need it, that speech there, I encourage people to read it. The President never said "Mission Accomplished." I realize that the banner said "Mission Accomplished." *That was specific to the mission of that ship. They were supposed to be deployed for six months* [italics added]. They were deployed well beyond that. I think they'd gone to both Iraq and Afghanistan. And that's what that banner was referring to. But I'm not going to—

*Q: The President did say, "In the battle of Iraq, the United States and our allies have prevailed."*
PERINO: We did prevail, in terms of toppling the Iraqi army and Saddam Hussein. And several months later, 12 million Iraqis voted for a new government and a constitution. And things looked very promising. And the President did believe that at the end of 2006, he would be announcing basically what was in the Baker-Hamilton report. Unfortunately, the sectarian violence had grown to the extent that the President, in the fall of 2006, underwent an extensive review to decide on a new strategy in Iraq, of which he announced on January 10, 2007. And the President believes that helping the Iraqi people now is critical.

## *The Hunt for WMDs: 2003–2005*
### George W. Bush
### ARI FLEISCHER/SCOTT MCCLELLAN

From the day George W. Bush took office in 2001, his intelligence team, led by CIA's George Tenet, briefed him regularly on threats to national security. But even with all of their discussions and planning, what Bush and—for that matter, anybody else in America—could not have known, was that the threat of terrorism would become a nightmarish reality on September 11, 2001. When al Qaeda attacked America, it came as an enormous shock to the country's psyche.

Although talk about weapons of mass destruction had been on the front burner of both the Clinton and Bush administrations, nobody in government could have anticipated Osama bin Laden ordering his trained terrorists to hijack airplanes to fly into the World Trade Towers and the Pentagon, and killing more than 3,000 people. The time had come for the Bush administration to start gearing up for an all-out attack on the perpetrators of this historic wound to America's pride.

On January 29, 2002, in a speech to Congress, Bush began to lay the initial groundwork for his campaign to send troops to Afghanistan and Iraq by accusing Iraq of being part of an international "Axis of Evil," the other nations being Iran and North Korea. Bush said: "Iraq continues to flaunt its hostility toward America and to support terror. The Iraqi regime has plotted to develop anthrax and nerve gas and nuclear weapons for over a decade. . . . This is a regime that has something to hide from the civilized world." It was clear that the top echelons of the White House were aiming their sights at Iraq.

The Bush administration spent much of 2002 discussing exactly how to pressure Saddam Hussein to give up his WMDs. It was not until November 8, 2002, that UN Security Council Resolution 1441 said that Iraq "remains in material breach of its obligations" under various UN resolutions and gave the country "a final opportunity to comply with its disarmament program."

The tension continued to build until, on November 27, 2002, the UN sent inspectors back into Iraq and they once again began to search out weapons of mass destruction. A week later, at a briefing on December 2, a White House correspondent asked White House Press Secretary Ari Fleischer: "Weapons inspectors in Iraq have now visited a couple of sites that both the President and Prime Minister Tony Blair pointed specifically as possible to sources of new construction and new development of Iraqi weapons programs. It doesn't seem they found anything. What's the President's assessment of Iraqi cooperation?"

Fleischer said the president's assessment of Iraqi cooperation was that it was far, far too soon to say. He said the inspection regime was just beginning. "They will continue to increase their numbers and their efforts. And the President has not reached any conclusions; it's too early to reach any conclusions," said Fleischer, adding: "I think it's fair to say the President has gone into this with a 'can-do' attitude to preserve the peace, and if it hadn't been for the President's efforts and leadership and willingness to state facts realistically, there would be no inspectors inside Iraq, would there be? There wouldn't have. It was the President who caused this to happen."

Another reporter put Fleischer squarely on the spot: "Has Iraq ever threatened the United States?" The press secretary replied: "Only when they shoot at our pilots. Only when they attack their neighbors and America's interests abroad."

*Q: You're assuming in your answer that they have weapons of mass destruction which they are hiding. They say they do not; you say that they do.*

FLEISCHER: I think the history of people who accept Saddam Hussein at face value do not take his word as accurate because they have been deceived by Saddam Hussein before. Saddam Hussein does not exactly have a track record of telling the world the truth. So he, on December 8th [2002], has to indicate whether he has weapons. Let's see what he says. If he declares he has none, then we will know that Saddam Hussein is once again misleading the world.

*Q: How will you know?*

FLEISCHER: We have intelligence information about what Saddam Hussein possesses.

*Q: So you say that you do have information that he has these weapons.*

FLEISCHER: It's no secret. We've said many times—you've heard the President say repeatedly that he has chemical and biological weapons, and he has missiles that can reach in excess of 150 kilometers, all three of which are violations of his sworn commitments to the United Nations. If Saddam Hussein indicates that he has weapons of mass destruction and that he is violating United Nations resolutions, then we will know that Saddam Hussein again deceived the world. If he said he doesn't have any, then I think that we will find out whether or not Saddam Hussein is saying something that we believe will be verifiably false.

On December 7, 2002—one day before the deadline— Iraq delivered a 12,000-page WMD report to the UN in response to Resolution 1441. UN Chief Inspector Hans Blix said the information provided by Iraq was largely "recycled material." In early January 2003, Blix reported that UN inspectors had not found any "smoking guns" in Iraq. Nonetheless, John Negroponte, then U.S. ambassador to the United Nations, said: "There is still no evidence that Iraq has fundamentally changed its approach from one of deceit to a genuine attempt to be forthcoming in meeting the council's demand that it disarm."

Meanwhile, Fleischer came under growing pressure from the press for the Bush administration to show some results on the hunt for WMDs. One reporter asked: "The chief nuclear inspector said just now that his team needs a few more months to complete their work. Is the President willing to wait a few more months?" Fleischer replied, simply: "The process is running out of time." Another reporter asked: "Ari, if you've concluded the Iraqis aren't complying with the inspectors, why not call a halt now, why not—you know—get on with it?" Fleischer responded: "Because, as the President said, it's important to continue to consult, to work with world leaders about how to address the growing problem of Saddam Hussein's failure to comply with the inspectors; the problem of Saddam Hussein continuing to have in his possession biological weapons and chemical weapons which he has not accounted for. And we will continue to consult per the President's promise."

Then came the administration's February 1, 2003, grand presentation at the United Nations. It was reminiscent in the eyes of some veteran correspondents of United Nations Ambassador Adlai Stevenson's "show and tell" of missiles poised in Cuba ready to be launched at the United States during the fall of the 1962 Cuban Missile Crisis. This time it was Secretary of State Colin Powell who put his reputation as a distinguished lifelong military career man who had served in combat, as well as an adviser to previous presidents, on the line.

Citing evidence he said was obtained by American intelligence, he told the United Nations in no uncertain terms that Iraq had failed "to come clean and disarm." In an impressive presentation, Powell showed a stunning array of photos, videotapes, maps, and other evidence that Iraq was, indeed, building up its supply of weapons of mass destruction. "My colleagues," referring to the members of the United Nations, he said,

> every statement I make today is backed up by sources, solid sources. These are not assertions. What we're giving you are facts and conclusions based on solid intelligence. . . . Iraq has now placed itself in danger of the serious consequences called for in U.N. Resolution 1441. And this body places itself in danger of irrelevance if it allows Iraq to continue to defy its will without responding effectively and immediately.

"The issue before us," he said solemnly, "is not how much time we are willing to give the inspectors to be frustrated by Iraqi obstruction. But, how much longer are we willing to put up with Iraq's noncompliance before we, as a council, we, as the United Nations, say: 'Enough. Enough.'"

Administration officials, the press, and the public were all impressed. Who would not believe Colin Powell, a man of proven character and integrity?

Again, in his State of the Union address on February 5, 2003, Bush charged that Iraq was trying to develop nuclear weapons. He stated unequivocally: *"The British government has learned that Saddam Hussein recently sought significant quantities of uranium from Africa"* [italics added]. Those sixteen words would come back to haunt Bush and his entire effort to build a consensus to go to war. It later became known that the president had based his statement on discredited intelligence.

The Bush administration's rationale for going to war in the aftermath of the attacks rested almost entirely on the claim—backed up by Powell's "evidence" at the United Nations—that Saddam Hussein possessed weapons of mass destruction—including nuclear arms—that he had been developing since the end of the Gulf War in 1991.

Although Iraq reluctantly submitted to international inspections and claimed it had destroyed its stockpiles and means of WMD production, Saddam Hussein's refusal to allow inspectors to fully inspect his country made it difficult for outsiders to tell exactly what Iraq was doing, if anything, about its stockpile of WMDs. As a result, on February 14, 2003, UN weapons inspectors led by Hans Blix reported to the UN Security Council that they had not discovered any biological, chemical, or nuclear weapons activities. But, proscribed missile programs were discovered and disabled. Blix expressed frustration with Iraq's failure to account for the vast stores of chemical and biological agents it was known to have at one point. "This is perhaps the most important problem we are facing. Although I can understand that it may not be easy for Iraq in all cases to provide the evidence needed, it is not the task of the inspectors to find it."

On that same day, February 14, 2003, Fleischer's briefing brought out some of the most penetrating questions he had been asked up to that point:

*Q: Ari, despite the Secretary of State's presentation, it seems rather clear that this administration ran into a brick wall of opposition today at the United Nations. What does the President make of that and what's the next step?*

FLEISCHER: I think that's a rather over-dramatic interpretation of what you've heard from New York today. Number one, let's start with some of the statements that you've heard. I think there is universal agreement that force is a last resort. That is valid for the United States. And the President remains hopeful that Iraq will, indeed, disarm and therefore avert the need for force to be used to disarm him. But in the end, the process set forward by the United Nations and all 15 members of the Security Council unanimously is aimed at the disarmament of Saddam Hussein. Nowhere did the world receive any comfort today in New York that Saddam Hussein has shown the inspectors that he has disarmed. Quite the contrary.

*Q: Okay. What's the evidence that it's an over-dramatization? I mean, you heard from the allies, including those who have the ability to veto a second resolution, that they don't support the timetable put forth by the United States and this administration, that they want to see inspections continue. The administration disagrees with that. So does the President not sense that there is a groundswell of opposition against the diplomacy that we're engaged in. And if so, what's he going to do about it?*

FLEISCHER: What remains important is the fundamental facing of the fact—and considering especially the two new pieces of evidence that Hans Blix brought forward this morning about whether or not Saddam Hussein has disarmed.

*Q: Did Hans Blix disappoint the President with his presentation? Did he think that Dr. Blix, perhaps, understated the lack of Iraqi noncompliance in the President's view?*

FLEISCHER: No, I think the report from Hans Blix was very diplomatic with its bottom line being that the world has no confidence that Saddam Hussein has disarmed. And that's what this is about. As Secretary Powell just indicated, this is not about whether U-2s fly. This is not about whether Mirages fly. This is about whether Saddam Hussein's claim that he has disarmed is itself a mirage.

*Q: Ari, what does the President want the Security Council to do now? Does he want another resolution specifically authorizing force? Or is he willing to settle for something watered down that everybody can agree on?*

FLEISCHER: Well, the President wants the world to study carefully what Mr. Blix said. There are important things that Mr. Blix revealed to the world this morning that the United Nations Security Council has to consider, the members of the Security Council have to consider. And I think it's likely that they will. The President has made clear he is open to another resolution.

*Q: Authorizing force?*

FLEISCHER: The exact words I think will be discussed. But already the United Nations Security Council has said that if Iraq fails to comply with Security Council Resolution 1441, which ordered Iraq to fully and immediately disarm, there would be serious consequences.

*Q: When would you expect the U.S. to submit a resolution to the U.N. for action for authorizing the use of military force? Does Blix's statement today change the timing in the U.S. view?*

FLEISCHER: Mr. Blix reported to the world today that the issues of anthrax, nerve agent, VX, and long-range missiles deserve to be taken seriously by Iraq, rather than brushed aside. Those are Mr. Blix's words about weapons that kill. Then he added in a crucial sentence: "It is not the task of the inspectors to find it; it is the task of Iraq to provide it." So when you listened to Mr. Blix describe the very fact that the weapons that kill are, one, proven to be in the hands of Iraq in a proscribed manner, and the weapons of mass destruction that kill even more—the anthrax, the nerve agent, the VX—are unaccounted for, the world still has great cause for concern about Saddam Hussein possessing weapons.

*Q: And what's the timing on submitting a resolution, days?*

FLEISCHER: The timing will be something the United States, in concert with our allies, will determine. I think it's too soon to say at this point. I think it typically happens after presentations of this importance are made to the Security Council as the member states take time to study them, to absorb them, to think about what it means that now we have three categories of missiles that are proscribed; that Iraq has not accounted for the VX, the nerve agents; and this new sentence—it is not the task of the inspectors to find it.

*Q: So if Iraq meets this test, that would be a substantive step forward in actual, factual disarmament on the ground that they destroyed missiles?*

FLEISCHER: Let me raise another issue that is related to this, because the threat to the world doesn't only come from these missiles, which Hans Blix cited this morning in his remarks. The threat to the world comes from what Hans Blix said the world has no confidence that Saddam Hussein has destroyed, which is what [the inspectors] found in the late 1990s. . . . This comes 12 years late and 26,000 liters of anthrax short; 12 years late and 38,000 liters of botulin short; 12 years late and 30,000 unfilled chemical munitions short. It's not just about one weapon system that Iraq possesses to wreak havoc and to kill people in the neighborhood, including Americans, including our allies and including risks that could be transferred to terrorists. It's not just one system, Terry.

*Q: Is there a link between Al Qaeda and Iraq?*

FLEISCHER: Sure, the President has said that. The night before Blix was scheduled to report on inspection efforts in Iraq, Bush held a news conference in which he again said Iraq is hiding something. He said: "These are not the actions of a regime that is disarming. These are the actions of a regime engaged in a willful charade. These are the actions of a regime that systematically and deliberately is defying the world."

Nonetheless, on March 20, 2003, Bush ordered the U.S. military and other members of an American-led coalition to invade Iraq. Baghdad fell on April 9 and, as he would come to regret, Bush declared "an end to major combat operations" on May 1, 2003, aboard a U.S. Navy vessel at sea. Shortly afterward, the Pentagon announced the formation of the Iraq Survey Group (ISG) to search for weapons of mass destruction.

Ari Fleischer once again told reporters: "There is no doubt that the regime of Saddam Hussein possesses weapons of mass destruction. As this operation continues, those weapons will be identified, found, along with the people who have produced them and who guard them. . . . This is a war to disarm the Iraqi regime from its weapons of mass destruction." He was immediately asked whether the mission could be considered a success. His response: "The President has every confidence, as the American people do, in the men and women of our military to achieve their objective, which is to disarm the Iraqi regime.

He has every confidence that will be done. But I'm just not, as a general matter of principle, going to provide a daily and nightly tick-tock like that. But when I say the President has every confidence, it's for good reason."

*Q: Ari, you've emphasized the support that the coalition is getting, but there's been substantial criticism, as well, particularly from President [Vladimir] Putin of Russia. What's your response?*

FLEISCHER: Well, again, the President is very gratified by the growing list of nations that support the coalition's efforts. The differences that the President has had, and the United States has, with a few other nations are well-known. There is nothing new to that. The President understands and respects the opinions of leaders like President Putin. Nevertheless, that will not deter the United States and the coalition of the willing from disarming the Iraqi regime.

The day after the invasion, Fleischer kept the reporters up to date by stating: "There is no doubt that the regime of Saddam Hussein possesses weapons of mass destruction. As this operation continues, those weapons will be identified, found, along with the people who have produced them and who guard them."

The hunt for the missing WMDs took on a bizarre twist when Bush exhibited questionable taste on March 26, 2004, at the sixtieth annual dinner of the Radio and Television Correspondents' Association, narrating a slide show of himself comically trying to find the WMDs under the furniture in his office. He was generally panned by the press for dealing with the WMD topic in such a lighthearted way. For some of the press, it offered an unflattering window into Bush's mind. In a skit on the stage, Bush looked for the WMDs under his desk, demonstrating he could joke about something as serious as the WMDs.[41]

On April 10, 2003, Fleischer said of the search for WMDs: "We are learning more as we interrogate or have discussions with Iraqi scientists and people within the Iraqi structure, that perhaps he destroyed some, perhaps he dispersed some. And so we will find them. I think you have always heard, and you continue to hear from officials, a measure of high confidence that, indeed, the weapons of mass destruction will be found."

On May 6, Bush continued his upbeat forecast: "I'm not surprised if we begin to uncover the weapons program of Saddam Hussein. I'm not surprised if we begin to uncover the weapons program of Saddam Hussein because he had a weapons program." After the press continued to hound the White House press secretaries about the weapons of mass destruction, on October 2, 2003—after months of looking—the Iraq Survey Group (ISG) inspector David Kay told Congress in an interim report that his American team of weapons inspectors had yet to find any evidence of WMDs. Kay said: "We have not yet found stocks of weapons, but we are not yet at the point where we can say definitively either that such weapon stocks do not exist, or that they existed before the war." Kay subsequently resigned, stating that: "My summary view, based on what I've seen, is that we are very unlikely to find large stockpiles of weapons. I don't think they exist."

That did not deter the president or his press secretaries from continuing to tell reporters there definitely were weapons. However, on July 9, 2004, the Report of the Select Committee on Intelligence on the U.S. Intelligence Community's Prewar Intelligence faulted America's ability to gauge Iraq's capabilities before the war. Senator Pat Roberts (R-Kansas) said:

> Before the war, the U.S. intelligence community told the president, as well as the Congress, that Saddam Hussein had stockpiles of chemical and biological weapons, and if left unchecked, would probably have a nuclear weapon during this decade. Well, today we know these assessments were wrong. They were also unreasonable and largely unsupported by the available intelligence.

This conclusion was also supported by the Iraq Survey Group on September 30, 2004, when it released its final report. Chief Inspector Charles Duelfer testified before Congress that after 16 months of investigation, he concluded that Saddam Hussein had no chemical weapons, no biological weapons, and no capacity to make nuclear weapons.

This, effectively, ended the hunt for WMDs.

Finally, on January 12, 2005, White House spokesman Scott McClellan, parsing his words, admitted to reporters that the *"physical search" for WMD, having found no weapons, "was over"* [italics added].

That conclusion was confirmed on March 31, 2005, when the Commission on the Intelligence Capabilities of the United States Regarding Weapons of Mass Destruction delivered its report, stating the failure to find WMD in Iraq as one of the "most public—and most damaging—intelligence failures in recent American history." The report, which was commissioned by President Bush, concluded that wide-ranging reform of the intelligence bureaucracy was needed to guard against global WMD threats.

That is exactly what the president did. The rest of the story is unfolding still.

The deliberate manner in which the Bush spokesmen tried to rationalize the "Mission Accomplished" event on May 1, 2003, and every year since, is part and parcel of this administration's all-out effort to spin almost anything that it wants to. David Gergen takes a critical—and perhaps realistic—view of the White House. "This [Bush] administration," he said, "has engaged in secrecy at a level we have not seen in over 30 years. Unfortunately, I have to bring up the name of Richard Nixon because we haven't seen it since the days of Nixon."[42] Gergen should know. He worked for Presidents Nixon, Ford, George H.W. Bush, and Clinton.

## NOTES

1. Transcript of Early press briefing at the White House, December 4, 1941.

2. Transcript of Early press briefing at the White House, December 6, 1941.

3. Goodwin, Doris Kearns. *No Ordinary Time, Franklin and Eleanor Roosevelt: The Home Front in World War II* (New York: Simon & Schuster, 1994), p. 289. From the book by Sherwood, Robert F., *Roosevelt and Hopkins: An Intimate History* (New York: Harper, 1948), p. 431.

4. Transcript of Early press briefing, December 7, 1941.

5. *The New York Times*, May 28, 1941.

6. "Navy Had War Tip, On December 3, '41; File Missing," *The New York Times*, December 12, 1941, p. 1. The article reported that in a document marked "Top Secret Report" three days before the attack an intercepted Japanese message which, when translated, said: "War with the United States, war with Britain, including the NEI (Netherlands East Indies), except peace with Russia . . . The Japanese message of Dec. 3, the report asserted, was picked up by a monitoring station operating under the Federal Communications Commission, was translated and made available to the Navy during the evening of December 3. This communication, the report went on, was known as the 'winds execute message,' a code dispatch implementing the Japanese decision to break off diplomatic relations [with the U.S.]. This 'winds execute' message has now disappeared from the Navy file and cannot be found despite the extensive search for it," the Army board said, adding that it was turned over to the director of Naval Communications for use as evidence before a Congressional committee investigating how the Pearl Harbor attack occurred. "There, therefore, can be no question that that between the dates of Dec. 4 and Dec. 6 the imminence of war on the following Saturday and Sunday, December 6 and December 7, was clear-cut and decisive."

7. On December 8, 1941, in at attempt to show candor and build trust, Press Secretary Early released the following information to the White House press corps: The Japanese attack resulted in: 2,335 military and 68 civilians killed, 1,143 military

and 35 civilians wounded, 2 battleships sunk, 4 battleships damaged, 3 cruisers damaged, 3 destroyers sunk, 2 other ships sunk, 188 planes destroyed, 155 planes damaged, 55 airmen, 9 submariners killed and 1 captured, 29 planes destroyed, and 4 mini-submarines sunk.

8. *The New York Times*, December 10, 1941, p. 1A.

9. Excerpted from transcript of President Roosevelt's December 11, 1941, speech to Congress requesting recognition of a State of War existing between the United States and Germany and the United States and Italy, December 11, 1941.

10. In December 1941, Price published a pamphlet setting out the guidelines by which he hoped the news media would abide in determining what war-related news was fit to print and what was not. Price stressed that the main question he wanted the press to ask itself about every story it considered publishing was: "Is this information I would like to have if I were the enemy?" The Office of Censorship was closed down on August 14, 1945.

11. From transcript of Early's briefing to press, December 17, 1941.

12. Baruch, Michael and Martha Joyner Kumar. *Portraying The President: The White House and The News Media* (Baltimore: Johns Hopkins University Press, 1981), p. 23.

13. Levin, Linda Lotridge. *The Making of FDR: The Story of Stephen T. Early, America's First Modern Presidential Press Secretary* (Amherst, NY: Prometheus Books, 2007).

14. Levy, Daniel and Susan A. Brink. *A Change of Heart, How The Framingham Heart Study Helped Unravel the Mysteries of Cardiovascular Disease* (New York: Alfred A. Knopf, 2005), pp. 19–20. Levy's study of heart ailments argued that Roosevelt reportedly had been suffering from clogging of his arteries and severe blood pressure elevation levels—all of which eventually contributed to a heart attack. Despite this, Early perpetuated the White House spin that FDR was in good health and was able to run for a fourth term and carry out all of his duties. The press rarely questioned Early's flat denial of a mysterious illness during his entire time in the White House. Early had, in fact, realized that FDR's health was failing—almost anyone who saw him regularly could see the deep circles under his eyes and his thinning, pale face. In fact, recently in books written about his last in his waning years, it has become clear that Early and FDR's other aides were in denial. Moreover, there was an unwritten, unspoken pact between FDR, other political figures, and the press not to write about his handicap from the time he took office. Early's take on FDR's being paralyzed from the waist down as a result of having polio was simple: It was not newsworthy. And the press, reporters, and photographers accepted his embargo. He even went as far as to rule out any photos of FDR in his wheelchair. Yet another view of Steve Early's going to "extraordinary lengths" to deny any reports of FDR's ill health throughout his time in office. In the last year and a half of FDR's life, Early saw to it that Roosevelt did not appear that much in public. According to one account, "His [FDR's] skillful press assistant, Steve Early, made full use of releases, statements, short press conferences and radio talks. As a result Roosevelt continued to dominate the news through the war."

[Gallagher, Hugh Gregory. *FDR's Splendid Deception: The Moving Story of Roosevelt's Massive Disability and the Intense Efforts to Conceal It From the Public* (New York: Dodd, Mead & Company, 1985), pp. 94–95, 185–191]. But, according to the author, FDR was deeply depressed, fatigued, and suffered from headaches, indigestion, and various ailments. "In the case of Franklin Roosevelt, it seems undeniable that depressive neurosis—a state of reactive depression—was a condition of the last year and a half of his life." FDR's condition grew so bad that he actually lost the use of his hands and, toward the end, he was so weak he was unable to negotiate around a room. By carefully hiding FDR's failing health and keeping up the image of a strong leader merely working hard, one could argue that Early was spinning the health story from start to finish. But as he saw it, that was not only his job but also his duty to his commander-in-chief.

15. Daniels, Jonathan. *White House Witness, 1942–1945* (New York: Doubleday & Company, 1975), p. 2.

16. Freidel, Frank. "Introduction,"in Jonathan Daniels, *White House Witness*, p. xii.

17. Ibid., *White House Witness*, pp. 284–285.

18. Tebbel, John, and Sarah Miles Watts. *The Press and the Presidency: From George Washington to Ronald Reagan* (New York: Oxford University Press, 1985), p. 440.

19. "The President's Press Conference," article by Henry Ehrlich, Washington correspondent for the *Herald*, May 23, 1937.

20. *The New York Times*, August 12, 1951.

21. Truman, Harry S. *Years of Decisions* (New York: Doubleday & Company, 1955), p. 47.

22. *The New York Times*, August 8, 1951, p. 7.

23. Pollard, James. *Presidents and The Press* (Washington, D.C.: Public Affairs Press, 1964), p. 26. Ross had been a boyhood friend of Truman's. After graduating from the University of Missouri-Columbia in 1908, he became the first professor of the newly formed Missouri School of Journalism. He came to Washington in 1918 as the chief Washington correspondent for the *St. Louis Post-Dispatch*. He won the 1932 Pulitzer Prize for his article titled, "The Country's Plight, What Can Be Done About It?," a discussion of the economic situation of the United States. In 1934 he became the editorial page editor for the *Post-Dispatch*, and then in 1939 became a contributing editor for the paper until Truman asked him to become his press secretary in 1945. Despite Ross's personal relationship with Truman, he was to be criticized by reporters of not running a tight ship in coordinating press releases, not being aware of everything going on in the presidency, not burnishing the president's image—that is, not using what we could call "spin" today—not being aware of the need for spot news, and being hard of hearing (Wikipedia, www.wikipedia.org).

24. *The New York Times*, June 30, 1950.

25. Courtesy of the Harry S. Truman Library, Independence, MO. Oral History interview by Jerry N. Hess with Edward T. Folliard, Washington, D.C., August 20, 1970.

26. Courtesy of Harry S. Truman Library, Independence, MO. Oral History interview by Jerry N. Hess with Roger Tubby, Washington, D.C., February 10, 1970.

27. Wikipedia, www.wikipedia.org. When Pierre Salinger resigned as press secretary in August 1964, Reedy was named to the position. During the escalation of the American involvement in Vietnam beginning in March 1965, press questions over the veracity of the Johnson Administration's public assessments of the war led to charges of a so-called credibility gap. In July 1965 Reedy took a leave of absence over his disagreement with Johnson's Vietnam policies. He was replaced by Bill Moyers, a longtime friend of Johnson's from Texas. In 1968, he returned to the White House to work as a special assistant shortly before Johnson's surprise announcement that he would not seek reelection.

28. *The New York Times*, August 8, 1964, p. 1.

29. *The New York Times*, August 6, 1973.

30. Reedy, George E. *From Johnson to Reagan* (New York: NAL Books, 1970), pp. 20–21.

31. There is an apocryphal story about Reedy that has been passed on through subsequent press secretaries that goes like this:

> These days we have to be thankful for any help we get. When you are starving you take anything you get. It's like the time George Reedy, the press secretary for LBJ, was sent to the hospital for a strict diet reduction. When his office staff sent him a big basket of flowers, Reedy acknowledged the gift with this telegram: "Thanks for the flowers. They were delicious."

32. Tebbel and Watts, *The Press and the Presidency: From George Washington To Ronald Reagan* (Oxford University Press, N.Y. and Oxford, 1985), pp. 491–497.

33. Moyers, Bill. *Moyers on America, Journalism, and Democracy* (New York: New Press, 2004), p. 99.

34. From transcript of Moyers's press briefing, February 7, 1965.

35. *The New York Times*, April 16, 1968.

36. Tebbel and Watts, *The Press and the Presidency*, pp. 495-496.

37. *The New York Times*, July 31, 1968.

38. Pamphlet, "The Presidency and The Press," edited by Hoyt Purvis, from transcript of seminar at the Lyndon B. Johnson School of Public Affairs, 1976.

39. Fleischer, Ari. *Taking Heat: The President, The Press, and My Years in the White House* (New York: William Morrow, 2005), p. 347.

40. *The New York Times*, October 29, 2003.

41. BBC News report, July 26, 2004:

> At a black-tie dinner for journalists, Mr. Bush narrated a slide show poking fun at himself and other members of his administration. One pictured Mr. Bush looking under a piece of furniture in the Oval Office, at which the

president remarked: "Those weapons of mass destruction have got to be here somewhere." After another one, showing him scouring the corner of a room, Mr. Bush said: "No, no weapons over there," he said. And as a third picture, this time showing him leaning over, appeared on the screen the president was heard to say: "Maybe under here?" The audience at Wednesday's 60th annual dinner of the Radio and Television Correspondents' Association obviously thought the quips hilarious—there were laughs all round—but the next morning, in the cold light of day, things looked far less amusing. The joke about the fruitless search for Iraqi WMDs so far, Washington's prime justification for the U.S.-led invasion, has been branded as tasteless and ill-judged. Mr. Bush's election challenger, [Democratic] Senator John Kerry, described the president's attitude as 'stunningly cavalier' and added: "If George Bush thinks his deceptive rationale for going to war is a laughing matter, then he's even more out of touch than we thought," he said in a written statement. "Unfortunately for the president, this is not a joke."

42. CNN "Reliable Sources," Howard Kurtz, March 12, 2006.

# CHAPTER 2

---

## COLD WAR

---

### The Birth of the UN: 1945
Harry S. Truman
CHARLES ROSS

Only two presidents in U.S. history have tried to establish a world organization whose mission was world peace. Woodrow Wilson was the first when the constitution of the League of Nations was adopted by the Paris Peace Conference in April 1919, with the League's headquarters in Geneva, Switzerland. However, after the U.S. Congress failed to ratify the Versailles Treaty, the United States never became a member of the League of Nations. Others joined but later left. It became, in effect, a powerless paper establishment and did not convene at all during World War II.

The other president who tried to bring the nations of the world into one viable organization was, of course, Harry S. Truman. Perhaps the single most important event in the history of the United Nations was the Conference on International Organization 5 (UNCIO) in San Francisco, California, from April 25 to June 26, 1945.

A plucky, sharp-talking man who seemed to grasp the presidency with confidence, Truman recalled in his memoirs that, "My first act as President of the United States had been to keep the peace. Within a few minutes of my taking the oath of office, I announced that the United States would take part in the San Francisco conference [to approve a United Nations Charter] with no delay in the schedule or change in the arrangements."[1] Truman was praised by internationalists in the United States for his strong support of the United Nations after a war that had turned the trend toward isolationism in America. Even the doubters in Congress believed there was a need for an international body.

Still, it took courage—and a professional press secretary—to make the splash that Truman wanted to make at this conference when he closed it with a rousing speech on May 14, 1945. Thanks to the promotion of this event for many weeks by the White House press office, the people of San Francisco had turned out on June 25, 1945, "a million strong," as Truman put it, to greet him and the U.S. delegation. The next afternoon, he attended the official signing of the Charter. "The Charter of the United Nations," he said to the delegation, "which you have just signed, is a solid structure upon which we can build a better world. History will honor you for it. Between victory in Europe and the final victory in Japan, in this most destructive of wars, you have won a victory against war itself."[2]

Soon after Truman called on his recently appointed press secretary, Charles G. Ross, an old high school friend from Independence, Missouri—who had just joined his administration—to help draft a message he wished to send to Congress on the UN Charter. Truman had persuaded Joseph Pulitzer, publisher of the *St. Louis Post-Dispatch*, to give Ross a two-year leave of absence to work for his old friend, Harry Truman.

When the White House has good news, one of the best ways a press secretary can serve a president is to lay back and let the story tell itself. Ross did just that. He further recommended that Truman's comments last no more than five minutes—keep it short, simple, and to the point. Ross piqued the interest of reporters before the message was to be delivered by telling them it would be a blockbuster.

It was. On July 27, 1945, with assurance from the Senate leaders that the Charter would be ratified, Truman won a big victory when the Senate did, in fact, pass it by a stunning margin of eighty-nine to two. Deeply gratified, Truman once again asked Ross to assist him in preparing a statement for the press the next day to be released simultaneously in Washington and in Berlin, where Truman was located because of a scheduled meeting with General Secretary Stalin.

Once again, Truman took Ross's advice and kept the message succinct. It read: "It is deeply gratifying that the Senate has ratified the United Nations Charter by virtually unanimous vote. The action of the Senate substantially advances the cause of world peace."[3] Later on in 1945, in a letter to his mother in Missouri, Truman wrote: "Charlie Ross said I'd shown I'd rather be right than President, and I told him I'd rather be anything but President."[4]

*Recognition of the State of Israel: 1948*
Harry S. Truman
CHARLES ROSS

Sixty years ago—on Friday, May 14, 1948—a milestone in the history of the newly formed state of Israel took place when the United States of America officially recognized it as an independent, free, democratic society. Much of the credit for persuading Truman to make this historic move goes to his friend and adviser, Clark Clifford. As Harvard University historian Michael Beschloss, in his book *Presidential Courage: Brave Leaders and How They Changed America* (2007), wrote:

> If the U.S. granted legitimacy, so would its allies, allowing the Jewish state to survive. . . . Truman's ultimate decision about a Jewish state—one of the most significant foreign policy decisions in U.S. history—emerged from a storm of cross pressures to court the Jewish vote in an election year and diplomats afraid to rile the Arabs. He felt compassion for the Holocaust survivors still in European camps and reverence for Biblical history.[5]

The brevity of the statement Truman signed once again came on the advice of his press secretary, Charles Ross, who himself became something of a newsmaker when he summoned White House reporters who were on duty to his office in the White House and told them: "The Jewish state has been proclaimed at 6:11 E.D.T." He followed with his own statement, which came at the end of a long day during which the White House had maintained a stone-cold silence on developments in Palestine although reporters knew something was afoot. It read:

> The desire of the United States to obtain a truce in Palestine will in no way be lessened by the proclamation of a Jewish state. We hope that the new Jewish state will join with the Security Council Truce Commission in redoubling its efforts to bring an end to the fighting—which has been throughout the United Nations's consideration of Palestine a principal objective of the Government.

Ross had also written a detailed press release, which he handed out to reporters in the hope that they would play the story as big news—which it was—and put it in proper historical perspective. Ross did not need to sell this piece of news, but he wanted to make certain that the press understood its full import. He was, in effect, spinning it gently. His release read, in part, as follows: "At midnight on May 14, 1948, the Provisional Government of Israel proclaimed a new State of Israel. On that same date, the United States, in the person of President Truman, recognized the provisional Jewish government as de facto authority of the Jewish state."[6] Ross's statement went on to give the complete history of the region dating back to 1917, leaving no doubt in anyone's mind of the importance of Truman's action in history.

The press had a field day with the story, with *The New York Times* running the story on Page 1 on May 15, 1948. However, on that very same day, the first day of Israeli independence, Arab armies invaded Israel and, tragically, the first Arab-Israeli War began and would continue—on and off—until modern times. With the beginning of this war—which Truman had known might occur in response to his recognition of Israel—Truman's press secretary was asked by reporters about the timing of the announcement. Ross told them that the recognition was "not a matter of snap judgment," but that, on the contrary, Truman had had it in mind for some time. However, he said it was "impossible to fix a time-table on Truman's approaches to his decision."

The press, meanwhile, reported that the decision had not been final until the day before the announcement. Ross explained that it had been reached in consultation with Secretary of State George C. Marshall and Undersecretary of State Robert A. Lovett. And, Ross explained, Truman took the action after he had received by messenger a letter from Eliahu Epstein, agent of the provisional Israeli government, requesting recognition. Asked for public reaction in this country, Ross told reporters that some 500 telegrams had arrived at the White House immediately after the announcement and that they were "very heavily" in favor of it.[7]

---

## The Bay of Pigs: 1961
### John F. Kennedy
### PIERRE SALINGER

---

There could no greater challenge to a brand new press secretary than trying to manufacture "good" news from the misguided Bay of Pigs invasion of Cuban exiles on April 17, 1961. President John F. Kennedy had officially approved it upon assuming office. Even though the plan had been drawn up under his predecessor, Dwight D. Eisenhower, the invasion was Kennedy's to inherit and to implement. Enter Press Secretary Pierre Salinger, who was not even a party to the decision and was kept completely in the dark until it was launched.

"My awareness of the first major crisis of the Kennedy administration began quietly enough with a telephone call from the President." Salinger writes, "JFK's voice was grave.[8] 'I want you to stick close to home tonight [April 16, 1961], Pierre. You may have some inquiries from the press about a military affair in the Caribbean. If you do, just say that you know only what you've read in the newspapers.' . . . The

President's cryptic call was my first official knowledge of the Bay of Pigs." Salinger found out later that no press officer in government— the Department of State, the CIA, the Pentagon, or any other agency— had any knowledge of the impending event.

Salinger's first awareness with the event was on that Monday morning when he saw Kennedy for five minutes. Kennedy told him only that: "We'll have no comment on what's happening down there. We're watching developments. That's all," he said. It was clear to Salinger that he had better remain tight-lipped with the media. But over the next seventy-two hours, Salinger reported, he was in and out of Kennedy's office a hundred times armed with the latest wire services flashes. Early reports from the beachhead landings by Cuban exiles were bad and getting progressively worse. Kennedy shook his head in dismay.

Five years later, in 1966, when Salinger wrote his personal account of the event, he was still loyal to his boss—in a way, one can conclude, which involved spinning history. Salinger observed: "JFK, who had been willing to risk his own life to save a single shipmate when PT 109 was cut in half by a Japanese destroyer off the Solomons, felt a personal responsibility for every one of the 1,400 Cuban exiles who were facing [Fidel] Castro's jet planes and Russian-built tanks."

Salinger's press briefing on April 17 was difficult, to say the least. Unfortunately, he had to fend off most of the reporters' questions because he did not know the answers. Such was the price he paid for not being informed in the first place. Some presidents, like Kennedy, chose not to keep press secretaries fully informed for fear that the information would leak or that a spokesman would be compelled to say "No comment," which was tantamount to a "Yes." So, when asked to comment on the Cuban situation at this briefing, Salinger simply said he had no knowledge of the story.

The next day, nonetheless, on April 18, 1961, *The New York Times's* late edition carried a story on Page 1 with a three-column head:

ANTI-CASTRO UNITS LAND IN CUBA;
REPORT FIGHTING AT BEACHHEAD;
RUSK SAYS U.S. WON'T INTERVENE.

The story reported that rebel troops opposed to Premier Fidel Castro landed before dawn the day before on the swampy southern coast of Cuba in Las Villas Province. The attack, which was supported from the air, was announced by the rebels and confirmed by the Cuban State Department. The only comment from the U.S. government came from the U.S. State Department, where Secretary of State Dean Rusk was extremely cautious in his remarks at his news conference. "What happens in Cuba," he said, "is for the Cuban people to decide." He added, however, that the administration was "not indifferent" to the intrusion of the "Communist conspiracy" into this hemisphere and promised to "work together with other governments to meet efforts by this conspiracy to extend its penetration."[9]

Later on the evening of April 18, Kennedy gave a televised speech to the nation to clarify the U.S. position on the invasion and to icily warn Russian Premier Nikita Khrushchev not to intervene. Kennedy left no doubt as to where America stood when he said, "The great revolution in the history of man, past and present and future, is the revolution of those determined to be free." Khrushchev replied immediately, challenging the U.S. position that it had an arms-length relationship with the rebels, and went on to say: "It's no secret to anyone that the armed bands which invaded [Cuba] had been trained, equipped and armed by the United States of America. . . . I earnestly appeal to you, Mr. President, to call a halt to the aggression." He warned that the Soviet Union would come to the aid of Cuba, if necessary.

At his press briefing on April 19, 1961, Salinger was questioned by newsmen and struggled to respond to their questions by giving vague answers or referring them to the State Department. A few examples:

*Q: Has the White House received any reaction this morning to the president's message to Mr. Khrushchev and the exchange of messages between them?*

SALINGER: We have received a great number of telegrams, all of which supported the President in his message to Khrushchev. We did not receive one single message, which voiced opposition to the stand he [Kennedy] took.

Asked about whether or not the United States was protecting American newsmen in Cuba, Salinger said: "We have made representations, as we have in the case of the newspapermen, to the Swiss government to find out just what the situation is."[10]

After three days, Salinger recalled, Kennedy asked him to come into the Oval Office. Salinger said that when he first glanced at the president, "His face was drawn and ashen. 'How could that crowd at CIA and the Pentagon be that wrong?'" Then, Salinger wrote, parenthetically: "While the President did make this statement privately to close associates, he was firm that as far as the public was concerned, failure of the operation was his responsibility and his alone." The rebel brigade began surrendering on April 19.

Salinger's only opportunity to gain any credibility for his boss from the entire episode was to flatly admit that the president—and nobody else—took full responsibility for the debacle. This, in itself, was not only the right thing to do but it gave Salinger an "alibi" in hindsight. The reporters realized that Salinger was not informed about the invasion beforehand and that's why he was either evasive or said that he did not know the answers to their questions in the days leading up to the rebel attack.

Still, there was some fallout from the press after the fact about keeping *them* totally in the dark. The adversaries were the president and the press and the issue was freedom of information. It was not a new fight at all—merely a resumption of the hostilities between presidents and the press dating back to George Washington. There had been one hundred days of comparative calm—the cease-fire the press traditionally observes to allow a new president to study the battle terrain and deploy his forces. It came to an explosive end only ten days after the Bay of Pigs. This incident showed how difficult—if not impossible—it is for a free, open, and democratic society to mount a covert operation against an enemy that generally operates in secrecy. Salinger told reporters that JFK's major concern was protecting the lives of the band of Cuban exiles who were about to invade their homeland. The press secretary conceded that the public had a right to know what its government is doing. Nonetheless, in this case, he said, he would do the same thing again. He also said that he thought the struggle between the press and government is necessary and provided a checks and balances system between the two powerful institutions. In this instance, one can argue that the White House had the best interests of the American public in mind when it kept the crisis secret as long as it could. In ensuing years, of course, future presidents continued to stonewall the press using a number of excuses, including executive privilege and national security.

---

### The Cuban Missile Crisis: 1962
#### John F. Kennedy
#### PIERRE SALINGER

---

Historians have said that the closest the United States and the Soviet Union came to an all-out nuclear war began on the morning of October

16, 1962. From a press secretary's point of view, it unfolded this way: Press Secretary Pierre Salinger was summoned to the president's Oval Office. "The President was in a black mood," recalls Salinger, a husky, outspoken, cigar-smoking member of Kennedy's closest advisors—a group the press labeled The Irish Mafia.

Salinger had worked as a reporter for the *San Francisco Chronicle* and as a contributing editor to *Collier's* magazine in the 1940s and 1950s before joining John F. Kennedy during the 1960 campaign. Salinger is best remembered by the press for eliminating Jim Hagerty's unwritten rule that reporters should get the press secretary's approval before interviewing any high government officials. That alone boosted Salinger's standing among the press. While taking his work very seriously, Salinger was reportedly one of the two people that JFK looked to lighten things up. He and another close aide, Dave Powers, were seen as court jesters by the president and his inner circle.

On this particular day, however, Salinger knew there was no time for small talk. Kennedy lacked his usual smile and his morning greeting, "What's up?" Salinger began to clear a number of announcements he wanted to make with Kennedy, who all the while was "drumming his teeth impatiently with his fingertips" and, for him, acting a little tense. He abruptly cut Salinger off by saying, with a deadly serious look on his face: "I haven't time to hear the rest of it. But I have one you can put on top of the list. I'm going to see [Soviet Minister of Foreign Affairs] Andrei Gromyko here Thursday." Salinger told the president reporters would want to know why Gromyko had called.[11]

"I don't know what he wants," JFK replied. "He's coming on his initiative, not mine." Then he added: "There's another thing. I expect a lot of traffic through here this week—[Secretary of State Dean] Rusk, [Secretary of Defense Robert] McNamara, [UN Ambassador Adlai] Stevenson, the Chiefs of Staff. If the press tries to read something significant into it, you're to deny that anything special is going on." Salinger did not ask any questions. "When he [Kennedy] was ready to tell me he would," Salinger wrote.[12]

That same morning, Kennedy asked his brother, [Attorney General] Robert F. Kennedy to come into his office. Robert Kennedy recalled:

> He said only that we were facing great trouble. He told me that a U-2 reconnaissance plane had just finished a photographic mission and that the intelligence community had become convinced that Russia was placing missiles and atomic weapons in Cuba. That was the beginning of the Cuban Missile Crisis—a confrontation between two giant nuclear nations, the U.S. and the U.S.S.R., which brought the world to the abyss of nuclear destruction and the

end of mankind. From that moment in President Kennedy's office until Sunday morning, October 28, that was my life—and for Americans and Russians, for the whole world, it was their life as well.[13]

And so the story of what could have been, as Robert Kennedy put it, "the end of mankind," began to unfold. He was not exaggerating.

Meanwhile, the next day, October 17, behind the scenes in the war room both Kennedys and their top advisors pored over U-2 photos showing at least sixteen and up to thirty-two missiles that had a capacity to be fired over a range of a thousand miles. Salinger kept the emerging news—although he still did not know what was happening despite the sudden appearance of a lot of brass in the White House—as a mystery at his press briefing on Wednesday, October 18, 1961. He could not tell reporters what they wanted to know simply because he did not know either. But he kept that to himself. This is always a rough challenge for a press secretary, who is not used to being kept in the dark. A partial transcript showing his lack of knowledge follows:

*Q: Could we talk about the summit for a minute?*
SALINGER: What summit?

*Q: A possible summit meeting. The President said at one of his news conferences he would be happy to meet with Mr. Khrushchev if he came here. Is [Ambassador to the Soviet Union Foy Kohler] empowered to say to Premier Khrushchev that the President would meet him if he came here?*
SALINGER: I have no comment whatsoever on Mr. Kohler's discussion with Mr. Khrushchev, except to say that the stories I read this morning were highly speculative.

*Q: Can you pinpoint precisely? There are many stories that are very long.*
SALINGER: They are long and speculative. FOR BACKGROUND: The speculative nature I am referring to is whether Mr. Khrushchev is coming or not.

*Q: For guidance, is what you are trying to tell us is that you regard the stories on Khrushchev coming to this country a little too hard at this point?*
SALINGER: FOR BACKGROUND. That is right.

*Q: Does the President have any fixed agenda or is he just open to whatever Gromyko wants?*
SALINGER: There is no agenda for the meeting, which was requested by the Soviet government.

*Q: Do you anticipate anything joint [statement] coming out ot this meeting?*
SALINGER: I would think not. Possibly we will have something to say about it.

Meanwhile, Kennedy kept to his schedule and met on Wednesday, October 17, with Soviet Foreign Minister Andrei Gromyko. Ironically, it was a longstanding appointment that had been made before the missile crisis arose. At first, Gromyko's stated purpose in meeting with Kennedy was that he wanted to appeal to the American president to lessen tensions in relation to Cuba. "President Kennedy listened, astonished, but also with some admiration for the boldness of Gromyko's position," recalled Robert Kennedy.[14]

Playing his cards close to his vest, Kennedy warned Gromyko that there would be serious consequences if the Soviet Union placed missiles or offensive weapons within Cuba. Gromyko denied the presence of any Soviet weaponry on the island and assured Kennedy the United States should not be concerned.

Salinger accompanied Kennedy on Wednesday, October 17, to Connecticut where the president spoke in behalf of Democratic candidates in the upcoming election. For the rest of the week, the president maintained his public schedule, leaving on Friday morning, October 19, for stops in Ohio, Illinois, Missouri, New Mexico, Nevada, and California. That Friday night, Salinger received two alarming calls at his hotel in Chicago—the first from a State Department spokesman warning him of the second call, which came shortly thereafter, from Carleton V. Kent, a reporter with the *Chicago Sun-Times*. "Pierre," said the reporter, "We have it on good authority that the 18th Parachute Corps is standing by for a jump on Cuba. I want a comment from the White House." Salinger went directly to Kennedy's hotel room and told him of the call from the reporter. Kennedy told Salinger to call the reporter back and tell him he was wrong—that the United States was not planning to invade Cuba. Salinger then decided to talk with Kennedy aide Ken O'Donnell who was staying in the hotel's Presidential Suite, whom he knew had been present at all of the strategy sessions with JFK every day during the week of October 16. "You're going to have to cut me in pretty quick," Salinger said. "I'm flying blind with the press."[15]

O'Donnell said all he could tell Salinger was that the president may have to develop a cold tomorrow. If that happened, he added, the trip would have to be called off and the president would head back to Washington. O'Donnell also cautioned Salinger to stay away from reporters, if he could. Salinger could not do that, however, because he had dinner plans with some staffers from the *Chicago Sun-Times* and it would look even more suspicious if he did not show up. It was not easy going for Salinger. All went well until one reporter casually asked toward the end of dinner: "How's your supply of Cuban cigars holding out, Pierre?" Salinger replied, coolly, but in his usual gruff voice: "Haven't been able to find one in months." His newspaper colleague said: "The way things are looking, you had better get used to the domestic variety."

Saturday morning, October 20—still in the dark—Salinger met with the press and outlined the schedule for the weekend. During the briefing, he was interrupted by a Kennedy staffer who told him that Kennedy wanted to see him right away. He headed directly to the presidential suite, where he found the president with Rear Admiral George C. Barkley, the White House physician, near the president. "The President was playing it straight," Salinger recalls thinking. Kennedy told him that he did, indeed, have a temperature and that he should cancel the rest of the trip with the reporters waiting downstairs in busses. The president then handed Salinger a piece of hotel stationary with the following written on it: "*99.2 degrees temperature. Upper respiratory infection. Doctor says he should return to Washington*"

Presidential press secretaries are sometimes tested by their own bosses. Even though he sat next to the president in his private compartment on Air Force One on the trip back to Washington, Salinger learned nothing more. He did turn to the president and asked if he really had a bad cold. The president, he said, mumbled something. "His unprintable answer sent a chill through me."[16]

When they returned to the White House on Saturday, October 20, Kennedy asked Salinger to stay around even though it was the weekend. Salinger held an abbreviated press briefing and sent his staff home. But the afternoon was far from over. Salinger received numerous calls from the press, and proceeded to issue a series of "no comments" until Saturday night, at about 10 P.M. Salinger got a call from Edward T. Folliard, political correspondent for *The Washington Post*, who told Salinger that the columnist Walter Lippmann had told Al Friendly, managing editor of the *Post*, that the nation was on the brink of war. Salinger passed this along to Kennedy, who was angered by what he heard. "This town is a sieve," he said. Then: "Pierre, how much longer do you think this thing can hold?"

"Whatever the story is," Pierre responded, "too many good reporters are chasing it for it to hold much longer. I would say through tonight and maybe tomorrow."

Then—at long last—the president told Salinger, "All right, Pierre I'll have [National Security Assistant McGeorge] Bundy fill you in on the whole thing." Salinger was undoubtedly relieved. After five full days of watching the hectic scene around him, with only rumors and whispers and questions from the media, he finally would find out what was up. Salinger knew why he had been left "out of the loop"—to protect him from lying. Still it was hard for him—or for any press secretary—to carry on as usual when he knew something big was about to happen and *cannot* ask. Sure enough, when he met with Bundy in "the Situation Room" of the White House, as Salinger put it: "Mac didn't pull any punches. He told me we were, at that very moment, on the brink of nuclear war."[17]

He told Salinger the administration had "absolute evidence"—and showed him aerial photographs—that proved beyond any doubt that the Soviets had built offensive nuclear missiles in Cuba, which could destroy many of the cities on the East Coast of America. Behind the scenes on Sunday, October 21, after learning that an air strike against the missile sites could result in ten to twenty thousand casualties, and that another U-2 flight discovered bombers and cruise missile sites along Cuba's northern shores, Kennedy decided on a naval blockade of Cuba. When confronted with questions regarding rumors of offensive weapons in Cuba, Kennedy asked the press not to report the story until after he addressed the American public. On Monday, October 22, despite being urged by Senate leaders to call for air strikes, President Kennedy announced to the public his resolve to implement a naval blockade only. A U.S. military alert was set and Castro mobilized all of Cuba's military forces.

On Monday, October 22, at noon, Salinger knew the word was getting out and decided to preempt any questions by opening his briefing with an announcement that Kennedy would address the nation that night. He confirmed that the president would make an address to the nation at 7 P.M. on the subject of the highest national urgency. Salinger then disclosed that the president had called a meeting of his National Security Council, a second meeting with his Cabinet, and a third with congressional leaders from both parties. The press secretary was then peppered with questions about the names of different high-ranking officials and whether or not they would be in attendance. Salinger confirmed the names, disclosed that Kennedy had not been in touch with Premier Khrushchev, and declined to answer a question as to whether or not Kennedy had put U.S. troops in Berlin on alert.

Later that afternoon, shortly after 4 P.M., Salinger held a second press briefing where reporters continued to press him about the president's speech. One reporter stated: "It has been suggested that the President's cold was a diplomatic illness. To put it another way, that it was a phony. I would like to have your answer to that question." Again, Salinger declined to comment, but confirmed that Kennedy definitely had a temperature in Chicago. But he added that he had recovered. Salinger wrote in his book *With Kennedy* (1966), about his press briefings during this time of high anxiety. The transcripts of his press briefings, he said, do not record incredulous glances, but they were the general reaction to his comments.

Meanwhile, as the 7 P.M. hour approached, the president was preparing to give his speech—described to reporters as "the most important of his life" by Salinger—in the Cabinet Room. At exactly 7 P.M. the president's face appeared on the TV screen. He got right to the point, stating that the United States had "unmistakable evidence" that a series of offensive missile sites was in preparation on the island and that the purpose of these bases could be none other than to provide a nuclear strike capability against the Western Hemisphere. Kennedy said the action constituted "an explicit threat to the peace and security of all the Americas" and it was "a deliberately provocative and unjustified change in the status quo which cannot be accepted by this country, if our courage and our commitments are ever to be trusted again by either friend or foe." He followed with an announcement that there would be "a strict quarantine on all offensive military equipment under shipment to Cuba."

"Then," said Salinger, "came the most chilling paragraph in the speech: 'It shall be the policy of this nation to regard any nuclear missile launched from Cuba against any nation in the Western Hemisphere as an attack by the Soviet Union on the United States, requiring a full retaliatory response upon the Soviet Union.'" Kennedy also stressed that the blockade was only a first step and that he had directed Defense Secretary Robert McNamara to make all the preparations that might be necessary to invade Cuba.

Salinger later reported that the number of newspapermen in the White House that night was the most in his time as press secretary, surpassed only by those present right after Kennedy's assassination and funeral. He said he must have taken 100 questions in fifteen minutes. He confirmed that the president and vice president were canceling all political tours for the duration, but in answer to the question: Would he speculate on the next move if the blockade did not succeed? Replied Salinger: "I am not in charge of speculation. That's your job."[18]

Salinger then wrote: "The next six days were the most anxious and active of my life and, certainly the grimmest of the thousand days of John F. Kennedy's presidency. But I never knew him to be more in command of himself or of events. And I can never forget his courage, his smile, and his optimism that this crisis, too, would pass."[19]

Behind the scenes, on Tuesday, October 23, at the White House, the top officials and the president reviewed the latest intelligence from Cuba and decided on a proclamation and implementation of the quarantine. Robert Kennedy expressed irritation about the failure of U.S. intelligence to discover the missiles earlier. "Now we are closing the barn door after the horse is gone." McNamara indicated that a ship carrying offensive weapons would have to be stopped and perhaps disabled. But Kennedy stated that the Soviets would likely turn around such ships on their own to avoid a confrontation.

JFK argued that the only way the placement of the missiles could have been prevented would have been by invading Cuba six months or one, two, or even three years before. "What we are doing," he said, "is throwing down a card on the table in a game which we don't know the ending of." McNamara reviewed plans for destroying any surface-to-air missile (SAM) site that shot down a U-2; JFK added that when taking out the SAM site, the U.S. should simultaneously announce that if another plane was brought down all the missile sites would be destroyed.

When a U-2 was actually brought down by a missile from a missile site four days later, JFK decided not to issue the order. Bundy suggested that the president should delegate the authority to order an air strike against a missile site to the secretary of Defense. JFK did not object but insisted that there must be absolute verification that the plane was brought down by hostile military action and not as the result of an accident. There was discussion of the need for hard photographic evidence to help convince the public especially, in Latin America, that the missiles were real.[20]

While negotiations with the Russians continued, Salinger continued to face the press. On Tuesday, October 23, he was asked by the veteran White House correspondent Helen Thomas: "There has been no formal communication by the Soviet Union to the White House?" Salinger replied: "The wire services report that the American ambassador to the Soviet Union, Mr. Kohler, was called to the Soviet Foreign

Office this morning and given a statement. The statement was released simultaneously by the wires and is being carried on the wires now, but we have not received the formal text as it was received by Mr. Kohler, as of now."

In answer to a barrage of questions, Salinger said that there would be "no comment" until the text of the Kohler communiqué was received, the White House would not be closed down to tourists although extra security measures were being taken; no reservists were being called up at that time; and that there had not yet been any incidents at sea or at Guantanamo, the U.S. base in Cuba; the White House was receiving letters and telegrams that were running twelve to one in favor of the president's action, and there was a chance some of the reconnaissance photos of the missiles would be released; he was "not a military expert" and could not therefore explain why the Cubans did not camouflage the missile sites; and, finally, that the proclamation to which Kennedy referred earlier had not yet been released.

At another briefing in the early evening, Salinger read aloud the text of the proclamation Kennedy had signed. It was titled "Interdiction of the Delivery of Offensive Weapons to Cuba" and essentially announced that, effective 2 P.M. Eastern Daylight Time on Thursday, the armed forces under command of the president were "directed to interdict . . . the delivery of offensive weapons and associated material to Cuba."

While this drama was unfolding, Kennedy had started to arrange for the photos of the Cuban missile sites to be given to UN Ambassador Adlai Stevenson to be used at the United Nations. Here is where Salinger played a key role: On Tuesday, October 23, Salinger had urged the president, personally, along with Don Wilson, of the United States Information Agency, to make the photos public at the United Nations and for publication in the media. Stevenson would use them with brilliant timing the next day. Salinger, meanwhile, in his briefing on Wednesday, October 24, in response to questions, said he did not want to comment on when the first contact with any [Soviet] ship was expected, whether there were any plans to evacuate the White House, whether or not there was a build-up of Soviet troops, and there was little more he could say.

Later that day, he met with the reporters again and informed them for "Background Information"—information that could be attributed to a "White House official" but not to Salinger—that he had met with the heads of two major American wire services and the heads of three networks to discuss the subject of national security and that the Defense Department was issuing a directive to its commands that spelled out what information they were not to give out. He added:

> This is not a binding matter on editors. In other words, they can either take our advice or reject it as they see fit, but it was felt that if the editors had in front of them a memorandum of the categories of information which we consider to be not in the national interest to print at this time, it would be helpful to them in making these judgments that we ask them to make.

Simultaneously, at the United Nations, Ambassador Adlai Stevenson addressed the Security Council and before a large contingent confronted Russian Ambassador V. A. Zorin. For Stevenson, as history would see it, this was his finest moment. He pounded Zorin for an admission that the missiles existed, something Zorin refused to acknowledge. Then came Stevenson's famous challenge:

STEVENSON: You are in the courtroom of world opinion right now, and you can answer yes or no. You have denied that they exist, and I want to know whether I have understood you correctly.

ZORIN: Continue with your statement. You will have my answer in due course.

STEVENSON. I am prepared to wait for your answer until hell freezes over if that's your decision. And I am prepared to present the evidence in this room.

With that, the self-assured Stevenson showed photos of the Soviet missiles and sites projected onto a large screen. The impact was palpable. Nothing more had to be said. It was all there for the world to see. And for the press to report. Salinger did not have to elaborate, let alone spin this news. His best course of action was to let it speak for itself.

At Salinger's press conference, a reporter came up with a tricky question: "Pierre, on this subject, *The New York Times* carried a report that the White House had requested certain newspapers, and they didn't specify which ones, to withhold information about the government's intended action in the Cuban crisis, and that the papers withheld it at their request. Can you say whether that is true or not?" Salinger confirmed the story, but denied the administration was practicing wholesale censorship.

The following day, Thursday, October 25, he explained the Defense Department had put out a statement disclosing that a dozen or more

Soviet ships had turned back or changed course; that these ships were all ships which we had indications of or suspected that they carried material which was contraband under the terms of the president's interdiction; that a Soviet tanker was permitted through the blockade that morning after the Navy satisfied itself that is was not carrying any material which was contraband material. Under questioning, he conceded that there was no telephone "hotline" between the White House and the Kremlin, and confirmed that six Soviet vessels had turned back. On Thursday, October 25, 1961, Salinger told reporters there was a clear indication that the quarantine would go on until all the other missile bases were dismantled.

At the next briefing, on Friday, October 26, Salinger was still under fire. Responding to questions, he said the White House had received the letter from Bertrand Russell and that Kennedy had answered it, but that neither would be made public; that UN Ambassador Adlai Stevenson had gone to New York to meet with the Secretary General U Thant and the United Nations's top officials; that he would not comment on any exchanges President Kennedy had been having with world leaders; that he would not comment on a report in the European press that the crisis had eased; that he would not comment on any date set for the dismantling of the missiles; and that there had been no telephone communication between Kennedy and Khrushchev.

Salinger did, however, read a statement that brought the reporters up to date. It read as follows:

> The development of ballistic missile sites in Cuba continues at a rapid pace. Through the process of continued surveillance directed by the President, additional evidence has been acquired which clearly reflects that as of Thursday, October 25, definite build-ups in these offensive missile sites continue to be made. The activity at these sites apparently is directed at achieving full operational capability as soon as possible. There is evidence of that as of yesterday October 25th.

The next day, Saturday, October 27, he also disclosed that in addition to one previous message from the Kremlin, a second one was on the way, and that he would not make either public at that time [October 27]. Salinger opened the briefing by reading a White House statement that several inconsistent proposals had been made by the USSR within the last 24 hours, work on the offensive weapons was still proceeding at a rapid pace, and that the U.S. position is that before an "urgent preliminary" consideration of any proposals takes place, work on the Cuban bases must stop; offensive weapons must be rendered inoperable; and further shipments must cease, subject to international verification.

On that very same Saturday afternoon the most crucial meeting of Kennedy and his advisors took place at the White House. It was the twelfth day of the agonizing event. Bobby Kennedy put it this way in his memoir *Thirteen Days*:

> Those hours in the Cabinet Room that Saturday afternoon in October could never be erased from the minds of any of us. We saw as never before the meaning and responsibility involved in the power of the United States, the power of the President, the responsibility we had to people around the globe who had never heard of us, who had never heard of our country or the men sitting in that room determining their fate, making a decision which would influence whether they would live or die.[21]

At his briefing on Sunday, October 28—the thirteenth day of the ordeal—Salinger made public the president's answer to Chairman Khrushchev's message. Salinger said Kennedy welcomed the Soviet leader's "statesmanlike decision" to stop building bases in Cuba, and to dismantle offensive weapons and return them to the Soviet Union under UN verification. He quoted Kennedy as saying: "It is my earnest hope that the governments of the world can, with a solution of the Cuban Missile Crisis, turn their urgent attention to the compelling necessity for ending the arms race and reducing world tensions."

On Monday, October 29, Salinger announced that Kennedy had formed a "coordinating committee" to spend full time on the Cuban Missile Crisis, to be chaired by John J. McCloy, of the United States Mission to the United Nations. He indicated the team would go to the United Nations to bring the crisis to an end. He could not, however, respond to a question as to whether the Cubans were dismantling the missile bases, but explained the issue had now shifted to the United Nations. Salinger also announced that, at the request of UN General Secretary General U Thant, there would be a two-day suspension of the quarantine on Cuba in order to permit the UN Secretary to visit the area.

On Tuesday, October 30, the press continued to be testy because Salinger referred most of the questions about the military situation in Cuba to the Defense Department spokesman Arthur Sylvester. Then came an example of how the White House press corps can try the patience of a press secretary: When asked why U Thant was going to

Cuba, Salinger said: "I suggest you ask him. I can't speak for the Secretary General." The reporter said: "You can speak for the United States government. That is all I want. What do you see as his role?" Again Salinger replied, somewhat testy, "I would suggest you ask him what his role is." The reporter became insistent. "I am not interested in what he says. I am interested in what you say." Salinger replied again: "I suggest you ask him the questions."

Finally, Salinger employed another technique press secretaries put to use: announcing in advance he would not comment on a specific subject. Immediately, he was asked about whether or not the president considered and rejected an invasion of Cuba or smashing the bases before he determined on the blockade. Salinger replied: "I think that in the weeks that are going to be ahead, we are going to see a lot of stories in newspapers about various things that are either supposed to have happened during the last week or supposed to have happened now. I think I will just make it a policy not to comment on any of these stories."

At 8:30 P.M., Salinger held his third briefing on October 31 and told the reporters that the two-day suspension of the quarantine would come to an end at "daybreak tomorrow" and the quarantine would be reinstituted (Thursday, November 1). Then he added: "In the absence of effective UN arrangements, the Hemisphere nations have the responsibility for continuing surveillance." On Thursday, in response to questions, he repeated that the surveillance would continue under the Hemisphere nations. On Friday, November 2, he knocked down reports that the Red Cross would be inspecting the Soviet ships and that "Guantanamo is not a discussible subject as far as we are concerned." On Wednesday, November 7, a reporter told Salinger that Khrushchev said the United States reported some evidence of Soviet missiles with nuclear warhead capability on their way back to Russia. Could he comment? The press secretary said he would reply "On Background" that there were indications that the missiles were rapidly being shipped out of Cuba as deck cargo.

On November 8, Salinger read a Defense Department announcement that the U.S. government had confirmed through aerial reconnaissance that medium-range ballistic missiles and intermediate-range ballistic missile equipment was being removed from Cuba and that within the next twenty-four hours it expected to obtain additional confirmation through observation of Soviet vessels by U.S. naval vessels. He told reporters "on background" that the provisions of the action were included in the exchange of letters between the president and Khrushchev.

Transcripts of Salinger's press conferences and careful readings of the events following those thirteen days—from October 16 to October 28—show that the news on the historic confrontation continued to trickle out exactly what happened behind the scenes, and who said what to whom. The thirteen days that Robert Kennedy chronicled passed, and with it the closest this nation has come to a nuclear war. Salinger believed he did not need a press conference to spell out the significance of it all.

Political pundits, looking back on the crisis shortly afterward, wrote that it was the result of a series of miscalculations based on unrealistic policies for well over two decades before it came to a head in 1962. And, perhaps it had been precipitated by the Bay of Pigs failure, which had occurred the year before. But these are observations that only historians, not journalists covering military crises, have the wisdom to make.

## The Iran Hostage Crisis: 1979–1980
### Jimmy Carter–Ronald Reagan
### JODY POWELL/JAMES BRADY

One of the most notorious foreign policy blunders in modern American history occurred on April 25, 1980. Eight American crewmen in helicopters collided while attempting to rescue fifty-two hostages held in Iran since November 4, 1979, when Iranian militants, described by Iran as "students," stormed the United States Embassy in Tehran and took them captive. This terrorist act touched off the most difficult crisis of the Jimmy Carter presidency and began a personal ordeal for Carter and the American people that would last for 444 days until the inauguration of his successor, Ronald Reagan. It also resulted in the resignation of Secretary of State Cyrus Vance a few days later because, he claimed, the president refused to accept his advice warning against the mission.

This, of course, was a major blow to the president. Until then, Carter had been pursuing a policy, articulated by Jody Powell, his press secretary, of restraint aimed at the safe return of the hostages. Powell was a longtime friend of Carter's and a member of the so-called Georgia Mafia. He began working for Carter in 1968 as a twenty-five-year-old fresh-faced wannabe politician with a master's degree in political science. He had been an all-around assistant to Carter when Carter served as governor of Georgia. By 1980, the thirty-seven-year-old Powell had become a seasoned political veteran beyond his years. He stressed to the White House press corps during this crisis that the president was putting the safety of the prisoners as his first priority rather than worrying on how it would reflect on his own political fortunes.[22] And, indeed, this policy did hurt Carter considerably because a growing number of Americans grew impatient with him for not taking any action and, when he did, bungling it.

The first word on the disaster came from the White House early in the morning of April 25. It gave few details of the botched mission, except to say that it had failed and that the eight American crewmen had died in Iran after the mission was called off.

"The mission was terminated because of equipment failure," said the White House statement issued at 1 A.M. Attempting to dispel any impression that this was not an aggressive military attack, the statement was careful to mention that the mission "was not motivated by hostility toward Iran or the Iranian people and there were no Iranian casualties."

Powell made certain that this angle was included because in the two weeks prior to the attempted rescue Carter had talked about possible military action against Iran but only if economic and political sanctions against Iran failed to bring about any change in its policy of keeping the hostages. Powell, who along with the president emphasized that the mission had a humanitarian and not a military goal, reportedly played a role in advising the president to immediately assume responsibility for the incident—the wiser course at the outset—rather than looking for scapegoats under him. The White House statement continued: "[The president] accepts full responsibility for the decision to attempt the rescue."[23]

This policy is rarely followed at the highest levels of government, but in this case both Powell and Carter knew that the president's reputation for honesty and candor was on the line and, therefore, it was the right thing for him to do. The general public respects a commander-in-chief who raises his hand high when bad news is released. Powell also made it clear that—despite the failure of the rescue mission—the president's goal in the ensuing weeks and months would be to strengthen efforts among the allies to put more pressure on Iran through economic and diplomatic sanctions. In light of the mishap, it was the only way the press secretary could spin the failed mission in a positive way.[24]

The plan, according to intelligence officials in Washington, had been for the helicopters to fly into Tehran, an operation called "Desert 1," rescue the Americans from the embassy and then fly them to a rendezvous point, dubbed "Desert 2." While disclaiming any military implications, "White House officials" [this a term often used by a press secretary when he or she does not wish to be identified by name] were quoted in *The New York Times* as saying that the White House had no apology to make for withholding the administration's plans to ensure the secrecy of the mission.

Shortly after noon on April 25, Jody Powell held a press briefing. He specifically said he would limit his comments to "on background" for attribution to an "administration official." Following, excerpts from this background briefing that show Powell facing up to the setback but, at the same time, trying to play it down and specifically contrasting the "courteous" behavior of the American soldiers toward some Iranians they came across after the crash to that of the Iranian "students" who took the fifty-two American hostages in the first place—in effect, a touch of spin to slightly mollify a bad situation. Powell denied that there had been any quid pro quo with the Iranian government that would have allowed the United States to carry out the mission.

Asked if, as a result of the failure, the president would have to suffer politically for it, Powell neatly sidestepped with the reply: "That is something for the voters to judge. That is not exactly our major concern right now." The next day, in an effort to stir up some controversy at Powell's daily briefing—not unusual during a time of crisis—one reporter asked: "There are reports in the paper that say some European officials think the President should resign. Did the President have his resignation written up?" Powell, who did not ordinarily show his emotions, stared at the questioner and said firmly: "No!"

Would he consider resigning? "No!" And that was the end of that.

On Monday, April 28, Secretary of State Cyrus Vance, confirming a rumor that had been circulating for some time, resigned. In a handwritten note to the president after a weekend of what Vance described as "anguished debate" in his own mind, Vance wrote: "I have the greatest respect and admiration for you and it is with a heavy heart that I submit my resignation." Carter responded immediately with a handwritten note of his own which read, in part: "Because you could not support my decision regarding the rescue operation in Iran, you have made the correct decision to resign. I know this is a matter of principle with you, and I respect the reasons you have expressed to me."[25]

Vance was immediately replaced by Warren M. Christopher, the deputy secretary of State. It was later learned that Vance had planned to resign and had told Carter on April 21, 1980—three days before the actual rescue attempt—that he would leave if the president went ahead with the mission. Powell stressed to reporters that there was no personal animosity between the two men. In fact, interviewed on the Public Broadcasting Service's program *The MacNeil-Lehrer Report*, Powell reinforced the fact that Vance had made his views known to the president beforehand and that his resignation was one of principle rather than a disagreement over details.

The resignation was clearly a setback for Carter, but Powell tried to minimize the political damage by flatly stating the facts in an unemotional way. In an attempt to ward off further criticism, Powell quietly warned that, "Everyone with an ax to grind will sharpen it on this issue." The only remaining political fallout from the whole affair came a few months later in October 1980 when reports were circulating in the media that—as a result of some encouraging statements from Iranian leaders—the hostages might be released before the year was out.[26] In an attempt to dampen expectations of a quick end to the crisis, Powell told White House reporters, "We are all best served by not drawing overly optimistic conclusions." He was right, of course. The hostages were not released until January 21, 1981, after Ronald Reagan had taken the oath as president.

The entire episode was so well handled by Powell that one reporter, in an analysis of the episode headlined "The Power of the Press Secretary" after the fact, wrote:

> Jody Powell's presentation of the Carter Adminstration's positions draws him—more than previous White House press aides—into shaping those positions. Never before has an American Presidential press secretary wielded such power. Mr. Powell's constant presence is itself an important factor. He is now the only person besides Mr. Carter himself who is playing a senior role at both the White House and the Carter-Mondale re-election committee, blending the politics with the substantive task of running the government.[27]

Praise from anyone in the White House press corps is rare—but in this instance, many longtime Washington insiders believed that Powell deserved it.

The hostage crisis appeared to be over on the first official work day of the Reagan administration, Reagan's new press secretary James S. (Jim) Brady was exactly the right man to ensure a smooth transition between administrations. He was an easygoing, ruddy-cheeked, well-built man with humility, a good sense of humor, and a friendly way with the press: He made them feel important. A former advertising and public relations expert in the private sector, he served in a number of capacities in government during the Nixon and Ford administrations, and as a press officer for a senator and for a presidential candidate He had a reputation as a hardworking, honest, straightforward guy who got along well with the press. Reagan named him press secretary on January 20, 1981, and he picked up exactly where Powell had left off with the hostages crisis. During his very first briefing on January 21, 1981, Brady told the White House press corps at 1:33 P.M. that former President Carter had sent a message to express "my joy and pleasure at the release of the Americans."

Brady then responded to a question about why President Reagan had signed an executive memorandum to all department heads in agencies that asked for offers of resignation letters from every non-career employee, all of which would be handled on a "case by case" basis, as well as rescinding pending nominations left over from the Carter administration. This immediately stirred up the press corps, but it gave Brady a perfect opening to spin one of the themes Reagan had campaigned on during his campaign—being tough on waste, fraud, and mismanagement in the federal government. The briefing read, in part:

Q: Why is he [Reagan] going to get rid of them, if that's an important objective?
BRADY: One of the cutting edges of what we've done during the entire campaign, as you know, is to put a great deal of stock in getting rid of fraud, waste, and mismanagement, and we want to find out—in many cases, and they'll be announced soon—people that are meaner-than-a-junkyard-dog when it comes to ferreting out fraud, waste and mismanagement. And this will be the Reagan team of inspectors-general that replace these people.

Q: Jim, how do you get rid of these guys?
BRADY: I don't know. That will be reviewed.

Q: What are the procedures for getting rid of them, Jim?
BRADY: The law, as I understand it, requires—you know, it's easy to get rid of them, but in the law it says that you have to do it with consultation with the Hill, which was done last evening.

On January 22, Brady returned to the subject of the hostages. Considering that it was his first week on the job—and the White House staff was far from working smoothly—it is instructive to read what he did, what he said, and how he managed to make the entire hostage return positive front page news. Brady's logistics under fire offer an insider's view of what a White House press secretary faces during his initial week in office—especially a week in which major, worldwide news was being made on the run. First, he read aloud a statement from the president welcoming the hostages to freedom and promising them they would be quickly reunited with their families. He also read another statement from President Carter, who was returning from Wiesbaden Germany where he had visited with what he called "the liberated Americans."

The press—always anxious to push the news cycle—pressed Brady over and over again for when, where, and who would hold the press conferences when it involved the hostages. Considering the initial onslaught—and the daily uncertainty of the plans in the White House—Brady held up well during his first few days. It was, after all, in the collective interest of all Americans to find out how these hostages were feeling after 444 days in captivity. It was Brady's job to spin what had been a disaster into a "good news" story.

Brady—still bracing himself under the pressure from scores of reporters—had some good news for them. He told the press on Sunday, January 25, that the families of the freed Americans would arrive at the White House and be greeted by the president and Vice President George H.W. Bush. He emphasized to the media: "I think it'll be a very private moment, a delicate moment. We are going to have some people in there to record the color. But it is just—at this point—not appropriate to have klieg lights at what has to be a very, very emotional and trying time for these people." At noon on Sunday, Brady held yet another briefing after the Reagans had met with the hostages and their families, opening with a comment intended to soften up the reporters: "Going up in the elevator, and looking at Mrs. Reagan," he told them,

> I'd characterize it by saying it was probably a pretty good day for Kleenex. The President said it was a very moving experience. He said that he was very proud of the families that were there, for all they've been through, and that the nation was looking forward to honoring the 52 hostages in the East Room of the White House—a place that holds a maximum of 700 people.

On Monday, January 26, 1981, Brady put a bipartisan twist to the event by disclosing that former President Carter had called Reagan and said "he felt strongly that the sole honor of greeting the returned

Americans belongs now to the sitting President and that he would not be attending the ceremony." Brady assured the press that all of the hostages were "free to speak" and there would be no restrictions whatsoever put on the press interviewing any of them. He added that the hostages would be seated on chairs and be given "full honors" and the president would give each of them a miniature American flag gift set—a small flag in a rosewood box with a plaque on the top, and the ceremony would conclude with the playing of the national anthem by the U.S. Army Band.

All of Brady's hard work—a virtual miracle during the first week of a new administration when nothing had been set up properly and yet one of the biggest stories in many years was breaking—paid off. The next day, Tuesday, January 27, Reagan addressed the former hostages in an emotion-charged ceremony promising them that he would take "swift and effective retribution" *against any attacks on American government employees in foreign lands* [Italics added]. Although no new foreign policy was announced that day, the president's statement was intended to warn all nations that there would be swift action taken if any of them ever seized American government employees in the future and took them hostage. It was, in effect, a clear signal that he would be a lot tougher on Iran—or any other country that willfully captured Americans—than his predecessor was.

The full day of ceremonies included an address by Reagan to the returning hostages and led Vice President Bush to exclaim: "It's the most emotional experience of our lives. You could feel it build until the point when it hurt inside. It was the greatest event I've ever seen," he added, referring to the turnout of an estimated 265,000 Washingtonians cheering and wearing yellow ribbons as they watched the motorcade carrying the returning hostages through the city. The Reagans, teary-eyed, watched the entire spectacle from a window in the White House, and when the hostages came into the Blue Room of the White House, according to one newspaper report, "Mrs. Reagan suddenly exclaimed, 'Oh, I can't stand this!' and began hugging and kissing the freed Americans." Jim Brady stood by quietly, knowing that he had done his job.

*"Star Wars"—The Strategic Defense Initiative (SDI): 1981*
Ronald Reagan
JAMES BRADY/LARRY SPEAKES/MARLIN FITZWATER

Ronald Reagan had come into office in 1981 with an image of a man who was amiable, homespun, and likeable. Not a man to be burdened with too many details, he gave the impression of knowing what he wanted in the big picture, of knowing how to delegate authority and responsibility, and of being upbeat and optimistic about his country. But make no mistake—he was also a self-described cowboy who could be tough and determined—even stubborn—when he needed to be. To complement his striking stature as a tall, plain-spoken man whose personality dominated anywhere he went, he hired Jim Brady, a Kansan who spoke openly and honestly in a low-key manner, and stayed—with one or two exceptions—well in the background to the presidential "folk hero" for whom he worked.

Brady's tour of duty was tragically cut short on March 30, 1981, when he was shot by an assassin's bullet intended for Reagan on a street in Washington, D.C. A wound to his head left him partially paralyzed for life and confined to a wheelchair. Even though Brady retained the press secretary title for the duration of Reagan's two terms in office, he never returned to work following the shooting. Reagan was also wounded—more seriously than first realized—but recovered quickly and maintained his good spirits throughout. Brady was succeeded by his deputy, Larry Speakes, as "acting press secretary." Speakes's credentials were also impeccable. He was a former newspaper reporter and editor, a press secretary to a U.S. senator, assistant press secretary to President Gerald R. Ford, worked on the staff of the Reagan-Bush team during the campaign, and was deputy spokesman for president-elect Reagan during the transition.

Reagan's tenure went relatively smoothly until March 8, 1983, when he forcefully delivered a blockbuster of a speech at the Annual Convention of the 4th National Association of Evangelicals, in Orlando, Florida, denouncing the Soviet Union as "an evil empire"—a catchy phrase that would become one of the earmarks of the Reagan years.

Reagan quickly followed that with an even more dramatic "Cold Warrior" speech on March 23, 1983, in which he announced that—in addition to a robust military program he had already pledged since he took office—the United States intended to exploit technologies in coming decades to develop an effective anti-missile system. In his televised speech, Reagan called his proposal "a vision of the future that offers hope." Reagan's plan was known as the Strategic Defense Initiative (SDI) and was dubbed "Star Wars" by the media. This announcement rendered obsolete the nation's decades-long policy of depending on massive retaliation by ballistic missiles to counter the nuclear threat of the Soviet Union.[28]

At a White House briefing the next day, as is often done in cases where highly technical information is being released, Speakes—together with an administration official talking on condition that he be referred to as a "senior administration official"—told reporters that the president's proposal to begin research on the anti-missile system should not be interpreted by the Russians as a threat and, he added, it did not violate the Anti-Ballistic Missile (ABM) Treaty. He added that the president said the Russians should not interpret this move as "first strike" capability. Spinning the news, the official said: "This is in no sense his intention." The official took great pains to emphasize that the plan would have no immediate affect but, in response to a reporter's question, said the president hoped research would be completed "by the turn of the century."

Asked at his 10 A.M. press briefing on March 24, what the reaction was to Reagan's speech, Speakes fielded this question smoothly and spun it to the president's advantage when he told reporters: "At 10:30 last night the telephone call count on the President's speech was—positive, 1,184, negative 242. It was the best response to any speech the President has made on television. The office opened again at 9:00 A.M. this morning manned by volunteers and they tell us the switchboard is lit solid—strong, strong."

Speakes was asked when the administration started measuring the president's popularity by the number of positive phone calls. Gearing his response to make the president look good, the press secretary replied:

> The genesis of the idea was that the President, as he does quite often, met with his national Security advisors, military and civilian. There are discussions as to what is the future of the arms situation of the world in view of the arms build-up. They gave him their assessment, which indicated that they were continuing the increase into the next century of offensive buildup, particularly in the missile category . . . and that he could, after their presentation, really see no end to this constant buildup by both sides. So it was his thinking, which is supported by all of his National Security community, that something needed to be done" [to determine the attitude of the general public].

Speakes also said the White House got a "favorable" reaction from the scientific community. Then, Speakes was brought down to earth with this question: "Larry, maybe I missed it, but whenever he [the president] was describing the maginot line in the sky—(laughter)—why didn't he come up with a really solid and concrete proposal giving some funding, giving a goal and outlining this?" Speakes took it in stride: "This is a start. You've got to start somewhere."

While SDI made news on Speakes's watch, it did not have the full impact that the Reagan administration had hoped it would. Looking back on this event, Speakes's successor as press secretary, Marlin Fitzwater, offered this view of the 1983 SDI speech:

> I believe that the news media largely missed the SDI story for two reasons: first, because the Soviet Union was so insular that few people truly understood their fear of SDI and what it meant to their view of the arms race; and second, because the U.S. media always thought "Star Wars" was only a concept. They didn't believe it would work, so why should the Soviets. In retrospect, we can see the remarkable portrait of an American president who changed the world through the sheer force of an idea, one that few people believed in but in which he believed so strongly that other nations had to take it seriously. How often has that happened in our history? Wilson and the League of Nations. Kennedy and going to the moon. Not often.[29]

Speakes remained with President Reagan until January 26, 1987, when he left to become vice president of communications at the investment firm of Merrill Lynch & Company. Upon his departure, Reagan presented Speakes with the Presidential Citizens Medal on January 30, 1987.[30] Summing up his time in the White House, Speakes told a reporter who asked him about how he perceived the press corps. "There is in the press corps, since Vietnam and Watergate, many times, an automatic presumption that Government is lying," he replied. "And a Government spokesman is forced day in and day out to prove he isn't lying. . . . Somehow we need to get away from this 'I gotcha' syndrome."[31]

In January 1987, Marlin Fitzwater took over as acting press secretary, although his title was upgraded to Assistant to the President for Press Relations. (As mentioned previously, the title of "Press Secretary" continued to be held by Jim Brady.) Fitzwater was also a perfect fit for Reagan because of his easygoing manner, his ability to poke fun at himself, and his reservoir of good will with the press accumulated over two decades in increasingly important federal government press jobs. He had served as Vice President George Bush's press secretary since April 1986.

Fitzwater served Reagan well, putting a positive spin—although he was a "natural," as newspaper reporters say—on Reagan's famous visit to Berlin on June 12, 1987, when the president stood in front of the Brandenberg Gate and demanded: "Tear down this wall, Mr. Gorbachev." That was Reagan's finest hour in terms of the image of bringing the

Cold War to an end. The wall finally did come down on November 10, 1989, and symbolized the end of what Reagan had called "the evil empire."

The likeable, easy-to-read Fitzwater had developed good working relationships with President Reagan and Vice President Bush and, as a result, started out with a lot of credibility with the press. Yet, as he admits, all was not smooth sailing. In a lesser-known event, Fitzwater—a good soldier who often took the blame for his boss's mistakes—recalls a press conference he set up for Reagan and General Secretary Mikhail Gorbachev at that summit in Washington, D.C., on December 7, 1987. When he saw a mob of reporters, Fitzwater headed for a side door so as not to be swarmed by the press. "The rule here," he recalled, "was the same as in any urban street situation: Never make eye contact with anyone you don't want to deal with. Reporters were shouting at me but I never looked back."[32]

Some time prior to the press conference, Fitzwater had invited Gennadi Gerasimov, Gorbachev's press secretary, to join him at the summit press briefings. Gerasimov had agreed. And preparing for the meeting, Fitzwater had spent a lot of time with the press, building up a public image of supporting Gorbachev and his reforms in Russia. Unfortunately, just five days before the summit, a report from the administration was released detailing Soviet violations of existing arms agreements.

Asked about it in his daily press briefing, Fitzwater offhandedly commented: "This is not a summit or session to be taken lightly between old friends. This is a summit between old enemies." As Fitzwater tells the story in his book:

> You could hear the "gotcha" buttons going off all over the room. Those are the shuffling, sneezing, and stifled laughs that occur when you have made a mistake that the press knows they can exploit, that can be shortened to one brief headline that will hold the president up to ridicule . . . I was aghast with myself. We had spent days, weeks, and thousands of words in briefings by every general who had ever touched a missile, trying to cultivate a positive public relationship with the Soviets. Now my slip of the tongue would be used to anger Gorbachev.[33]

He was right. Within minutes the Associated Press played it straight and sent out a wire story with the following lead: "White House spokesman Marlin Fitzwater said today that President Reagan's tough rhetoric towards the Soviet Union reflects his belief that his upcoming meeting with Soviet leader Mikhail S. Gorbachev is 'a summit between old enemies, not friends.'" That was followed in rapid fire by immediate dissemination of his remarks by the Federal News Service, the Foreign Press Center, and around the world. Then, to make things worse, a few reporters called the Soviet embassy in Washington for response to Fitzwater's inflammatory statement. Soon enough, a copy of the story was sent to the Foreign Ministry and advisers to Gorbachev who, in turn, passed it along to their leader who—according to Fitzwater's account—tucked it into his pocket to be used at an appropriate moment.

That moment came soon enough. At about noon on December 7, a red-faced Fitzwater and Gerasimov called a joint press briefing in the Marriott Hotel, where the summit was to take place. "It was like a carnival," reported Fitzwater, with reporters smiling and laughing, photographers strolling in front of the podium, couriers waiting in the back of the ballroom with their bicycle helmets on, and USIA employees standing along the walls, just watching the show. "As we reached the podium, someone in the audience said, 'Fifty dollars on Gerasimov.'"

The first question from a reporter was a request to sum up the U.S. position on Star Wars. His face red but smiling, Fitzwater replied: "The president's position on the Strategic Defense Initiative is clear. He has said that he intends to research, develop, and deploy such a system. That position is well known to the Soviets."

Fitzwater somehow got through the briefing and pointed out that he cared about "saying the right thing," not how he looked on television. Sure enough, that opened up another opportunity that the press jumped on. The *London Daily Telegraph's* correspondent sent out a story that began: "As Mr. Gorbachev flew across the Atlantic yesterday his spokesman, Mr. Gennadi Gerasimov, his face caked with television makeup, and Mr. Marlin Fitzwater, President Reagan's man, appeared before the world press to set the summit scene."

The contrast in styles was ironic. The Russian was tall and elegant in the manner of Cary Grant. The American, squat, ruddy-cheeked, and balding, had the look of a jolly Russian peasant. But that was only the beginning of trouble for the self-effacing Fitzwater whose embarrassing experience—one might use the cliché—raises the proverbial question: "Why do bad things happen to good people?"

The next morning, Reagan and Gorbachev offered welcoming comments on the South Lawn of the White House, then quickly moved indoors and retreated to the Oval Office. There were so many members of the press present that Fitzwater resorted to the procedure of selecting a pool reporter to do the questioning for all of the press. Fitzwater disdained the pool concept but admitted it was sometimes necessary because of space limitations. The idea angered the entire press corps, but every press secretary had to live with the arrangement for practical reasons. In this instance, Fitzwater selected Owen Ullmann of Knight-Ridder newspapers, an old friend of Fitzwater's for many years when he was an AP reporter in Detroit. "He would do a professional job," Fitzwater wrote of this event, "especially with 7,000 other reporters looking over his shoulder, but he didn't shy from the embarrassing question."

At the close of the photo sessions, after both leaders appeared to be optimistic about the outcome of the meeting, Ullmann literally shouted the inevitable question: "Old friends or old enemies?" As Fitzwater described his own reaction: "My heart jumped, and my legs weakened." Instantly, as Fitzwater tells it, "The president responded, 'Well, I think you can judge for yourself.' The Gipper had saved me again. But I looked up to see Gorbachev staring straight at me. He said nothing, and the press rushed from the Oval to get these first pictures on the wires."[34]

But Fitzwater was not out of the woods yet. When it came time to wind up the summit, both Reagan and Gorbachev shook the hands of all the aides who had worked so hard for them. "It was a kind of receiving line," Fitzwater recalls.

> As my turn came, Gorbachev's interpreter, Pavel Palazchenko, a slight, bald-headed fellow, leaned in to the general secretary and told him, "This is Marlin Fitzwater. He's the one who said we are old enemies." I was standing right in front of Gorbachev, holding his outstretched hands and looking him straight in the eye as Pavel's words, "old enemies," registered. Gorbachev's eyes instantly hardened, as if a switch had been turned, his hand pulled away, and his body muscles visibly flinched. He raised his right hand, squeezing it into a fist almost at the level of my face, and said "If you had said that in my country, I would scold you." His closed fist in front of my face scared me. I froze. Then, from somewhere, a low Kansas voice came out of me nervously, "Sometimes I get scolded in my country." But Gorbachev gave no sign at recognition. He lowered his hand, and turned to the next person in line. I stumbled away. It seemed to me the only time during the entire summit that he wavered from his obvious purpose of showing a new kind of Russian leader.[35]

And so ended a near-catastrophe—at least in Fitzwater's mind—and a wonderful anecdote that Fitzwater was only too happy to share with the public in his memoirs—showing, after all, that press secretaries sometimes have to spin their own way back into good graces with the press—not to mention world leaders.

## NOTES

1. Truman, Harry. *Memoirs of Harry S. Truman: Volume I, Years of Decisions* (New York: Doubleday, 1955), p. 270.

2. *The New York Times*, June 26, 1945, p. 1.

3. Truman, *Memoirs*, p. 400.

4. Ibid., p. 560.

5. Beschloss, Michael. *Presidential Courage: Brave Leaders And How They Changed America 1789—1989* (New York: Simon & Schuster, 2007), pp. 196–197.

6. President Truman's statement recognizing the State of Israel, May 14, 1948. Charles Ross Papers, 1904–1967, Alphabetical Correspondence File: "Handwriting of the President," Courtesy of Harry S. Truman Library, National Archives and Record Administration.

7. *The New York Times*, May 16, 1948, p. 1.

8. Salinger, Pierre. *With Kennedy* (New York: Doubleday & Company, 1966), p. 145.

9. *The New York Times*, April 18, 1961, p. 1.

10. Transcript of press briefing by Pierre Salinger, April 19, 1961.

11. Salinger, *With Kennedy*, p. 249.

12. Ibid., pp.249–250

13. Kennedy, Robert. *Thirteen Days: A Memoir of the Cuban Missile Crisis* (New York: W.W. Norton & Company, 1969), p. 23.

14. Ibid., pp. 40–41.

15. Salinger, *With Kennedy*, p. 251.

16. Ibid., p. 252.

17. Ibid., p. 254.

18. Ibid., p. 267.

19. Ibid., p. 267.

20. JFK Library release notes prepared by Sheldon M. Stern.

21. Kennedy, *Thirteen Days*, p. 101.

22. A list of the prisoners, their ages, and their hometowns was made available to the press.

23. *The New York Times*, April 25, 1980, p. 1.

24. *The New York Times*, April 26 1980, p. 1.

25. *The New York Times*, April 29, 1980, p. 1.

26. *The New York Times*, October 24, 1980.

27. Weisman, Steven R. *The New York Times*, October 26, 1980.

28. *The New York Times*, March 24, 1981.

29. Fitzwater, Marlin. *Call the Briefing! Bush and Reagan, Sam and Helen: A Decade with Presidents and The Press* (New York: Random House, 1995), p. 131.

30. The citation reads as follows: "In journalism, politics, and Government, Larry Speakes has faithfully served the cause of truth and, in doing so, has served the cause of America. Veteran of the White House press office for 9 years under three administrations, conducting some 2,000 daily press briefings during this Administration, Larry Speakes has become a familiar sight to all of us. America has come to know him as a man cool under pressure, conscientiously working to get the facts out—a man whom the American people could always count on to tell them the truth. America is more knowledgeable because of Larry Speakes."

31. Boy, Gerald. "Q&A With Larry Speakes; Reflections Upon Leaving the White House," *The New York Times*, January 26, 1986.

32. Fitzwater, *Call the Briefing!*, pp. 131–132.

33. Ibid., p. 135.

34. Ibid., p. 143.

35. Ibid., pp. 149–150.

# CHAPTER 3

## PRESIDENTIAL SCANDALS

### The Watergate Affair: 1972–1974
#### Richard M. Nixon
#### RON ZIEGLER

[Author's Note: *The following passage is not intended to be comprehensive or to include all of the individuals who played a key role in the complex Watergate scandal. Instead, it is a report on the specific role that Press Secretary Ronald L. Ziegler played on behalf of President Richard M. Nixon, and includes numerous excerpts from his daily White House press briefings that— intentionally or otherwise—were examples of "spin."*]

It all started innocuously in the early morning of June 17, 1972, when five men attempted a break-in to electronically bug the offices of the Democratic National Committee in the sprawling Watergate hotel and office complex in Washington, D.C. An alert security guard called the police, who arrested the men at 2:30 A.M. It appeared at first glance to be a routine robbery—initially described in a press briefing shortly thereafter by White House press secretary Ron Ziegler as follows: "Certain elements may try to stretch this beyond what it is." He called it a "third rate burglary." A few days later, at a press conference, Nixon was asked this question: "It is reported that the people who bugged [Democratic] headquarters had a direct link to the White House. Have you had any sort of investigation made to determine whether this is true?" Nixon, having anticipated the question and—amazingly, citing his own press secretary as the source—replied: "Mr. Ziegler, and also Mr. [Attorney General John] Mitchell, speaking for the campaign committee, have responded to questions on this in great detail. They have stated my position and have also stated the facts accurately. This kind of activity as Mr. Ziegler has indicated, has no place whatever in our electoral process or in our governmental process. And, as Mr. Ziegler has stated, the White House has no involvement whatever in this particular incident."[1]

Ziegler's "third rate burglary" remark would come back to haunt him. A little more than two years later—after a badly bungled attempt by Nixon and his top aides to cover up the crime and its ensuing abuses of national security by Nixon staff members—a congressional inquiry brought to light other crimes. More than thirty high administration officials, Republican campaign officials, and Nixon campaign contributors pleaded guilty or were found guilty of breaking the law. Within two years, on August 8, 1974, Nixon resigned as he faced the almost-certain threat of impeachment by the Congress.

Even though many millions of words and archival material have been compiled about Watergate over the years and Ziegler himself appeared thirty-three times before Congress during its Watergate hearings, no evidence has ever been discovered that Ziegler himself was personally involved in the cover-up. Nonetheless, for a bright new press secretary who had been elated by Nixon's historic "comeback" victory in 1968, the ensuing two years had to be one of the worst public relations nightmares any press secretary has experienced in White House history.

For purposes of analyzing the scandal from the point of view of the press secretary to the president, we will focus on the story of a talented, well-educated, twenty-nine-year-old journeyman who was caught up in the scandal. Although Ziegler's actions were not illegal, he did parrot to the press and the world the untruthful words of Nixon and a number of his senior aides who wound up either going to prison or disgraced.

From the time Nixon took office in 1969 until 1972, Ziegler was described by well-known newspaperman and journalist David Wise as follows: "The job of Presidential press secretary seemed not to have taken the slightest toll on Ronald Ziegler in almost four years. . . . He was just as smooth-faced, and seemingly relaxed, as the day he moved into the White House. In his early thirties he retained something of the easy style of the high school jock who just scored the winning touchdown."[2]

Another veteran political expert and author, John Herbers, had a similar positive impression of Ziegler in 1972. He wrote:

> At thirty-four years of age, Ziegler had survived four years in one of the toughest jobs in Washington. The President and almost everyone in the official White House gave him high marks for the way he handled the press, putting out exactly what the President and his staff wanted, and no more, and he ran an efficient office, which meant that the media had quick and

easy access to that which was released. The mimeograph machine ran on time. If Ziegler minded conveying only what he was told to convey—and we know from the White House tapes he was a willing part in the regime—he never showed it. He was quite sure of himself in those days, very authoritative and very maddening to the reporter whose job was to know what was going on behind closed corridors and offices.[3]

Ziegler had no doubts how much his chief client, the president, detested the "liberal" media—in part because of his loss to John F. Kennedy in 1960 when he looked so bad on television and felt he was beaten on style rather than on substance. Consequently presidential assistants tried to convey to Ziegler the president's particular dislike of *The Washington Post* and *The New York Times*. In a memorandum dated May 30, 1970, from the president to Chief of Staff H.R. (Bob) Haldeman, he laid out his directive:

> I would like you to have a talk with [Herbert] Klein [director of communications] with regard to some very strict instructions . . . with regard to *The New York Times, no one* [ital Nixon's] from the White House staff under any circumstances is to answer any call or see anybody from *The New York Times*. With regard to *The Washington Post* Ziegler under no circumstances is to see anybody from *The Washington Post* and no one on the White House staff is to see anybody from *The Washington Post* or return any calls from them.[4]

Ziegler will no doubt be remembered as the presidential spokesman who unwittingly lied to the White House press corps—and to the world. Unfortunately, his legacy will always be inextricably tied to Watergate because he was loyal to his president—to a fault. He was not immediately accepted by the White House correspondents because he did not have a journalism background and he had only a limited knowledge of world affairs. As previously noted, his experience had been in advertising and public relations—especially the fine art of putting the best possible face on a story or, if necessary, offering complex, difficult-to-understand explanations. Because of his talent for sidestepping issues, the White House press nicknamed him "Zigzag," and his statements to the press were labeled "Ziegles." Furthermore, as one author writing about Ziegler put it: "Ziegler briefed reporters twice a day, but often the synopses were filled with trivia and obfuscations. Ziegler refused to admit he might not have an answer to a question, and sometimes his answers were ludicrous. Although he tried to please as much as aggravate, Ziegler drew mixed reviews from reporters."[5]

From the outset, Ziegler was at a disadvantage because he reported directly to presidential aide Bob Haldeman. So, his independence was tenuous because he did not have as much direct access to the president as the White House press corps would have wanted him to. Ziegler's tenure as press secretary was characterized by one of his successors, Marlin Fitzwater, as one that had "a tragic quality . . . His role was denigrated by the media and the public, and people kind of shied away from him."[6]

*The Washington Post's* investigative reporters Bob Woodward and Carl Bernstein, of course, broke the Watergate story that brought down the Nixon administration and won them and the newspaper a Pulitzer Prize. Known for his cool nerves, Ziegler defended the president to whom he gave complete, unquestioning loyalty, but his inability to either keep himself informed and to be shut out of the process eventually lowered his credibility to the point where the White House press corps could not believe almost anything he said. Ziegler was particularly incensed by Woodward and Bernstein. He drew considerable laughter from the press when he told reporters at the height of the crisis, "If my answers sound confusing, I think they are confusing because the questions are confusing and the situation is confusing."[7]

Ziegler's attempts at "spin" were not subtle; he simply denied what the press was printing or released such complex information that it could not be immediately understood. At the majority of his press briefings, reporters had to keep asking him the same question over and over and ask for further explanations because of his sometimes clumsy, unprofessional way of doing business. It worked—for a while.

Following the break-in, however, *The Washington Post* reported on September 29, 1972, that Attorney General John Mitchell controlled a secret Republican fund used to finance widespread intelligence-gathering operations against the Democrats; and that on October 10, 1972, FBI agents established that the Watergate break-in stemmed from a massive campaign of political spying and sabotage conducted by the Committee to Re-Elect the President (CREEP). Despite this adverse publicity, on November 7, 1972, Nixon was reelected in one of the largest landslides in American history, winning more then 60 percent of the vote against Democratic senator George McGovern. His victory confirmed Ziegler's belief that the president, indeed, was completely innocent of any wrongdoing.

Ziegler's press briefing on October 25, 1972, ran fifty-two minutes and the transcript shows that two-thirds of it was devoted to the press secretary's criticism of *The Washington Post*. Finally, after a long series of questions, Ziegler was asked why *The Washington Post*, in his words, was trying to "discredit" the Nixon administration. The press secretary then singled out Ben Bradlee, the executive editor, as the individual who was determined to fight Nixon.[8]

Nixon did not enjoy his victory for very long. On January 30, 1973, *The Washington Post* reported that former Nixon aides G. Gordon Liddy and James W. McCord Jr. were convicted of conspiracy, burglary, and wiretapping in the Watergate incident. *The Washington Post* stories continued: Although evidence over time began to point toward the Oval Office as the culprit in Watergate, Ziegler continued to fiercely defend Nixon. The next move on February 7, 1973, was by the U.S. Senate, which established a Select Committee, headed by North Carolina Democratic senator Sam J. Irvin Jr., to begin investigating the Watergate affair.

Following are a few examples from excerpts of his press briefing of March 7, 1973, when Ziegler tried in vain to contend with some tough questions from the press:

*Q: Ron, can you give us at least one reason why you say John Dean is not prepared to hold a press conference?*

ZIEGLER: It is his judgment that he does not feel it would be appropriate to do so.

*Q: Ron, given the public interest and our obvious interest in this whole matter of the Watergate affair and the whole matter of Mr. [L. Patrick] Gray's confirmation [as director of the FBI] hearing on the Hill, why do you not apprise yourself of the details, when on other issues, multitudinous as they may be during any given year, you manage somehow to get yourself very well briefed?*

ZIELGER: I apprise myself of those details of what I consider to be relevant and I don't consider Mr. Gray's testimony before the Senate Subcommittee, as they proceed with the process of advise and consent on a nomination that the President has made, to be a matter for him to address from here . . . I am not the person to provide you details on the Watergate hearing or the Watergate case when there has been a grand jury hearing, when there has been a trial, when there have been depositions taken that have been made public, and when those who wish to pursue this matter can take many other vehicles, it is not my role, it is not my position to get into a question and answer session on this.

In fairness, a majority of the press who covered Nixon believed that Ziegler could not have possibly had all the information in his head about all of the various ramifications of Watergate—even if he had been briefed about all of the details. Yet, the press kept coming. On March 26, 1973, for example, there was a front page story in *The New York Times* that reported that the White House acknowledged that John W. Dean III, Nixon's counsel, had asked L. Patrick Gray III, the acting director of the FBI, to "correct" the statement he had made previously about his allegation that Mr. Dean "probably" lied to federal agents investigating the Watergate case. Ziegler immediately stepped in, according to the newspaper story, stating: "The President nominated Mr. Gray and stands behind him. I don't say that, as it was reported the other day, hesitatingly. I say that straight out. The President supports him fully." Ziegler added: "The President has absolute and total confidence in Dean." All of which left the press totally confused—probably what Ziegler intended. However, it was the first crack in the White House hierarchy and a symptom of far worse developments to come. On March 29, 1973, Ziegler announced that Nixon would not testify either orally or in writing, to either the grand jury or the Senate committee investigating Watergate. "We feel it would be inappropriate," said Ziegler. "It would do violence to the separation of powers."

At a press briefing the next day, Ziegler became more aggressive. It opened this way on March 30, 1973:

ZIEGLER: Now, anticipating some of your questions this morning, I have prepared some notes here which I would like to state to you as a reiteration of general policy regarding the administration and White House positions regarding the inquiry into the Watergate matter: As all of you are aware, over the past week there have been a series of unsubstantiated or uncorroborated charges, which seeped from private sessions of the Senate Select Committee as they are having their initial meetings on this matter. These unsubstantiated charges have associated names of the White House staff with the Watergate matter. And it is evident that personal rights of individuals have been abused in very serious ways by procedures, which are less than orderly and judicial. I would like to remind all of you here and call to your attention that it has been our position in the past and it remains the White House position that the public media and the White House briefing room are not the places to try and conduct an analysis of these charges or to make judgments regarding individuals in response to what are unsubstantiated and uncorroborated charges. . . . The purpose of this policy is the opposite of covering up information. It is the policy which has been set with the objective to get the true facts in an orderly way.'

At the same time, Ziegler also said the president had issued an order to all members of his staff to testify if called before a federal grand jury that was continuing to look into the Watergate raid. Ziegler said that with respect to both the court and the congressional inquiries into political espionage, Nixon was willing to cooperate in any way that did not do "violence to the separation of powers" in either investigation. But he added that appearances of his White House staff would be limited to sessions closed to the public. Thus, for the first time, the White House appeared to be showing concerns about the bipartisan attacks on the administration's conduct in the Watergate case. In a conciliatory tone, Ziegler said he wanted to "dispel the myth" that "we seek to cover up."

There was one particular day than stands out as an example of how relentless the reporters could be and how defenseless—and defensive—Ziegler was. Before Ziegler's briefing, on the morning of April 17, 1973, Nixon—appearing determined to put an end to the growing Watergate scandal and to make it appear that he, personally, was not involved in any way—made two announcements. The first was that there had been "major findings" in the case. He said he told a hastily called press conference at the White House that an agreement had been reached between the White House and the Senate Select Committee investigating Watergate that would, at once, preserve "the separation of powers" [between the legislative branch and the executive branch] which would make his aides available to testify to the Senate investigating committee while, at the same time, promising limited testimony from any of his White House aides. In reading his statement—no questions were allowed—he said he would take action against any government employee involved in the case. Reading a statement that he would, no doubt, come to regret, he said, "No individual holding office in the past or in the present, in a position of major importance in the Administration, should be given immunity from prosecution. I condemn any attempt to cover up this case, no matter who is involved."

Nixon's second announcement pertained directly to the break-in case itself. He said, "If any person in the executive branch is indicted by the grand jury, my policy will be to immediately suspend him. If convicted he will, of course, be automatically discharged." Nixon pledged to aid the judicial process "in all appropriate ways."

Nixon also disclosed "executive privilege was expressly reserved and may be asserted during the course of the questioning of any staff member." The president said he agreed to have the hearings televised and that all staffers would appear voluntarily and testify under oath and that television reporters would cover hearings in which only wrongdoing had been charged.

Within minutes after Nixon's unscheduled and dramatic appearance on April 17, 1973, Ziegler held an informal briefing in which he stated— much to the astonishment of the entire White House press corps—that Nixon's [and, presumably Ziegler's] past statements denying any involvement by White House staff members were now "inoperative"—a phrase that would come to haunt Ziegler for the remainder of his tenure and which, arguably, came to define his own place in history as a press secretary with little or no credibility. Ziegler suddenly reversed all of his previous statements denying any wrongdoing by the president and his aides when he told the White House press corps that the president had released a revised statement about the Watergate affair indicating that the White House staff had fully cooperated with an internal investigation made by John Dean, and that the U.S. Attorney's office was also proceeding with an investigation. "This [Nixon's comment that morning] is the operative statement," he said. "The others [up to now] are inoperative." Ziegler had made literally thousands of White House statements but this comment ["inoperative"] was the only one that people remembered through the intervening years—presumably because it was so striking a turnabout.

Some excerpts from that embarrassing briefing would subsequently be recalled by succeeding press secretaries as the nadir in White House press relations:

*Q: Ron, on March 2nd [1973], the President said that the investigation conducted by Mr. [John] Dean [counsel to the President] indicates that no one on the White House staff, at the time he conducted the investigation, was involved or had knowledge of the Watergate matter. Does that still stand?*

ZIEGLER: Well, of course, that was a statement made prior to the President's statement issued today and the President's statement today is the operative statement.

The others are inoperative.

*Q: Is the President still convinced of John Dean's innocence?*
ZIEGLER: I am not going to address myself to any individual.

*Q: Has there been any changes in the duty of John Dean? Is he continuing to function as counsel to the President just as he has been?*
ZIEGLER: I am not going to focus on any individual today.

*Q: In the past, the President has denied, you have denied, that the White House has denied involvement of White House staff members in the Watergate affair. The statement today, which is the "operative" statement, does not make such a denial. Therefore a normal inference would be that someone on the White House staff has been found to be involved. Is that a correct inference?*

ZIEGLER: The reason I dwelled on this before is the fact that the comments made previously were based on information available previously. I would caution you against drawing any conclusions beyond the statement by the President and any conclusion such as you suggested in your inference.

*Q: You have a new investigation going. Is it typical White House procedure that while it is ongoing—you started it, you have reason to start it—you just continue to deny things?*

ZIEGLER: I think you had better look at the record before you draw such a broad sweeping emotional comment.

*Q: On March 26, Ron, you said, "It is totally false that Mr. Dean had any prior knowledge of the Watergate matter." Now how does today's statement by the President make that statement inoperative?*

ZIEGLER: Sir, I am not going to, as skillfully as you have asked the question, attempt to focus this on one individual.

*Q: I have a procedural question, Ron. The President's statement [today] says, "Real progress has been made in finding the truth." Can we assume from that that when the investigation is finished, that the President or the Justice Department will announce whatever was found out through that investigation?*

ZIEGLER: I cannot predict how that will be handled.

Nixon launched a counteroffensive the next day on April 18, 1973, by announcing he wanted to see the guilty found and tried. He took a preemptive strategy. "Get the possible culprits before a grand jury and let the courts work their will, settle the civil suits out of court: above all, demolish the subsidiary issue that has become paramount in recent days: The White House cover-up." In a news analysis in *The New York Times*, reporter R. W. Apple Jr. wrote: "Having done all this, so the thinking goes, there is little to worry about from the Senate's investigation, which certainly threatened to do more damage politically than any other conceivable proceeding."[9]

On April 18, 1973, Ziegler's press briefing continued to center around Nixon's statements and made Ziegler's job even more difficult. A reporter brought up the president's statement in October 1972, referring to the activities at the Watergate as "political skullduggery" and said it was "reprehensible." Did Nixon still feel that way?

Ziegler quickly cut off that line of questioning by stating:

> I am not going to "no comment." I am just not going to provide you any answer. I don't think it would be appropriate from the standpoint of individuals, the rights of individuals, and also I think it would be unwise and unfair, in human terms, to answer questions that by their nature suggest or make reference to not only individuals, but individuals located in one place or another. *So I will simply say to you that my position in the briefing will not be to provide answers to any questions on this* subject [italics added].

At this point, the briefing became unusually personal and nasty. It was one of the classic battles between a press secretary and White House reporters. One reporter angrily stated: "Ron, last October I quoted you as saying that there was no question but that the financing of the burglary came from the committee. I think I have some human rights, shall we say, to have you apologize at the present time for being inaccurate and unwise." Ziegler stubbornly held his ground. "Sir, I responded to your questions at that time, and my remarks stand on the record."

The reporter shot back: "Were you inaccurate? Did you make the statement to me at that time relative to the source of the money to finance the burglary at Watergate? I am asking you. This is a matter of personal privilege. It doesn't get into any defendants or any of the things you have tried to deal with." Ziegler again: "My answer to your question is that I responded to you at that time and I have nothing further to say." The reporter persisted: "Well, you did not respond adequately. You should apologize, I think, in having challenged an accurate story." This was followed by the most egregious charge a reporter can publicly make against a press secretary: lying. "If that is your kind of response," the reporter said, "We all have a right to say the statement will not be operative because it was a lie when you said it and it is a lie now."

Another reporter chimed in: "Ron. Do you think the White House creditability has suffered through your denials for ten months, the White House—in the name of the White House and suddenly you say everything we have said before is 'inoperative'?" Ziegler stuck to his guns. "I think, as I said earlier, the comments that we have made here at the White House, in my view, will stand the test of time." Then came another personal insult: "Do you feel free to stand up there and lie and put out misinformation and then come around later and just say it is all 'inoperative'? That is what you are doing. You are not entitled to any credibility at all when you do that."

Ziegler, clearly uncomfortable with the way things were going, finally tried to put the issue to rest. "I will answer your question finally on the entire subject of what is operative and what is inoperative without my attempting to get into dissecting it all this time, by simply saying that the President's statement of yesterday was clear. It has set a course for an action which is being followed and the position that I will follow in these briefings on this subject is the one that was outlined to you earlier."

That did not help. The reporter accused Ziegler, as the president's spokesman, of not doing his job by refusing to answer any questions on the topic of Watergate and asked if "the muzzle is on you in this area?" Yet another newsman, incredulous about what he was hearing, asked: "Is it possible that your non-response to Watergate questions could proceed all the way through the indictments ands trial and appeals for the next year, or two years?" Ziegler turned away and, looking at the assembled mass of reporters, asked plaintively if there were any other questions. The reporters continued their pursuit. Said one: "Ron, very seriously, are you at all concerned that you might appear to be somewhat suspicious, when on the one hand, in effect you are lowering the curtain on questions about the Watergate affair now; yet, for months you have been willing to refer to individuals on the White House staff and tell us that the President has confidence in them. Are you at all concerned about a question surrounding your posture?"

The press would not let up. Here's the remaining Q&A:

ZIEGLER: I think I have already responded to that question in several ways, and I will have to ask for the next question.

*Q: Is the president's intensive inquiry continuing, or now concluded?*
ZIEGLER: I will ask for the next question.

*Q: Did anyone in the Justice Department or on the White House staff talk to Gordon Liddy after he refused to talk to the grand jury?*
ZIEGLER: I will ask for the next question.

*Q: Speaking of history, do you think that the "third rate burglary" comment of yours last June or July will stand up to the test of time?*

ZIEGLER: I think that is quite obvious. It has already withstood the test of time (laughter.)

There was little doubt that, in football terms, the reporters were "piling on" the press secretary who, because of his blind loyalty to Nixon, was going to pay the ultimate price in the eyes of the media: total loss of credibility. Nonetheless, to his credit, he kept his balance and his sense of humor about his job. The next day, April 19, 1973, the press continued peppering Ziegler with pointed questions:

*Q: Mr. Dean has just issued a statement from his office saying that he will not be a scapegoat in the Watergate affair. I wonder if there is any special significance attached to the fact that he issued the statement privately; that it did not come from your office. Why did he do it that way?*

ZIEGLER: I think the President's statement of the 17th made it quite clear that the process which is now in motion is not a process to find a scapegoat. The process now in mention is a process to find the truth in this matter.

*Q: Ron, I have been standing back here under the impression, and drawing the impression, that under the circumstances of the last few days, you must have the world's worst job. I was wondering how you might characterize it yourself?*

ZEIGLER: My job? I love it.

*Q: You love it?*

ZEILGER: I enjoy it. I like working here.

*Q: You like all this??*

ZIEGLER: Well, we go through difficult periods in the briefing room, from time to time, but I understand that.

*Q: Ron, has the President been informed of Mr. Dean's statement [about not being a scapegoat]?*

ZEIGLER: Yes, he has been.

*Q: What is his reaction?*

ZEIGLER: Gentlemen, I am not going to take any further questions on this subject.

By this time momentum for impeachment was starting to build. Nixon's top staffers—H. R. Haldeman, John Erlichman, and Attorney General Richard Kleindienst—resigned over the scandal, and the president fired John W. Dean III on April 30, 1973. Ziegler, much to his credit, called Bob Woodward and Carl Bernstein that day at *The Washington Post* and apologized to them. Unfortunately, at the same time, Ziegler also had to cope with newspaper reports that the FBI was putting guards on the files of three senior White House officials who were leaving the administration because of the Watergate case—Dean, Ehrlichman, and Haldeman. Haldeman was immediately succeeded by Alexander M. Haig Jr., vice chief of staff to the Army, as assistant to the president. Neither Haldeman nor Dean was allowed to examine or remove any papers from their offices unless an FBI agent was present, the story said.

This was another huge challenge for Ziegler to face. He tried to spin his way out of this by saying that "the safeguarding procedure," was not meant "to cast aspersions on any individual."[10] In fact, he added, all three staffers agreed to the procedure. But, as the April 30, 1973, *The New York Times* reported: "Their acquiescence could not obscure the fall from grace of the two men who, until their resignations yesterday, had more access to the President than any other public official. Now they are unable to look at their papers alone." With these top aides now out of commission, Ziegler, in effect, became the public face of a presidency struggling for survival—and he wanted to survive, as well.[11]

On that same day, April 30, 1973, Nixon took to national television and told the nation that he accepted responsibility for what had happened in the Watergate case, even though he had no knowledge of political espionage or attempts to cover it up, but he alleged wrongdoing on the part of those he had delegated to run his 1972 presidential campaign and those whom he appointed to investigate the matter. Nixon said that because of his preoccupation with foreign policy matters, he had delegated most of the responsibility for the 1972 campaign to subordinates. But he accepted full responsibility for those who he described as "people whose zeal exceeded their judgment."[12]

According to Irvin, however, "The speech was cleverly contrived to present the speaker [President Nixon] to the nation as a dedicated, harassed, and overburdened President, who had been engrossed throughout the presidential campaign in 1972 in efforts to obtain prosperity and peace with honor in Southeast Asia for Americans and peace for all the world." Irvin argued that Nixon, by reason of such efforts had been "justifiably ignorant" at all times before March 21, 1973, of the true nature of the Watergate affair and the possibility of any involvement of any of his political or governmental aides in it. He had learned for the first time since March 21, 1973, because of new investigations supervised by Nixon, that "some of his political or governmental aides may have participated in the Watergate break-in and in subsequent efforts to hide the identities and activities of those responsible for it from law enforcement officers."[13]

Much to Ziegler's satisfaction, however, *The Times* reported, "Nixon obliquely but stoutly defended the press secretary in his television speech, asserting that Mr. Ziegler's early denials of White House complicity, like Mr. Nixon's own, had been based on inadequate investigation." The speech was interpreted as an emotional appeal to save the integrity of his presidency, according to *The Times*. "Tonight," Nixon asked with a grave expression on his face, "I ask for your prayers to help me in everything that I do. God bless America and God bless each and every one of you." With Nixon rapidly backtracking, Ziegler's believability sunk even further and reporters continued to refer to his words, almost daily, as "Ziegles."

On May 1, 1973, in responding to a question from a reporter, Ziegler—who had refused to issue any apology up to that time—said: "Mistakes were made during this period, " referring to the eighteen months during which the Watergate affair broke. "I was overenthusiastic." The press secretary said his comments were "an overstatement . . . particularly if you look at it in context of developments that have taken place." He said that both reporters had vigorously pursued the story and deserved credit. "When you're wrong, we're wrong," Ziegler said, "and I would have to say I was in that case and other cases."[14]

Some cynical White House–watchers in the media felt his contriteness was too little, too late, but on the whole he was praised for finally stepping up to what had been a continuing series of embarrassing statements about what proved to be *The Washington Post*'s accurate stories. That one statement alone by Ziegler may well have contained the most honest words that he uttered during the entire controversy—and it brought him kudos from the press, starting with Katherine Graham, publisher of *The Post*, who responded: "We appreciate it and accept it with pleasure," adding that "the Administration was trying to undermine the credulity of the press for the last 10 months."[15]

On May 18, 1973, the Senate Watergate Committee began its nationally televised hearings. Attorney General–designate Elliot Richardson named former solicitor general Archibald Cox the Justice Department's special prosecutor for Watergate. During the course of his briefing that day, Ziegler continued his drumbeat defending Nixon: "The President did not participate or have any knowledge of activities relating to the cover-up." Ziegler, ever consistent, said Nixon was going to continue with his work as president. "He was elected to lead this country in 1972 and that he will do." He brushed aside questions about Nixon considering resigning.

On May 22, 1973, a bombshell was dropped: Two of Nixon's lawyers, Leonard Garment and Fred Buzhardt, held a press briefing run by Ziegler in which they handed out a statement from Nixon that conceded for the first time that there had been "wide-ranging" efforts in the White House to cover up the Watergate scandal, but he firmly denied any involvement on his own part. Nixon stated that he had no prior knowledge of the Watergate break-in, that he took no part in it, nor was he aware of any efforts to hide the truth, at no time did he authorize any offer of executive clemency for the Watergate defendants, nor did he know of such an offer, that he did not know until his own investigation of any effort to provide the Watergate defendants with money, and that at no time did he attempt, or authorize anyone else to attempt, to implicate the CIA in the matter.[16]

"With hindsight," Nixon wrote, "it is apparent that I should have given more heed to the warning signals I received along the way about a Watergate cover-up and less to the reassurances. It now appears that there were persons who may have gone beyond my directives, and sought to expand on my efforts to protect the national security operations in order to cover up any involvement they or certain others might have had in Watergate."[17]

On June 3, 1973, *The Washington Post* disclosed that Dean had told Watergate investigators that he discussed the Watergate cover-up with the president at least thirty-five times. On July 2, 1973, at a briefing, Ziegler repeated his statement,

> The President will not appear before the [Senate] committee or will not respond to any specific request to appear in such a forum to discuss the matter [Watergate] because he feels that he has the responsibility to maintain the prerogatives of the Executive branch. But as soon as the Watergate phase of the hearings is over, the President will address the matter, and he will do so in what he considers to be the appropriate forum at that time.

The press secretary said the president would not appear before the grand jury because "it would be constitutionally inappropriate."

On July 13, 1973, Alexander Butterfield, former presidential appointments secretary, revealed in congressional testimony that since 1971

Nixon had recorded all conversations and telephone calls in his office. Astonished by this revelation, investigators immediately requested the tapes. On July 23, 1973, Nixon refused to turn over the tapes to the Senate Watergate Committee or the special prosecutor. Nixon decided that he would not make the tapes available to the congressional impeachment inquiry or to the special prosecutor. "Perhaps this is Armageddon," he told Ziegler privately, "but I would rather leave fighting for principle." Ziegler continued to deny that Nixon had anything to do with Watergate and that he had no intention of resigning. "He is up for the battle," Ziegler said, "He intends to fight it, and he feels he has a personal and constitutional duty to do so."[18]

At a black-tie dinner on August 1, 1973, at—of all places Kakuel, Kansas—in the midst of offering a toast, Nixon suddenly said: "Let others spend their time dealing with murky, small, unimportant vicious little things. We have spent our time and will spend our time building a better world." Although the president did not use the word Watergate, sources in the White House press office who worked for Ziegler or his deputy, Gerald L. Warren, confirmed the president was referring to Watergate. It was just a week before the dinner that Nixon had decided to deny the Senate Watergate Committee's request for the tape recordings he had made of his conversations in the Oval Office. The president had also been heard telling members of his staff: "Let others wallow in Watergate. We are going to do our job."[19]

Ziegler, dedicated as he was to the president, was nevertheless the object of Nixon's displeasure one evening in August 1973 when the president made a stop in New Orleans en route to California. Faced with a barrage of reporters, an angry Nixon "brusquely grabbed Ziegler and shoved him at a group of trailing reporters just before giving a speech to a veterans' group." It was one of the few times that the press saw for themselves the dark side of Richard Nixon.[20] However, Nixon remained loyal to Ziegler. At the height of the Watergate crisis, Secretary of the Treasury John Connally, Secretary of Defense Melvin Laird, and Chief of Staff Al Haig all told him that Ziegler should leave, that he was not helping the cause. Nixon would later write: "I thought it unfair to Ziegler. So did [Secretary of State Henry] Kissinger, who said that we would regret it if we hurt innocent people in an effort to palliate the press."[21]

On October 20, 1973, the date of the infamous "Saturday Night Massacre," Nixon fired Archibald Cox and abolished the office of the special prosecutor, Attorney General Elliot Richardson and Deputy Attorney General William D. Ruckelshaus resigned, and pressure for impeachment of the president began to mount in Congress. In an unusual Saturday night briefing, Ziegler stated that the president had made the move "to avoid a constitutional confrontation by an action that would give the grand jury what it needs to proceed with its work with the least possible intrusion of Presidential privacy. That action taken by the President in the spirit of accommodation that has marked American constitutional history was accepted by responsible leaders in Congress and the country."

On December 7, 1973, the White House was asked to explain an eighteen and a half-minute gap in one of the subpoenaed tapes. The best explanation came from Chief of Staff Alexander Haig, who proposed that "some sinister force" had erased that segment. That mystery has never been cleared up and remains a footnote to history that will probably never be solved. The House of Representatives, after deliberation, voted to proceed with the presidential impeachment probe on February 6, 1974. On March 1, 1974, a federal grand jury indicted seven men, including Haldeman, Ehrlichman, Mitchell, and Special Counsel Charles Colson, for conspiracy to obstruct justice. This was the first time in history that so many trusted advisors of a president faced criminal accusations in a single indictment. Nixon put his own special spin on the news, saying that he hoped the trials "will move quickly and to a just conclusion."

On April 30, 1974, the White House released more than 1200 pages of edited transcripts of the Nixon tapes to the House Judiciary Committee, but the committee insisted that the tapes themselves must be turned over. The White House declined and the issue went to court. On July 24, 1974, the U.S. Supreme Court unanimously ruled that Nixon must turn over the tape recordings of sixty-four conversations, rejecting the president's claims of executive privilege.

On July 27, 1974, the House Judiciary Committee passed the first of three articles of impeachment by a vote of 27 to 11, charging obstruction of justice. Nixon's support virtually disappeared. Nonetheless, against all odds, Ziegler was defiant. He said the president still believed the full House of Representatives would reject any article of impeachment. "The President remains confident that the full House will recognize that there simply is not the evidence to support this or any other article of impeachment and will not vote to impeach. He is confident because he knows he has committed no impeachable offense," Ziegler said at a press briefing. In response to questions, however, Ziegler said the White House had not counted the votes in the House and added that the White House staff would not lobby against the president's impeachment among members of Congress. To some, the apparent optimism of both the president and his press secretary appeared to be an attempt to go down fighting, rather than making any concessions before the fact. It was implausible, in light of what had been uncovered, that Nixon would be able to stem the tide against him.

Everything was now out in the open. The transcripts triggered a national reaction of disbelief; for the first time, the masses of Americans got an inside look at the White House's political apparatus and discovered that Nixon was a bitterly torn man, but nonetheless cynical, sometimes obscene, and far more desperate than anyone could have imagined. The tapes and the accompanying transcripts revealed that Nixon was, indeed, deeply involved in the cover-up and, as a result, his support in Congress evaporated.

Nixon's downfall became official when, on July 31, 1974, Representative Robert F. Drinan, Democrat of Massachusetts, introduced a resolution calling for the impeachment of Nixon "for high crimes and misdemeanors." That was the first action actually taken in the Congress because impeachment hearings started in the House under the constitution. Representative Peter W. Rodino Jr., New Jersey Democrat who was chairman of the House Judiciary Committee, said he would study the resolution before deciding whether to call for committee hearings and move ahead on impeachment.

And then it finally came: At 12:20 P.M. on August 8, 1974, Ziegler put out a brief, three-paragraph press release to the assembled press corps that read:

> I am aware of the intense interest of the American people and of you in this room concerning developments today and over the last few days. This has, of course, been a difficult time. The President of the United States will meet various Members of the bipartisan leadership of Congress here at the White House early this evening. Tonight at 9 o'clock Eastern Daylight Time, the President of the United States will address the nation on radio and television from his Oval office.

Finally, after Nixon told the nation he would resign his office at 11:02 P.M. on August 8, 1974, Ziegler held another briefing for reporters in which he somehow managed to spin Nixon's exit with high praise.

> As I said, earlier today, this has been a difficult day, and these have been difficult times. I would prefer only a personal observation, that the strength of

the President during this period and the strength, I believe, and the courage that he showed tonight has sustained the members of his staff who have served the President over the last five and one-half years and over the last years and months. All, I know, have respect for the President and the cause, which he has represented through the period of his Presidency. I just would like to take a minute myself to say goodbye, I hope, over the next few weeks, to have a chance to see each of you personally, but this is the last time we will be meeting in these circumstances. We have met, of course, in this setting many times, here and around the world. I have been proud to be President Nixon's press secretary over the past five and one-half years. I have tried to be professional, as all of you are professional, and I hope I have never under-estimated the difficulty of your jobs or the energy and intelligence you bring to them. We have been through many difficult times together and we have been through many historic times together. I know that I will remember the good ones and I hope you will, too. I would like to just conclude by saying that whatever our differences have been, I believe that there are no simple answers to the complex questions that this period poses but above all, I think I take away from this job a deep sense of respect for the diversity and strength of our country's freedom of expression and for our free press. Thank you very much.

The next day, August 9, 1974, even in defeat, Ziegler would not give up. He wanted to try the spin of all spins—that is, attempt to depict Nixon as a dignified statesman whose departure—a historic moment, because no previous president had ever resigned from office—would be recorded for all time as an example of the peaceful transition of power in a democracy. Ziegler persuaded Nixon to have his departure televised. He sold Nixon on that idea because he wanted the American people to see the president standing tall, waving his famous "V" sign as he walked up the steps of his helicopter, signaling that he left with dignity and his composure intact.

Having become one of Nixon's closest intimates, Ziegler remained with Nixon and was aboard the airplane that the president took to San Clemente as Gerald Ford was sworn into office. Ziegler worked with Nixon for almost a year after Nixon's resignation before moving into public relations jobs for trade associations. For years, Ziegler contin-ued to defend his boss, describing him as "the first American political exile." Ziegler himself proclaimed his own innocence as recently as 1995—eight years before he died on February 10, 2003, at the age of sixty-three—when he told "Larry King Live" that he "absolutely" had been kept in the dark. "Thank goodness," he said, adding, "I was one of the few members of the Nixon White House staff who was never indicted and I was not part of the cover-up."[22]

*Postscript*: In 1976, two years after he resigned, Ziegler was publicly questioned when he was as a member of a panel discussing the presidency and the press. He was asked about whether or not he was ever asked to evade the truth. The occasion was an academic discussion at the Lyndon B. Johnson School of Public Affairs. Ziegler replied:

> Now, there are times when a press secretary is faced and a President of the United States is faced with a situation where you cannot speak or cannot go into an issue and should not get into an issue, and that happens often. However, *press secretaries do find themselves in a situation where they do in fact lie* [italics added] because of the information that one of their colleagues gave them, which they felt to be true, and that ends up not to be true. So that is a dilemma that a press secretary faces.[23]

Thus, the one Nixon senior staff member who had survived Watergate, knew—with the benefit of hindsight—exactly what he had done, and had the courage to admit it. A majority of the other press secretaries analyzed in this book, however, would no doubt disagree with Ziegler's contention that press secretaries do, in fact, have to lie. Or perhaps spin has become the more acceptable term to use when they shade the truth. That is a judgment that those who have been members of the White House press corps are best qualified to make.

---

## Pardoning Richard M. Nixon: 1974
### Gerald R. Ford
#### JERALD terHORST

---

Soon after Richard N. Nixon resigned the presidency on August 9, 1974, Vice President Gerald R. Ford ushered in a new administration that was filled with high expectations. "My fellow Americans, our long national nightmare is over," he said—a phrase that will long be remembered. Ford selected as his first press secretary Jerald F. terHorst, Washington bureau chief for *The Detroit News*, a man who had developed a trusting relationship with Ford. TerHorst said at the time that he took on the new duties that he would be honest and up front with reporters. Ford agreed that terHorst was unique in being an active White House correspondent who had covered Ford as vice president.

Well regarded and personally likeable, terHorst seemed a nifty successor to the irascible and discredited Ronald Ziegler.

The atmosphere in the White House press room changed overnight. For the next thirty days, terHorst established a brand new rapport with his ex-colleagues while his boss, Gerald Ford, was riding high as the knight in shining armor. The press secretary could do no wrong and neither could the president.

At terHorst's first press briefing a 3:26 P.M, August 9, he assured reporters that the transition between the Nixon and Ford staffs would go smoothly. He announced a few appointments, including Arthur Greenspan to succeed Herbert Stein as head of the Federal Reserve Board. As for naming a vice president, terHorst told the reporters: "The President has uppermost on his mind this constitutional responsibility to pick a successor to himself as vice president." He hoped to have a nominee to submit to Congress possibly within a week or ten days. Accordingly, terHorst responded in the affirmative when asked if Haig would stay on as chief of staff. Then came a few unexpected, possibly inflammatory questions, which terHorst handled with aplomb.

*Q: Did former president Nixon sign a pardon for himself prior to leaving office?*

terHORST: Well, I am not here to speak for anyone but President Ford. I have no way of answering that question.

*Q: Does President Ford have any views on a grant of immunity to former President Nixon?*

terHORST: President Ford's position on the question of immunity for President Nixon is, I believe, if my memory serves correctly, was expressed by him in the hearings during his nomination on the Hill.

*Q: What did he [Ford] say on the Hill?*

terHORST: It was my understanding on the Hill he was negative on that question.

*Q: Do you plan to tape all the other [Presidential] meetings?*

terHORST: No. Tape will not be used in the Ford administration.

*Q: Any news on whether Nixon signed a pardon for himself?*

terHORST: I have been advised that President Nixon did not sign a pardon or any form of immunity for himself or anyone before he left office.

*Q: To follow up on that, can you check for us if President Ford's position as he stated on the Hill that he is not in favor of immunity?*
terHORST: Yes, I can assure you of that.

*Q: Thank you, Mr. Press Secretary.*

That's how the Ford administration's press relations started out. Up front and straightforward, as terHorst said it would be. And so it remained—for thirty-one days. That all changed on Sunday, September 9, 1974, when Ford, much to terHorst's astonishment—announced he had given former President Nixon a pardon for all federal crimes that Nixon "committed or may have committed or taken part in" while in office. Ford said the pardon was intended to spare Nixon and the nation further punishment as a result of the Watergate scandal. It was a pardon heard 'round the world—and with mixed reactions—mostly negative. Democratic politicians, in particular, condemned the pardon, which, ironically, instead of healing the nation provided even more partisanship and deep consternation in Washington political circles.

The reason for the shock and unfavorable press was Ford's apparent contradiction of himself only a month after taking office. TerHorst had regularly been asked about a possible pardon during the four weeks he was press secretary, and each time he replied that the president would not address the issue until the legal process had been completed. TerHorst himself did not learn of the pending pardon until the Saturday night before Ford announced it on Sunday. Many of his colleagues in the media believed that terHorst was angry about being left "out of the loop," and that by not including him as part of the decision, Ford had sent a message to the White House press corps that he [Ford] did not have full confidence in terHorst. That alone was enough for terHorst to resign.

I asked terHorst what his immediate reaction was:

> I was astonished.[24] It was a case of having quoted the President for weeks about his position on a pardon. He had told me: "When it comes to me I will deal with it. But I won't deal with it now. It has not come before me yet." That was the line I constantly repeated at almost every briefing I held. Certainly every time that question came up that was my standard line and Ford had never wavered from it. Almost immediately, I thought about resigning. I had just lost all of my credibility. Ford was declaring a double standard of justice—where you have justice at the top for an unindicted co-conspirator, which Richard Nixon was getting, and nobody else getting off. All of his

underlings went through the agony of trials and prison terms and were suffering as much if not more than Nixon because they had fewer resources to fall back on. And Ford was not doing anything for the several thousand guys and gals who went to Canada or Sweden to escape the draft.

I wrote out my resignation that Saturday night and showed it to my wife. The envelope was marked: "Eyes Only to the President's Attention."[25] When I finally had a chance I went in to see the President Sunday morning before the pardon was announced, I said, "Mr. President, this is my final day. I can't do this any more. I'm done. Tomorrow I will not be here." He said, "Jerry, I am sorry you feel that way." But he made no attempt to ask me to stay. There were others who did, however. One aide of Ford's handed my letter back to me a short while later and said, "You can't do this today." I said, "I'm sorry, I've done it." He stuck the letter in my pocket. We announced the pardon that morning. I then went back into the President's Oval Office and handed his secretary my letter and said, "Please put this back on the president's desk. I've not changed my mind."

I asked terHorst what advice he might have given Ford if he had had the chance and terHorst offered these insights:

If I had been asked, I would have said, "Mr. President, there are ways you can help the people to be on your side. You could raise the issue publicly and say, 'What do we do about Nixon? Does the American public really want to see him in court prosecuted for this or that? What should we do about dealing with this now that he is no longer in office?'" I think he could have gotten sympathy from a lot of people who would have made it possible for Ford to issue a pardon without acrimony and a big cloud over his head. But I never had the opportunity to help him overcome his Nixon problem. And he had a Nixon problem.

TerHorst told me that he believed press secretaries should, first, accurately portray what is happening in the White House and, second, the media expects them to be forthcoming. "It's a balancing act that is really almost impossible," he said. "I have on my living room wall my favorite picture of a trapeze artist in the middle of his walk with a stick on each side trying to keep his balance. That's how I felt all the time I was with Jerry Ford."[26]

Immediately after terHorst's resignation, Ford moved to replace him—no easy task in the new environment of trust and good fellowship that had been shaken by terHorst's resignation. Ford selected Ron Nessen, an experienced hand in Washington and an unflappable professional journalist. Nessen served five tours as an NBC war correspondent in Vietnam and later served as NBC News White House correspondent during the Johnson administration. When Ford announced his appointment, Nessen, at his first briefings, said with a smile: "I hope the White House press corps is ready for another Ron, I am a Ron, but not a Ziegler, I can tell you that." A new era in press relations was under way.

## The Iran-Contra Affair: 1986–1989
### Ronald Reagan
### LARRY SPEAKES/MARLIN FITZWATER

The Iran-Contra affair broke during a White House ceremony on November 13, 1986, when reporters asked President Reagan to comment on rumors that the United States had exchanged arms for hostages being held in Iran. He repudiated the rumor, then appeared on national television one week later to explain the administration's case, a case grounded in denial of any wrongdoing. "We did not," he declared in his conclusion, "repeat—did not trade weapons or anything else for hostages, nor will we."

However, on November 19, Reagan opened a press conference by announcing that he had based his earlier claims on a false chronology constructed by the National Security Council and the White House staff. He announced formation of the President's Special Review Board, known as the Tower Commission, headed by former Senator John Tower (R-TX), and included former Secretary of State Edmund Muskie (D-ME) and former national security adviser Brent Scowcroft. In late February 1987, the board concluded that the president was guilty of no crime but found that Reagan's informal or lax management allowed subordinates the freedom to carry out what turned out to be an illegal policy.

The White House confirmed a media report that "a secret plan had been hatched by the Reagan administration to provide up to $30 million to the Nicaraguan Contra rebels from profits gained by selling arms to Iran."[27] Although the whole affair remains somewhat of a mystery to this day, press secretaries Larry Speakes and then Marlin Fitzwater defended President Ronald Reagan throughout and explained it as "Reagan's Bay of Pigs."

"It was something he was sucked into," Speakes said, "and then it simply got out of control." Speakes said the attempt to make a strategic opening to Iran rapidly became an arms-for-hostages deal.

The thinking was, a few arms here, a few arms there, what will that hurt if we can get our hostages back? We were trying to show the powers-that-be in Iran that the Iranian "moderates" had some clout, by providing the moderates with weapons. You could deny that it was arms for hostages, although it really was. Reagan himself simply rationalized it by saying, "We were supplying arms to someone—Iran—who might influence those terrorists who were holding our hostages."[28]

When the story came to light, Reagan's loyal aides told the press that Reagan was not aware of the details of the arms-for-hostages deal because they wanted to give him deniability. On the other hand, Reagan's critics—and there were many—came to the conclusion after a commission had been appointed to investigate the affair, that his management style was too hands-off and that he should have known about it. Many of those eventually brought to justice—Lt. Col. Oliver North, Vice Admiral John M. Poindexter, Attorney General Edwin Meese, National Security Advisor Robert C. McFarlane—were later pardoned. As Speakes would have it, the transfer of funds to Iran was engineered by Reagan aides who simply did not tell the president what was happening. Although Reagan eventually took responsibility for the scandal, when all was said and done, Speakes later said that had John Poindexter gone to the president and said, "Mr. President, we want to take profits from the Iranian arms sale and give them to the Contras," Reagan would probably have agreed. However, said Speakes, if Poindexter added, "Mr. President, we have some doubts about the legality of this," Reagan might well have demanded "a full investigation by his legal, diplomatic, military and political advisers, and would have concluded that no one in the U.S. government could send money to the Contras unless Congress approved it."[29]

The scandal, basically, was made up of two separate and equally complex actions. The first was to placate moderates within the Iranian government in order to secure the release of American hostages held by pro-Iranian groups in Lebanon and to influence Iranian foreign policy in a pro-Western direction. The second was a plan to aid the Contras who were waging guerrilla war against the Sandinista government of Nicaragua. Both were a violation of a law that had been passed in Congress in 1983.

Speakes and his successor Fitzwater responded to the White House press corps during the press coverage of the scandal. They were candid in their replies to questions but, at the same time, continued to deny any wrongdoing on Reagan's part. Both did their best to defend Reagan's stature and reputation and—for the most part—succeeded.

Here are some examples of how they did it in their White House press briefings:

On November 14, 1998, Speakes tried to spin the president's position as he faced a barrage of questions. The reporters were relentless. Here's a sampling of how aggressively they went after the press secretary and, therefore, the president:

*Q: Larry, has the President decided not to send any more weapons to Iran— for what reason? Was it the public disclosure? Or was it the fact that there's little hope for the hostages?*

SPEAKES: Our idea was to establish a relationship with the Iranians that would permit us to become credible as an arbiter, perhaps, in the war against Iraq. Everything the President did, including the condoning the shipment, was in his opinion, done in the best interest of the United States foreign policy, and that was his sole criteria for making decisions on this entire matter.

On November 17, at a press briefing, a reporter asked Speakes:

*Q: Has the President decided not to send any more weapons to Iran—for what reason? Was it the public disclosure? Or was it the fact that there is little hope for the hostages?*

SPEAKES: Well, the original purpose was to establish—to be credible—in our dealings with Iran to indicate that the decisions that were—the discussions that were taking place did, in fact, have the President's backing. Our idea was to establish a relationship with the Iranians that would permit us to become credible as an arbiter, perhaps, in the Iran-Iraq war.

*Q: Larry, called into question as much as the blips in the foreign policy have been the question of the White House credibility. That's been splashed all over and since the President's speech. What is your finding? What are the soundings in the White House as to White House credibility today in the country?*

SPEAKES: We have not done any polling on the subject. It is our belief that we've had an opportunity to tell our story. It is up to us now to explain fully and totally, which we have done, what we did and why we did it and what our goals were.

*Q: So there doesn't seem to be a vast skepticism?*

SPEAKES: I don't think the skepticism is quite as vast as it's made out. If you look at the number of people that have spoken out on the record against it, there is not that many. In fact, you can count them—the members of Congress, I believe I'd be safe to say, on the fingers of one hand.

*Q: Is the President concerned that he has a real credibility problem now? Or does he think that it's all over?*
SPEAKES: Well, there is one way to combat that, and that's the truth, and we've told the truth.

*Q: I am asking about the group that is holding the latest three Americans to be kidnapped.*
SPEAKES: We believe that is the radical group that wishes to continue to prosecute the war.

In January of 1987, Speakes left the administration to take a job in the private sector. He was replaced by Marlin Fitzwater. At the outset of his briefing on February 25, 1987, Fitzwater announced that the Tower Commission, which had been investigating Iran-Contra, would release its report on February 26, 1987, and that Reagan would lead off the press conference. He said he believed the president had not seen it but he was clear on what he wanted to say because he had had two discussions with the Board and that the Board was aware of the president's position that would be laid out in the report. Fitzwater went on to point out that the president's position remained the same: He was not aware of any arms-for-hostages transaction. But asked if he could not remember whether or not he approved arms to Iran, Fitzwater replied: "There is no question about his approving the arms sale and that is part of our overture to Iran. . . . We have said from the very beginning that we were reaching out to elements in Iran to try to establish a relationship in a post-Khomeni era and that arms sales became a part of that effort and it was approved by the President." The new press secretary repeated that Reagan didn't believe he broke any laws or deceived the American public; that he had acted "entirely appropriately" and cited Reagan's own words in his State of the Union address:

> I do not believe it was wrong to try to establish contacts with a country of strategic importance, or try to save lives. And certainly, it was not wrong to try to secure freedom for our citizens held in barbaric captivity. But we did not achieve what we wished, and serious mistakes were made in trying to do so. We will get to the bottom of this, and I will take whatever action is called for.

Two days later, on February 27, 1987, Fitzwater addressed the subject of the Tower Commission report. In his first comment, he successfully used some light-handed spin to maintain the impression—consistently held by the president and his spokesmen—that the president had no knowledge of the arms-for-hostages plan and that he intended to take firm action. Fitzwater said the report chronicled the intricate management and staff failures in a comprehensive way that has made the president rightfully angry about the mismanagement described in the report, and that he intended to make changes as soon as possible. When asked, "Whose management? Isn't the President in charge?" the press secretary employed a highly successful technique in press relations, i.e., stepping up to the plate by emphasizing that the president had all along taken full responsibility for what his staff did. As for the report, Fitzwater spun that topic, as well, by saying: "I think we look at the report as an opportunity to make changes in a lot of areas." At this point, Fitzwater broke the ice with a touch of humor, denigrating himself.

Q: *When a chief of staff leaves [Donald Regan] this administration, it's expected that the people under him, which is virtually everybody, in senior positions around here, leave also.*
FITZWATER: That's the question I've been waiting for (Laughter).

Q: *Not, not you, Marlin.*
FITZWATER: Where's my 40-page script on how important the press secretary is? (Laughter)

On that same day, *The New York Times* published as its lead story the findings of the Tower Commission. It reported that the Commission portrayed Reagan today as "a confused and remote figure who failed to understand or control the secret arms deal with Iran," and who thus had to "take responsibility" for a policy that in the end caused chaos at home and embarrassment abroad. And the Tower Commission report said that the president clearly didn't understand the nature of this operation, who was involved, and what was happening.

On March 3, 1987, Fitzwater announced the president would give a speech to the nation that night. The headline in *The New York Times* the next day read: "THE REAGAN WHITE HOUSE CONCEDES MISTAKE IN ARMS-FOR-HOSTAGE POLICY; TAKES BLAME, VOWS CHANGES." The story reported that Reagan said that his policy toward Iran had deteriorated into a trade of arms-for-hostages and that he accepted full responsibility for the Iran-Contra affair.

The president adopted an unusually conciliatory tone in his television address, detailing a long series of mistakes and misjudgments made by his administration and vowing some changes in the way it worked. "What began as a strategic opening to Iran deteriorated in its implementation into trading arms for hostages," Reagan said. "This runs counter to my own beliefs, to Administration policy, and to the original strategy we had in mind. There are reasons why it happened, but no excuses. It was a mistake. I let my personal concern for the hostages spill over into the geopolitical strategy of reaching out to Iran."

At the next briefing on March 5, Fitzwater opened the session by spinning the overall impact of Reagan's speech: "The President set a tone of serious reflection and dedication to duty, and that's the path he intends to follow in the months ahead. As we say in Kansas, it's time to roll up your sleeves and get on with the business of government."

Reagan survived the scandal, and his approval ratings returned to previous levels; when the scandal broke in 1986, Reagan's approval rating plummeted to 46 percent, but he later finished strong with a December 1988 Gallup poll recording a 63 percent approval rating. One of the oldest—but often forgotten—lessons of public relations is to address a mistake immediately and, should you be wrong, say so. That is precisely the advice that Fitzwater gave to Reagan and, for the most part, it blunted any long-term damage it might have inflicted on Reagan's presidency. Of course, Reagan's ability to look and act sincerely contrite didn't hurt either.

## Monicagate: 1998–1999
### Bill Clinton
### Mike McCurry/Joe Lockhart

[Author's Note: *While there were many major figures who played roles in the Lewinsky scandal, for purposes of telling the story of what the press secretaries did, the majority of characters who were involved in this story were not included. Instead, the focus is on the press secretaries and how they handled the scandal at the outset and at its conclusion.*]

The judgment of history is still out on whether or not the sex scandal centering around President William Jefferson (Bill) Clinton—leading to his impeachment by the U.S. House of Representatives and acquittal by the Senate—will be the one thing historians remember most about the forty-second chief executive of the United States. What his legacy in history will be remains to be seen. Whatever the final determination—and it could be many years—it is abundantly clear that the press secretaries who had the painstaking role of speaking for him to the media in the worst of times did the best possible job under the circumstances to try and spin his image as a man under fire who remained firmly in full command until his last day in office.

The Lewinsky scandal was first revealed on January 17, 1998, on the *Drudge Report* Web site and was affirmed by the mainstream media on January 21 when *The Washington Post* published a story on it. Despite strong denials from Clinton, the story "had legs," leading Clinton to address the nation on January 26, 1998, in a White House press conference in which he issued his most forceful denial. Waving his forefinger at reporters, he stated: "I want to say one thing to the American people. I want you to listen to me. I'm going to say this again. I did not have sexual relations with that woman, Miss Lewinsky. I never told anybody to lie, not a single time; never. These allegations are false. And I need to go back to work for the American people."

Despite months of repeated denials, Clinton was called to testify before a grand jury (the first sitting president to do so) and he finally admitted in taped testimony on August 17, 1998, that he had had an "improper physical relationship" with Lewinsky. Independent counsel Kenneth Starr, who had been investigating Whitewater without success, made the case for impeachment before the U.S. House of Representatives, which formally impeached the president on December 19, 1998.

Polls at the time showed that the American public supported Clinton, with 60 percent opposing impeachment. He was subsequently then acquitted on two charges—perjury and obstruction of justice—stemming from the Lewinsky scandal by the U.S. Senate on February 12, 1999, with the necessary two-thirds majority not having been achieved. He served out the remainder of his term through January 20, 2001.

The transcripts of the press secretaries' briefings clearly show that both press secretaries Mike McCurry and Joe Lockhart were hamstrung by the fact that they did not know the truth. Nor did they attempt to find out, because neither wanted to be subpoenaed by a grand jury to testify. According to reports published since that time, Clinton elected not to discuss the matter with any of his close aides—at least those who were not attorneys—primarily because he sought to protect his trusted staff. Nonetheless, the ever-demanding White House press corps kept after both spokesmen. They either sidestepped some of the questions or used a little spin to tone down the criticism. For example, whenever the word "resignation" was used, the press secretary would immediately dismiss the possibility. There was no doubt that the press found it a fruitless task to quiz the press secretaries but they did, nonetheless, hoping for a breakthrough.

In his press briefing on January 21, 1998, McCurry did his best to answer questions, even though he had not spoken to the president about the Lewinsky affair. The reporters quibbled over the meaning of the phrase "improper relationship" but he pledged that the president would cooperate in any investigation.

In the period following the disclosure of the Lewinsky scandal and up to the actual congressional investigation as well as the results of the probe by the independent prosecutor, which led to the impeachment hearings, the press secretaries responded to many questions, but rarely offered any particulars for one reason: Neither of them were informed. Another Clinton aide, Lanny Davis, an attorney, was designated to answer legal questions and to be the front man on the Lewinsky case when it came to talk shows, TV interviews, and the like. Davis handled this assignment superbly, divulging very little because of "the ongoing investigations," but staunchly defending the president's innocence.

At a press briefing by Lockhart in the waning days of the investigation in 1999, it did not take long before the reporters got to the point: "Has the President considered resigning?" Raising his voice just a bit, Lockhart said, "No!" At another briefing, Lockhart was asked this question: "Does Clinton intend to do anything in response to Senator Joseph I. Lieberman's (D-CT) suggestion that 'heals the wounds of our national character' before the Starr report goes to Congress?"

Straight faced, Lockhart replied: "The President is a firm believer in healing." At the same time, he told reporters that the president had indicated the Starr investigation was something that the White House should not comment upon. McCurry said the president believed that it was within the province of the Senate and how they want to proceed and it's not something that the White House should pre-judge.

In the press briefing on February 12, 1999—the day Clinton was acquitted by the Senate—Lockhart was obviously relieved and, in answer to questions, told reporters that the president had not watched the hearing, that the end of the hearings had brought relief both to the president and to people at the White House; that Clinton's lawyers did a very credible job; and that the president was "pleased" by the outcome, but nevertheless wanted to move forward and work with Congress to get something accomplished. Asked if the president was going to "celebrate" that night, Lockhart wisely turned the question aside by saying the president felt the matter that had gone on for so long that he was relieved it was over, but there was really nothing to celebrate. Lockhart used this opportunity spin the story by stating that the one positive that came out of the probe could be that politicians will pull back somewhat on their personal attacks.

"We believe, as the President has talked about for six or seven years on the national stage, that we've fallen into a cycle of politics of personal destruction and we need to find a way out of it. And I think if both sides can look back at the events of the last year and take from that that the cycle needs to end and it needs to break, and by reaching across party lines we can do that now, that would be a positive," Lockhart explained.

Finally, asked if Clinton thought the impeachment would make any difference in his ability to do his job, Lockhart said: "I think the President has been doing his job, and that in large part is why the President continues to enjoy solid support from the American public and he'll continue to do that." When asked how Clinton kept going and did his work under the most trying of circumstances, Lockhart said:

> I think it's a couple things, and I talked to him about this. One is while accepting the responsibility for what he did, he believes and has said that the way to make it right is to rededicate himself to doing his job, doing the best he can. I think, secondly, the President believes that when all is said and done, when all of the partisan rancor has died down, the American public has a very good sense of fairness in what's going on. And I think he took some heart in that, and focused on doing his job. I don't think it's any more complicated than that.

Aside from the impeachment, why did Clinton get such a bad press during his entire eight years, even though he had highly qualified press spokesmen? White House observers believe that Clinton brought much of it on himself because of his indiscretion and that he strung out the Lewinsky scandal far too long before coming to grips with it. Helen Thomas summed it up this way:

> My impression is that this man, President Clinton, did not know one second—and I won't even say a minute—in the White House when he was not being investigated by the right-wing. He should have had the street smarts to know that he was the target. That was incredible—that he didn't realize that you don't play into their hands. Everything was under investigation.

Constantly. I don't know how they stood it. The resilience of that family [helped]. I think we [the press] should have been much more intuitive. Whitewater turned out to be really nothing in terms of the special prosecutor and so forth. I think the Clintons suffered a lot.[30]

*Postscript*: Looking back on that tension-filled period, McCurry said in an interview after he left office:

> I took the initiative when the story first broke in 1998. I knew there was great danger in having conversations that were not within the contents of a legal defense strategy or something like that, so the minute that story got out, I told my staff that we couldn't go and have private conversations with the president. That's not in our interests and not in the president's interests. And we will do all this through the lawyers and I am only going to say to the press what the lawyers have authorized. We have to always reference that the lawyers have approved this because that's the only thing that will protect us against getting a lot of subpoenas, which, in fact, turned out to be true. I never got subpoenaed by [Special Prosecutor] Kenneth Starr, unlike some of my colleagues. I think that's because they figured I would be a sympathetic person in the public eye and they didn't want to tangle with me. I also think they knew I was playing everything by the book. It was in my interest, to be sure, but it was also for the president. He had to have some place where he could design a legal strategy with his lawyers.
>
> We knew we did not know the full truth, but on the other hand we tended to believe his denial. It was a very firm denial that he did not have "sexual relations with that woman." We all pretty much took that to the bank and we figured well, maybe there's an elastic definition of "sexual relations," but we didn't know how elastic it was going to end up being.

When asked by the White House press corps for comments on a daily basis during the scandal, McCurry took the position that he couldn't comment because they were under investigation. "But," he points out,

> I was taken to task in some places for that position. For example, *The New York Times* editorial page asserted that for a president's press secretary to say he is not going to entertain questions on a certain subject was not acceptable. The paper was critical of the Clinton administration because we said at the outset that we would maintain a high standard. In effect they were saying, what's the deal now why, aren't you true to your word? That would be what I get from the tenor of my conversations with *The Times* executives.

We were under some personal pressure to comment because we were asked questions like: "Well, the president misled you guys." My only personal comment was that he apologized and it was appropriate he apologize but not more appropriate that he apologize to us than the American people. As for the impeachment, I was not there for that. That was under Joe Lockhart. I left in October of 1998 right after the mid-term election was winding down. It was exactly the right time to leave because Clinton had endured the Monica Lewinsky thing, he had made his testimony in front of the grand jury. It was clear that he was not going to pay much of a political price for this because the American public was ready to move on. That was when the organization moveon.org was formed. People were saying it is time for the country to move on. My assumption, and I think the conventional thinking, was that the Republicans were gong to drop the whole business after the mid-term elections and get back to some normal order of business. I remember having a conversation with Lockhart and saying to him "Well, you are going to have a good two-year run here because you will have a clean slate. I'm leaving, plus people are going to back off and give Clinton a little time." If I had been told that impeachment was in the offing and that there was going to be a battle royale beginning in 1999, I don't think I would have felt very good.[31]

For his part, Joe Lockhart took a slightly different view. In an interview he pointed out that it was easier for him to step into McCurry's shoes because he had been McCurry's assistant press secretary. So he knew the score.

Mike's last year was my first year. Had I come in from outside, it might have been unbearable. But when I took over we were already in what had settled into a permanent crisis where you did not know where things were going from day to day. My challenge was to continue to look responsive to the press but also not to lose sight of what the President was interested in— anything but Lewinsky. [Lockhart began as deputy press secretary at the beginning of Clinton's second term, in January 1997. He was press secretary from Oct. 5, 1998, when Mike McCurry resigned to September 29, 2000.]

I would discuss the politics of the coverage of the subject with Clinton, but we never discussed the facts. That was something he and his lawyers did. He was the President first and foremost, but he also was an individual who had legal rights and I thought it was perfectly legitimate to say to the press that he is having discussions with his lawyers. The briefings I did in the aftermath of the Lewinsky story saddened me. I think that whole tawdry business did no one any good. There was some solace in the fact that we eventually were able to get back to doing the business of the American people even when the President was wrestling with a crisis that was purely personal.

People wanted my view, but I told them that was not important. The most important thing one has to remember in this job is: it's not about you. Reporters were attacking me, but it wasn't a personal debate. I was speaking for the President. When the Monica story first broke, part of me felt, here we go again, another one of those so-called scandals. In this one, however there was enough uncertainty in the way he reacted that gave me some pause. Personally, I knew there was some germ of truth in what he was being accused of. I was confident there was nothing criminal and that it was being blown way out of proportion. In the end, you know, like any other human being, of course, you are disappointed when someone doesn't tell you the truth.

My most gratifying moment was when we got toward the end and the independent counsel announced that the Whitewater investigation was closed due to insufficient evidence against the president. There was incredible frustration after five years of something being heavily covered on the front pages of every newspaper constantly when we all knew there was nothing to it. As for my comments being labeled "spin," that term is fairly pejorative. It comes out of a journalist's mouth. On the other hand, the biggest consumers of spin are journalists. There are lots of journalists who find it a lot easier to dissect the spin rather than roll up their sleeves and figure out what the President's policy is. It's harder work. I don't take much notice of what pundits say about spin. My job is standing up there and the journalist's job is to poke at the information to test the validity of it. Hopefully, at the end of the day, they write what the President says is accurate.[32]

## NOTES

1. Nixon, Richard. *The Memoirs of Richard Nixon* (New York: Grosset & Dunlap, 1978), p. 1001.

2. Wise, David. *The Politics of Lying, Government Deception, Secrecy, and Power* (New York: Random House, 1975), p. 245.

3. Herbers, John. *Thank You, Mr. President* (New York: W.W. Norton & Company, 1976), p. 39.

4. Oudes, Bruce (ed). *Richard Nixon's Secret Files* (New York: Harper & Row, 1988), pp. 125–126.

5. Leibovich, Louis W. *The Press and the Modern Presidency: Myths and Mindsets from Kennedy to Clinton* (Westport, CT: Praeger, 1998), p. 72.

6. *Guardian Newspapers*, February 11, 2003.

7. Ibid.

8. Sussman, Barry. *The Great Cover-Up: Nixon and the Scandal of Watergate* (New York: Thomas Y. Crowell, 1974), p. 127.

9. Apple Jr., J.W. *The New York Times*, April 19, 1973.

10. *The New York Times*, May 1, 1973.

11. Ibid.

12. Ibid.

13. Ervin Jr., Sam J. *The Whole Truth, The Watergate Conspiracy* (New York: Random House, 1980), p. 109.

14. *The New York Times*, May 1, 1973.

15. *The Washington Post*, May 3, 1973.

16. *The New York Times*, May 23, 1973.

17. Nixon, Richard. *The Memoirs of Richard Nixon* (New York: Grosset & Dunlap, 1978), p. 1004.

18. Ibid.

19. *The New York Times*, August 2, 1973.

20. Gold, Gerald (ed). *The Watergate Hearings, Break-in and Cover-up*, narrative by R.W. Apple, chronology by Linda Amster. (New York: Viking Press, 1973), p. 63.

21. Nixon, *Memoirs*, p. 857.

22. Condon Jr., George E. and Finlay Lewis. *Copley News Service*, February 10, 2003.

23. Pamphlet, "The Presidency And The Press," edited by Hoyt Purvis, from transcript of seminar at the Lyndon B. Johnson School of Public Affairs, 1976.

24. Author's interview with terHorst, June 15, 2006.

25. In his letter dated September 8, 1974, terHorst stated:

> Without a doubt this is the most difficult decision I have ever had to make. I cannot find words to adequately express my respect and admiration for you over the many years of our relationship and my belief that you could heal the wounds and soul of our country in this most critical time in our nation's history. . . . It is with great regret, after long soul-searching, that I must inform you that I cannot in good conscience support your decision to pardon former President Nixon even before he has been charged with the commission of any crime. As your spokesman, I do not know how I could credibly defend that action in the absence of a like decision to grant absolute pardon to the young men who evaded Vietnam military service as a matter of conscience and the absence of pardons for former aides and associates of Mr. Nixon who have been charged with crimes—and imprisoned—stemming from the same Watergate situation. These are also men whose reputations and families have been grievously injured. Try as I can, it is impossible to conclude that the former president is more deserving of mercy than persons of lesser station in life whose offenses have had far less effect on our national well being. Thus it is with heavy heart that I hereby tender my resignation as Press Secretary to the President, effective today. My prayers nonetheless remain with you, sir. Sincerely, Jerald F. terHorst.

26. Author's interview with terHorst, June 15, 2006.

27. Available online at www.wikipedia.org/.

28. Speakes, Larry. *Speaking Out: The Reagan Presidency From Inside the White House* (New York: Avon Books, 1988), p. 377.

29. Ibid., p. 378–379.

30. From an interview by Tim Russert on the "Meet the Press [TV Show]," June 10, 2007.

31. Author's interview with Mike McCurry, December 6, 2006.

32. Author's interview with Joe Lockhart, December 13, 2005.

Stephen T. Early, the first modern press
secretary, served President Franklin D.
Roosevelt from 1933 to Roosevelt's death on
April 12, 1945. He is shown working with
Roosevelt on January 2, 1941. In December 1950,
Early was called in to serve briefly as press
secretary to President Harry S. Truman. Truman
awarded Early the Medal of Merit for his
service to the country.
—*Courtesy of The Franklin D. Roosevelt Library.*

President Harry S. Truman, in his office on May 15, 1945,
accompanied by, left to right, Press Secretary Charles G. Ross,
and Press Secretary Jonathan Daniels, who succeeded Ross
from 1945–1950.

—*Courtesy of Harry S. Truman Library.*

James Leonard Reinsch, press secretary to President Harry S. Truman for a brief period in 1945–1946, helped Winston Churchill write his radio speech in March 1946, coining the phrase "Iron Curtain" in describing the barrier between the Western democracies and the Soviet bloc.
—*Courtesy of Harry S. Truman Library.*

President Harry S. Truman, center, with Press Secretary Joseph Short, left, and Roger Tubby, right, relaxing in Key West, Florida, on March 15, 1951.
—*Courtesy of Harry S. Truman Library.*

President Dwight D. Eisenhower accompanied
by Press Secretary James C. Hagerty, in
Washington, D.C. in 1959.
—*Courtesy of U.S. National Park Service and Dwight*
*D. Eisenhower Library.*

President John F. Kennedy confers with Press Secretary
Pierre Salinger on October 7, 1962.
—*Photo by Cecil Stoughton, courtesy of the John F. Kennedy
Presidential Library and Museum.*

Press Secretary Bill Moyers discusses the day's news
with President Lyndon B. Johnson in the Oval Office
at the White House on August 24, 1965.
—*Courtesy of the Lyndon Baines Johnson Library and Museum.*

Press Secretary George Reedy listens to President Lyndon B. Johnson in a Cabinet meeting in the White House on October 6, 1965.
—*Courtesy of the Lyndon Baines Johnson Library and Museum.*

Press Secretary George Christian, facing camera, talks with President Lyndon B. Johnson aboard Air Force One on June 25, 1967.
—*Courtesy of the Lyndon Baines Johnson Library and Museum.*

President Richard M. Nixon meets with Press Secretary Ron Ziegler in the Oval Office on November 24, 1970. Official White House Photograph.

President Gerald R. Ford talks with Press Secretary Jerald terHorst in the Oval Office on August 22, 1974. Following Ford's pardon of Richard Nixon on August 9, 1974, terHorst resigned on September 8, 1974, for reasons of personal conscience.
—*Courtesy of the Gerald R. Ford Presidential Library and Museum.*

Press Secretary Ron Nessen, foreground, responds to questions from the press on September 10, 1974, the day he was announced as press secretary, with President Gerald R. Ford at his side at the White House. Official White House Photograph.

Press Secretary Jody Powell spends an enjoyable moment with President Jimmy Carter in the White House soon after Carter assumed the presidency in 1977. Powell had been appointed on November 15, 1976. —*Courtesy of the Jimmy Carter Library.*

Press Secretary James Brady is shown with President Ronald Reagan, who named him to his post on February 24, 1981. One month later, on March 30, 1981, Brady was shot and seriously injured following an assassination attempt on President Reagan.
—*Courtesy of the Ronald Reagan Presidential Library.*

President Ronald Reagan, left, talks informally with his press secretary, Larry Speakes, on August 14, 1985, at the Reagan ranch in Santa Barbara, California.
—*Courtesy of the Ronald Reagan Presidential Library.*

Press Secretary Marlin Fitzwater enjoying a moment with President Ronald Reagan on January 12, 1987, in the Oval Office at the White House.
—*Courtesy of the Ronald Reagan Presidential Library.*

President George H. W. Bush talking things over with Press Secretary Marlin Fitzwater in the Oval Office of the White House on October 24, 1989. Official White House Photograph.

President Bill Clinton at a news conference on December 22, 1994, with his first press secretary, Dee Dee Myers, at his side. Official White House Photograph.

President Bill Clinton walks on the White House grounds with Press Secretary Mike McCurry, and the Clinton's cat, Socks, on March 6, 1997. Official White House Photograph.

President Bill Clinton strolling on the White House lawn on December 19, 1999, with Press Secretary Joe Lockhart. Official White House Photograph.

Press Secretary Jake Siewert awaits President Bill Clinton, who is answering questions from the press near the White House helicopter pad on June 22, 2000. Official White House Photograph.

President George W. Bush at his desk in the Oval Office getting some advice from his first press secretary, Ari Fleischer, early in 2001 after the long, drawn-out election of 2000. Official White House Photograph.

President George W. Bush, on April 26, 2006, thanks outgoing Press Secretary Scott McClellan, right, for his service and introduces his new press secretary, Tony Snow, left, in the James S. Brady Press Briefing Room. Official White House Photograph.

Dana Perino, press secretary to President George W. Bush, succeeded Tony Snow in September, 2007. She is only the second woman in history to hold that position. The first was Dee Dee Myers, President Bill Clinton's first press secretary in 1993. Offical White House Photograph.

# CHAPTER 4

## DOMESTIC CRISES

*School Integration at Little Rock, Arkansas: 1957*
Dwight D. Eisenhower
JAMES C. HAGERTY

The U.S. Supreme Court's landmark decision *Brown v. Board of Education*, handed down in 1954, found that the historic "separate but equal" clause was unconstitutional and the court ordered all public schools to be integrated "with all deliberate speed." In cities throughout the South, including Little Rock, Arkansas, the decision was accepted but the white establishment was not happy about enforcing the law and actually making it happen. Like other cities, the Little Rock, Arkansas, school board took three years to implement a plan that would least disrupt the community—integration in stages.

When the board laid out plans to integrate Central High School, some twenty-seven black students volunteered to attend the previously all-white high school, but when school was about to open, that number dropped to nine. Next, a group of white families, spurred on by a lawsuit filed by one parent, publicly expressed fear about sending their white children to a newly integrated school. Enter Governor Orval Faubus, who supported an injunction, only to be overruled by a federal court that ordered the integration to get under way. As the nine students prepared to enter Central High on September 2, 1957, Faubus ordered National Guardsmen to block the entrance to blacks and in a nationally televised speech that would become historic declared Central off limits to blacks and the all-black school, Horace Mann, off limits to whites. He warned that if the black students attempted to enter Central, "blood would run in the streets." The students were denied entry and a stalemate resulted.

However, on September 24, 1957, after the stalemate had stretched out for weeks, President Dwight D. Eisenhower decided to involve the federal government by sending Army troops to Little Rock to enforce the law of the land. That day, Press Secretary Jim Hagerty, accompanying the president who was on vacation in Newport, Rhode Island, sober-faced and looking in command, opened his daily briefing at 12:30 P.M. by stating: "At 12:22, the President signed an Executive Order, providing assistance for the removal of an obstruction of justice within the State of Arkansas."

He confirmed that the president had federalized the National Guard and the National Guard of Arkansas, and ordered the secretary of Defense [Charles Wilson] to "use the armed forces of the U.S. he deems necessary." He also said the president was in touch with his secretary of Defense and the Army chief of staff. Hagerty announced, too, that he had asked the TV and radio networks for time for the president that evening to talk to the nation from his office in Washington, D.C. Following are excerpts of that briefing:

*Q: Could you say what particular incident led up to this? The fact that the Negro children did not go to school?*
HAGERTY: No, it was the non-conformance, non-compliance with the [President's] Proclamation of yesterday.

*Q: The order to disperse, cease and desist?*
HAGERTY: That is correct.

*Q: In other words, the gathering of the mob?*
HAGERTY: And the reports that we had from Little Rock were that they did not desist or did not disperse and also that there was evidence, as we say here in the first, "Whereas the command contained in that Proclamation had not been obeyed and willful obstruction of enforcement of said court orders still exists and threatens to continue."

*Q: Who gave you that information, Jim?*
HAGERTY: The Department of Justice and the attorney general relayed it.

The president, acting through the chain of command, followed up by sending the 101st Airborne Division into Little Rock to guard the school and to make certain the black students entered peacefully. Nonetheless, white students around them insulted them and made them feel uncomfortable to the point where there was physical hostility. Despite being harassed, eight of the nine students finished the year and were the first blacks to graduate from Central High School.

---

## *Kent State Student Protestors Killed: 1970*
### Richard M. Nixon
### RON ZIEGLER

---

Press secretaries have employed just about every technique that one can think of, especially high-powered spin, to avoid bad publicity. But few were as unsuccessful as Ron Ziegler when he answered questions from the press about the four Kent State University students shot to death by the National Guard on May 4, 1970—the day that antiwar students held demonstrations across the country. Four were killed and at least eight others wounded. Asked by reporters if the violence might have arisen because some students felt the administration had turned a deaf ear to their grievances—indeed, Nixon had publicly called the demonstrators "bums"—Ziegler responded: "The president made clear in his speech Thursday [April 30] that the objectives of the action taken along the Cambodia-South Vietnam border is to bring a peaceful conclusion to the conflict in South Vietnam."

What Ziegler was trying to do, in effect, was to echo the president's position on demonstrators and shift the blame to the students themselves rather than the Guardsmen who, ironically, were not much older than the students they had shot. Some observers at the time attributed the shootings to the fact that the crowd of students were coming at them and that they, themselves, unnerved the Guardsmen and made them feel threatened. This interpretation was borne out by Nixon himself when he stated immediately after the shootings, "It is my hope that this tragic and unfortunate incident will strengthen the determination of all the nation's campuses, administrators, faculty and students alike to stand firmly for the right which exists in this country of peaceful dissent and just as strongly against the resort to violence as a means of such expression."

That statement was widely interpreted as Nixon condoning the shootings, although the demonstrators—especially those at Kent State—showed few signs of turning violent. Aside from the fact that they comprised a large number of students and were heading toward the Guardsmen, there was no discernable violence. To this day, no official body has found out exactly what caused the Guardsmen to fire and who gave the order if, indeed, anyone did. The adjutant of the Ohio National Guard in Columbus said in a statement at the time that the Guardsmen had been forced to shoot after a sniper opened fire against the troops from a nearby rooftop, and the crowd began to move to encircle the Guardsmen. He said the soldiers were under orders to take over and return any fire.

According to *The New York Times* account of the incident on May 5, 1970, reporter John Kifner, who filed the story from Kent State, wrote: "This reporter, who was with the group of students, did not see any indication of a sniper fire, nor was there the sound of gunfire audible before the Guard volley. Students, conceding that rocks had been thrown, heatedly denied that there was any sniper." Kifner described the scene:

> When the firing stopped, a slim girl, wearing a cowboy shirt and faded jeans, was lying face down on the road at the edge of the parking lot, blood pouring out, about 10 feet from this reporter. The youths stood stunned, many of them clustered in small groups staring at the bodies. A young man cradled one of the bleeding victims in his arms. Several girls began to cry. Many students who rushed to the scene seemed almost too shocked to react. Several gathered around an abstract steel sculpture in font of the building and looked at a .20-caliber bullet hole drilled though one of the plates.

On May 6, 1970, the president ordered a complete report on the fatal shootings after he had conferred with six students from Kent State. Ziegler told the White House press corps that the staff analysis of the Justice Department information would be prepared by John D. Ehrlichman, assistant to the president, and would recommend ways "to avoid similar incidents with the same tragic outcome." While Nixon took a hard line, so did Vice President Spiro Agnew, who was traveling around the area criticizing students for protesting the war. On the other hand, the whole topic became even more controversial when one of Nixon's own Cabinet members, Secretary of the Interior Walter J. Hickel, complained publicly in a letter to the president that his administration was turning its back on the youth of America and therefore, ironically, possibly contributing to anarchy and revolt.

He avoided blaming the president personally but suggested that the administration make contact with those who opposed the war in order to lessen the tension. The Hickel letter was seen as a deep-seated sense of frustration that was known to be shared by several members of Mr. Nixon's Cabinet. "It was symbolic," Hickel wrote, "also of an even deeper discontent that is evident in the lower ranks of the government and is inspiring widespread talk of resignation and protest, according to columnist Max Frankel, of *The New York Times*."[1]

The story also took note of the fact, incidentally, that Hickel's son had announced that he would take part in a demonstration at the University of San Francisco the next day. Frankel reported that Hickel and his son conferred about the letter the secretary had written. "He is a very progressive thinker," the younger Hickel said about his father. *The New York Times*, in an editorial titled "Death on the Campus," took Nixon apart for making his insensitive comments. It read:

> The deplorably unfeeling statement by the President of the United States— through an intermediary [Ron Ziegler] certainly does not provide either any answer or any comfort—nor does it show any compassion or even understanding. Mr. Nixon says that the needless deaths "should remind us all once again that when dissent turns to violence it invites tragedy," which of course is true but turns this tragedy upside down by placing the blame on the victims instead of the killers. The way this dreadful incident was handled could hardly have been better calculated to drive the mass of moderate students—the great majority—over to the side of the alienated. It is nothing short of a disaster for the United States, and it is doubly tragic that the President does not seem to realize that this is so.[2]

Given all of this turmoil, Ziegler's original spin that the demonstrators themselves were somehow the troublemakers did not go down well with the Washington press corps. In fact, it backfired. However, most White House observers would agree that there was not much a press secretary could do—other than meet with those Kent State students—to save his president when the president himself lacked the ability to reach out and understand where the young people were coming from.

The Kent State killings have been under investigation for years because of how they have come to symbolize forceful repression of the right to protest. After two decades of investigations and lawsuits all the way up to the U.S. Supreme Court in 1990, the victims' families [those killed or wounded] settled out of court. The state of Ohio awarded them a total of $675,000, to be split thirteen ways, and the defendants [the National Guardsmen] signed a "statement of regret."

Some of the families involved claimed the statement was an apology, but the defendants and their attorneys disputed that.

### Air Traffic Controllers' Strike: 1981
#### Ronald Reagan
#### LARRY SPEAKES

During the summer of President Ronald Reagan's first year in office, the Professional Air Traffic Controllers Organization (PATCO), the union representing the controllers employed by the Federal Aviation Administration, called a strike to start on August 3, 1981, to demand higher wages, a shorter work week, and better retirement benefits. The threat of a strike became a test of Reagan's famous willpower and his stated position that unions alone would not determine what happens in labor-management disputes. Emphasizing that it was illegal for them to strike, Reagan left no doubt beforehand that if the controllers went out, they would be fired. There would be no compromises—there would be "no amnesty" for those participating in a walkout, nor would there be any negotiations during a strike. Some economists and federal officials predicted that a prolonged strike would have a devastating national economic impact.

The decision to fire the controllers had been made a few days earlier and, according to White House Press Secretary Larry Speakes,[3] the president was firm from the outset. Reagan's announcement that he would fire the controllers if they went out on strike came on a Monday, March 3, at a press conference in the White House Rose Garden. Reagan issued a stern ultimatum: The workers on strike must report to work within forty-eight hours or face dismissal from their jobs. As federal employees, the controllers were subject to a no-strike clause in their contracts. The derivation of this law stemmed from a congressional action in 1955 that made such strikes a crime punishable by a fine or one year of incarceration. This law was tested but upheld by the Supreme Court in 1971.

Speakes recalled in an interview, "I told the press that the President was doing the right thing—he is enforcing the law."[4] The press secretary had to emphasize—or spin—the news to blame the union for breaking the law. "I told the press that everything would be alright and that the striking controllers would be replaced as quickly as possible. I said the president would not bend. It was a show of strength. I said that it's good for the country; we need to have more people like Reagan who put the public interest before anything else," he recalled.

Speakes said it was the decisive manner in which Reagan handled the strike that convinced many Americans that he was the kind of leader the country needed—a strong president, unlike his predecessor, Jimmy Carter, who was viewed as weak and indecisive. The press bought the press secretary's logic, as did the public. The controllers may well have thought that Reagan was bluffing, but the reporters who covered him at the White House knew better.

After the 12,000 striking members disobeyed President Reagan's ultimatum to return to their posts, they were fired. The union was decertified by the government as the controllers' bargaining agent and fines and criminal charges were filed against union leaders. Meanwhile, to soften the public image of the government acting too harshly, Speakes went to great lengths to reassure the press that Reagan—in light of his own background as a union leader in his early Hollywood days—was not anti-union. He said that Reagan took no pleasure in letting the controllers go. The press secretary pointed out that Reagan was the first president to be a lifetime member of the AFL-CIO, and that the president was well aware that PATCO had been one of the few unions to support his presidential bid. "I supported unions and the rights of workers to organize and bargain collectively," Speakes wrote in his memoirs, "but no president could tolerate an illegal strike by Federal employees."[5]

By August 31, when Speakes held a briefing for the White House press corps, the subject was just about played out. But there were one or two reporters who clung to the story. One asked why Reagan had not agreed to talk with Lane Kirkland, president of the AFL-CIO, about the strike. The question: "Why isn't the President going to show some compassion towards the air controllers?" Speakes's ready reply: "Because they broke the law." The next question: "Richard Nixon did, too, but one of our former bosses [Gerald Ford] pardoned him." Speakes, with a smile, shot back: "Yes, I remember that."

For Reagan, there were no shades of gray when it came to the law: He either enforced it or he did not. Reagan, never shy about taking action, simply issued the order. There was little public support for the strikers.

The Transportation Department had assured the president that the Federal Aviation Authority's contingency plan would go into effect right away—thus minimizing the strike's impact on the public and business interests. Approximately 3,000 supervisors joined 2,000 non-striking controllers and 900 military controllers in manning airport towers. The FAA ordered airlines at major airports to reduce scheduled flights by 50 percent during peak hours for safety reasons. Nearly sixty small airport towers were scheduled to be shut down indefinitely. More than 45,000 people applied within four weeks after the strike began. In a matter of weeks, approximately 80 percent of airline flights were operating as scheduled, while air freight remained virtually unaffected, according to airline officials.

Perhaps the main reason that Speakes's tactic with the press was successful was that the public did not support the strikers. Instead, it sided with the government and, in doing so, helped Speakes to enhance Reagan's image as a strong and courageous leader. It did not take long before full service was restored and by 1984, air traffic increased by 6 percent while there were still 20 percent fewer controllers than had been on the job prior to the walkout.

The outcome constituted a singular victory for the president of the United States who, arguably because of his background as a union member and leader, received the overwhelming support of the people. It also showed how a professional secretary can take advantage of the situation and spin it in the president's favor. [Author's Note: *It should be noted that President Bill Clinton reinstated the dismissed air traffic controllers in 1993, but many observers believed Reagan's success in breaking this strike demonstrated the increasing trend toward lessening the power of unions across America.*]

---

## *Los Angeles Riots in Watts: 1992*
### George H.W. Bush
### MARLIN FITZWATER

---

Race relations has, for generations, played an important, if not controversial role, in the body politic of America. History has shown that, in many instances, violence erupts when a black person is involved with confrontation with police. Such was the case on March 3, 1991, when Rodney King led police on a high-speed chase. At the time, King was on parole from an assault and robbery conviction. Police said King resisted arrest even after pulling over, and was therefore beaten to the ground by the police. What made this normally routine arrest national news was the fact that the entire brutal episode was videotaped by a bystander. That's all that was needed to inflame the black community, which already had been expressing anger about police brutality in the black community of South Central Los Angeles. The cops involved were eventually charged with the use of excessive force in the beating.

Due to the media coverage of the beating, the trial was covered by the national media, as well. Members of the black community waited for what they were sure would be a guilty verdict, but on April 9, 1992, three of the officers were acquitted. The verdict triggered a violent four-day riot in Los Angeles—one of the worst racial-driven upheavals in the history of the city. People took to the streets in other cities across the nation as well. On the third day of the trial—May 1, 1992—King made a plea in public to the TV cameras that, surprisingly, became a cliché for those involved with race relations across the country. He asked, simply: "People, I just want to say, you know, can't we all just get along?"

On that same day, at his White House press briefing, Press Secretary Marlin Fitzwater tried to calm the waters with his opening remarks: "There are encouraging reports that the situation in Los Angeles is improving," he said quietly. "We are encouraged by this, but share the concern of everyone who is working to restore order in Los Angeles and other areas." Fitzwater told reporters that in response to requests for assistance by Mayor Tom Bradley and Governor Pete Wilson, President George H.W. Bush had ordered some 1,000 law enforcement officers to go to Los Angeles, and that the U.S. Army would move some 4,000 troops from Fort Ord, California, to a staging area nearby. If necessary, Fitzwater said the president was prepared to federalize the National Guard. Bush had already publicly called the riots "a tragic situation that cannot be allowed to continue. The rule of law defines our freedom. The forces of repression, suppression, and anarchy cannot be allowed to continue."

In the Q&A session with reporters, Fitzwater was asked: "What is the President doing in terms of cooling this thing off?" Fitzwater, always calm in a crisis, replied: "He wants to hear from leaders of various minority groups from the Small Business Administration and others that will be helping to reestablish businesses, to help people readjust when this is over and to hopefully bring it to a swift conclusion."

On May 4, in his press briefing, in an effort to offer more reassurance that the president was still actively involved in solving the crisis, Fitzwater reported that Los Angeles was "relatively calm, with only sporadic incidents," that the attorney general reported the total federal presence to be 12,430, including the regular military, federalized National Guard, and civilian law enforcement authorities, and that President Bush "praised the responsiveness and effectiveness of our military and civilian leaders responding to the emergency."

Fitzwater also told newsmen that the president had taken the additional step of asking David Kearns, deputy secretary of education and former chairman of the board of Xerox, to lead a small group of officials to Los Angeles to meet with local leaders and "to assist their needs." Kearns, Fitzwater said, was deeply involved in education and was "a very respected leader." In time, order was restored and, with the help of Fitzwater, the news that the Bush administration had responded quickly and effectively to the riot appeared in the media, offering a favorable spin to what was, obviously, a very challenging situation. When a riot occurs, the best a press secretary can do is to keep the public calm and constantly reassure everyone that the White House is on top of the situation. In this, Fitzwater succeeded.

---

### September 11, 2001
### George W. Bush
### ARI FLEISCHER

---

At the moment when the worst attack on America in our history occurred—with two hijacked passenger airplanes purposely being flown into the Twin Towers in Manhattan killing some 3,000 people, a third crashing into the Pentagon in Washington, D.C., and a fourth into a mountainside in Shanksville, Pennsylvania, as a result of heroism on the part the doomed passengers. At the time (9 A.M.), President George W. Bush was in a Sarasota, Florida, school. He had delivered a speech and was visiting a second-grade classroom of youngsters, where he was reading them a book, "My Pet Goat."

White House Chief of Staff Andrew Card walked into the classroom and whispered into the president's ear, telling him a plane had crashed into the World Trade Center. The president paused for a moment, continued to read, but then got up and quietly left the classroom. According to reports from those on the scene, Bush seemed stunned but calm. The president delayed addressing the tragedy until he received more information. At about 9:30 he was briefed by National Security Advisor Condoleezza Rice. After getting on Air Force One at 10 A.M. heading to Louisiana, the president called Vice President Dick Cheney and ordered America's military on a high alert status.

Upon arriving at Barksdale Air Force Base, Louisiana, before noon, he made several telephone calls to government officials, including Secretary of Defense Donald Rumsfeld. Shortly after 1 P.M. Bush said, "Make no mistake: The United States will hunt down and punish those responsible for these cowardly acts." Fifteen minutes later, Bush headed for the U.S. Strategic Command at an Air Force Base in Nebraska, talking to Cheney in Washington by phone. A half-hour later, Bush left for Washington, working with several aides on his nationally televised prime-time speech that night, in which he vowed "to find those responsible and bring them to justice."

While this was happening, a pool reporter for the press was being briefed by Press Secretary Ari Fleischer, starting at 1:47 P.M. Fleischer wasted no words and kept the reporter fully informed. Fleischer matter-of-factly gave out action-oriented information intended to keep the nation calm in the midst of the worst shock it had experienced since Pearl Harbor. Fleischer emphasized what was being done to help families of victims of the tragedy, how the president had taken charge, and how capably and swiftly the president and the federal government's agencies were acting to respond to the profound, premeditated wound to America's pride. The nation's generations-old self-confidence had been severely shaken, since it had always felt protected by an ocean on either side.

Fleischer's briefings that day and on the ensuing days provide a textbook example of how to reassure a shocked nation of governmental vigilance and response. He kept up a steady drumbeat of positive messages that served him, the president, and the nation well in terms of avoiding panic or losing faith in those sworn to protect the public.

For example, he told reporters that the president's first priority was the families of the victims killed in the attacks in New York and Washington, D.C.; the president was making dozens of phone calls to leaders around the world seeking support for a worldwide, unified front against terrorism; that Bush was receiving bipartisan support from both Houses of Congress in drawing up plans for a retaliation of some kind; that the president himself was coordinating all government agencies in an effort to safeguard the nation; that from that point on it would not be "business as usual" in Washington, D.C.; that the American people could expect the president would talk to them honestly as events unfolded and that his "resolve is clear and strong and that America is united"; and, finally, that the United States and its allies would "track down and destroy those who had perpetuated that unspeakable act of aggression against innocent Americans."

The story is best told by reading excerpts of the press secretary's briefings, starting the day of the attack on September 11, 2001:

FLEISCHER: While on the ground at Barksdale, the President spoke to the Vice President several times—the Vice President, of course, being at the operations center at the White House. He spoke with the Secretary of Defense; he spoke to Senator [Charles] Schumer (D-N.Y.); he had spoken to his wife prior to landing in Louisiana.

*Q: Do you know where she is?*
FLEISCHER: She's at a secure facility.

*Q: And his daughters?*
FLEISCHER: They're also at a secure location.

*Q: Are they with her?*
FLEISCHER: No, no, they're at their respective schools. There will be a National Security Council meeting later this afternoon, in which the President will participate via teleconference. And, needless to say, all elements of the United States government are now doing their part, not only to help those who have been hurt, but also to collect information, to analyze it and to provide it to the President.

*Q: Does the President now know anything more about who is responsible, the coordinated attack, and whether this is it or—*
FLEISCHER: That information is still being gathered and analyzed. I anticipate that will be an ongoing process for a little while. Often, at a time like this, information comes in, it turns out not to be true. The proper procedure is to carefully, thoroughly evaluate all information.

*Q: Had there been any warnings that the President knew of?*
FLEISCHER: No warnings.

*Q: Does the President—is he concerned about the fact that this attack of this severity happened with no warning?*
FLEISCHER: First things first: his concern is with the health and security of the American people and with the families of those who have lost their lives. There will come an appropriate time to do all appropriate look backs. His focus is on events this morning.

*Q: Has he been given any estimate of what the American casualties may be?*
FLEISCHER: I don't believe so.

*Q: Has he spoken with Mayor [Rudolph] Giuliani or Governor [George] Pataki?*
FLEISCHER: He spoke with Governor Pataki. He plans to speak with Mayor Giuliani.

*Q: Does the President feel hunted or in jeopardy? I mean, he is kind of trying to stay out of—*

FLEISCHER: The President is looking forward to returning to Washington. He understands at a time like this, caution must be taken; and he wants to get back to Washington.

*Q: What's he doing right now?*

FLEISCHER: He's talking to people on the phone from his cabin.

[Author's Note: *In a rare demonstration of appreciation for the press secretary's efforts, one reporter ended the briefing with these words: "Thank you for bringing us whatever you can, in terms of information on what he's doing." At a time like that, such a comment was music to Fleischer's ears.*]

In the ensuing days, Fleischer continued to give out the news calmly and factually in an effort to keep a lid on the fear that had spread across the nation and to reinforce the image of the president as a man of action on the international stage. He informed the press that the president had been making a series of phone calls to leaders around the world to rally an international coalition to combat terrorism; that he had spoken with Prime Minister Blair, Prime Minister Chretien, President Jacques Chirac, with Chancellor (Gerhard) Schroeder, with President Jiang of China, and twice with President Vladimir Putin; that the president would continue to reach out to leaders throughout the world to develop a coalition and send a message that the United States and the world stand united with all the freedom-loving countries to fight terrorism.

Fleischer spun his comments in a larger context, stressing that Bush felt "freedom and democracy are under attack and that the American people need to know that we are facing a different enemy than we have ever faced. Those are the President's words." Fleischer also confirmed that the White House viewed the attack as "an act of war" and it had "real and credible" information that the airplane that had flown into the Pentagon was originally intended to hit the White House; that Vice President Cheney remained in the White House but was removed to a secure area.

The press secretary emphasized that "the information that he had about Air Force One being a possible target was 'real and credible'"; and that, he added, was one of the reasons why Air Force One did not come back to Andrews Air Force Base, where some people thought it would. [Author's Note: *Fleischer made this point to deflect criticism from some quarters that the president should have returned to Washington after he first heard of the initial attack in New York.*] Asked about the level of killing in these attacks, if the president could assure the American people that his response would be commensurate with that, Flesicher repeated: "You have what the President said about how the United States will prevail. But I'm not going to speculate."

Did the press secretary know who was responsible for the attacks? At this point, Fleischer simply did not know so he replied: "The United States is in the process of gathering all the facts about this matter. The full resources of the federal government at all levels have been dedicated to this. And we will continue to gather those facts and ascertain all the information available."

One reporter asked if the White House was going to make an open-ended request to Congress for funding, or was there going to be a figure given to Congress? Fleischer: "No, the President thinks it's important that this not become an open-ended request. The President—and by the way, the meeting with the bipartisan congressional leaders was a very important and stirring meeting of patriotism. The outpouring of support, shoulder to shoulder, regardless of anybody's political party, was wonderful, it was impressive, and it should make every American proud."

Another reporter got to the heart of the matter when he asked: "Ari, all the fingers are being pointed at Osama bin Laden and Afghanistan; he is being supported by Taliban and bases in Pakistan. So are we talking about now going against Afghanistan or Pakistan? And if it happened, then it is all in the name of Islam. So is it time now for the United States not to wait anymore, more innocent people will be killed in the name of terrorism?" Fleischer demurred, not knowing for certain himself what the answer was. Another reporter then asked another penetrating question that would later become the focus of a congressional inquiry: "Is the President satisfied, and should the American people be satisfied, with the performance of the intelligence community in this country, given what happened?"

This was the first of what would become a series of challenges relating to the intelligence capability of the United States.

> The President believes that the intelligence community and the nation's military are the best in the world. And, clearly, something yesterday took place in New York that was not foreseen, that we had no specific information about. But the President's focus right now is on helping the families of those who have lost their lives and those who are suffering in this tragedy; and then on taking whatever the appropriate next steps should be.

He said Bush would look into the intelligence issue in due time and that Bush's earlier statement that "the actions against the soil of the

United States are what led the President to say that this was an act of war against the United States." The president had used that term in a nationwide address immediately after the attack, in which he said he would work with Congress on any appropriate measures he would take "at the appropriate time."

Fleischer stressed that this attack was different than any in past U.S. history and that the United States was dealing "at this point, with nameless, faceless people. And it is a different type of war than it was, say, when you knew the capitol of the country that attacked you. So we will continue to work with the Congress on appropriate language at the appropriate time."

Asked if the president was "angry," Fleischer thought for a moment and then took the opportunity to spin his answer making Bush seem to be resolute rather than angry. Said Fleischer: "I see him as determined. There's no question that the President has strong thoughts and strong feelings. He is focused on rallying our nation, on helping those who need help at this time—in New York and at the Pentagon—expressing his sorrow to the families involved, and ascertaining all facts and all information so that the United States can and will do the right thing."

Fleischer had all the right words. He added that Bush would consult with the Congress and with world leaders before taking any action.

> The President is going to continue to lead. But it's particularly important now to consult with the Congress. One of the greatest strengths of our country is that we are a Constitution-based democracy. Our Constitution and our nation have survived acts of terror and attacks on our nation before. And the President knows that the strength of our nation comes from that Constitution, which gives an important role to Congress.

In answer to a question about whether or not Bush, as a man of faith, had consulted with any clergy, Fleischer replied, candidly: "You know, I have not asked him that, so I do not know. I think it's fair to say that in all things, the President's religious faith sustains him, particularly at a time like now."

Fleischer also stated, in answer to questions, the Department of Transportation was fully addressing the issue of airline security. Asked when the president would be going to New York City to see what became known as "Ground Zero," Fleischer said:

> The President's heart goes out to those who live in New York, to the families who have lost loved ones and to all New Yorkers, and to all Americans who look at New York and see a beautiful skyline that is now altered. But the

President is also cognizant of the fact that nothing should be done that would in any way hinder the ability of those who are carrying out the rescue efforts to find survivors and get them out. And any time the President travels, it does create issues for people on the ground, and the President is not going to try to do anything that would make anything harder for the people who are carrying out their number one priority. So at the appropriate time, the President will go to New York. But the President's first focus is on making sure that the rescue workers are able to conduct their jobs.

He was asked again about the "act of war" phrase Bush had used, giving Fleischer yet another opportunity to spin his boss's image as follows: "I think there is no other way to describe it. And I think that's what the American people expect from their President." Fleischer described the attack as "a wake-up call to all concerned that terrorism must be combated in all its forms and in every way. And this presents people with an opportunity to work together now, to move beyond the disputes of the past. And we'll see what events unfold as a result of this."

Two days after the attack, reporters had more questions and Fleischer stepped up to them supplying the following information: The Department of Treasury, in conjunction with the Department of Justice, announced the deployment of agents from the U.S. Marshal Service, U.S. Border Control, and U.S. Customs at designated airport security checkpoints throughout the country as part of the heightened security measures that had gone into effect; the Secret Service expanded the security perimeter around the White House as a precautionary matter; the Department of Transportation ordered that national airspace would be reopened to commercial and private aviation, but only after implementing a more stringent level of security; the Department of Justice, in conjunction with the Department of Treasury, beefed up the security at the airports.

"Finally," Fleischer concluded, "Let me just say this: The President was very touched by his visit to the hospital [in Washington, D.C.]. At the hospital, he met with people who are in a burn unit now, who have survived. Some people are there as a result of the heroic actions they took in saving lives. The President met with one family where a mother stood by the bed of her son, in the company of the soldier who rescued her son. And she said, 'Mr. President, you have no idea how much this means to my family, that you are here.'" Fleischer added: "He and Mrs. Bush were very touched by the determination of our nation and its military, and all the people that were affected by this, and the people in

New York City." Fleischer explained that Bush would follow protocol and ask Congress for a resolution giving him the power to take military action, as a "show of unity" between the executive and legislative branches of government during a crisis. He also said Bush had been in touch with many foreign government leaders, including Pakistan, where the United States would need cooperation in the event of a counterstrike.

Would Bush need approval from Congress? "The Constitution vests in the President as Commander in Chief the authority to take actions he deems necessary to protect and defend the United States," said the press secretary. "The President is very encouraged as the result of working with Congress on this joint resolution, which is a real show of unity from the Congress. And the White House will work with Congress on that language."

Three days after the attack, on September 14, 2001, Bush went to Ground Zero in New York, dressed in a light jacket, collar open, and climbed a pile of rubble on which a New York City fireman, #164 on his helmet, stood. Bush put his left arm around the fireman and with a microphone in his right hand, in a firm voice, shouted clearly to the thousands of firemen, policemen, and other workers in the crowd—who were whistling and chanting "USA, USA, USA . . ."—

> I want you all to know that America today is on bended knees. In prayer for the people whose lives were lost here, for the workers who work here, for the families that mourn, this nation stands with the good people of New York City, New Jersey, and Connecticut as we mourn the loss of thousands of our citizens. (Pause, with noise from the cheering crowd getting louder). I can hear you. The rest of the world hears you. And the people who knocked these buildings down will hear all of us soon. (Crowd cheers increased in volume as it chanted in unison, "USA, USA, USA . . .") The nation sends its love and compassion (a man shouts out "God Bless America!!") to everybody who is here. Thank you for your hard work. Thank you for making the nation proud. And may God bless America. (Huge cheering follows for several minutes and again resuming its chanting of the phrase: "USA, USA, USA.")

During Bush's years, the president rarely, if ever, performed as well as he did that day. This was a rare case—for him—when no press secretary, no matter how talented, could possibly say a single word that would come close to giving America the image of a strong, compassionate president who showed that he was resolute, unbowed, and determined to fight back.

At his next press briefing, when a reporter pressed him on whether Bush would be required by law to go to Congress, Fleischer enlightened the press with some information he had obviously prepared beforehand: "There have been some 125 military actions that took place in the United States, and I believe only five involved declarations of war." When asked again about going to New York, Fleischer said it had become "appropriate" for the president to visit the city.

Subsequently, Fleischer was asked if the president expected greater cooperation from Congress on his domestic programs. Fleischer: "I think what you're going to see is Democrats and Republicans alike uniting on all kinds of areas. I can't guess with specificity what the domestic future will look like. But based on the meeting the President had with the congressional leaders, I think it's fair to say that there is a different domestic mood. Our nation's leaders in Congress remain men and women of principle, and they will take the actions that they think are in the national interest. And I think as events unfold on the domestic front this fall, leaders of Congress and the rank and file of Congress will show those principles, and our government will unite."

*Hurricane Katrina: 2005*

George W. Bush

SCOTT McCLELLAN/TONY SNOW

They knew it was coming and it did, making it the worst natural disaster in U.S. history. From August 25 to August 30, 2005, in Florida, Mississippi, and Louisiana, Hurricane Katrina slammed into the Gulf Coast with 127 mile-per-hour winds and major storm surges, destroying hundreds of homes and businesses and causing massive flooding, especially in New Orleans where the levees failed.

At least 1,833 people died, with 1,464 of those in Louisiana, and about a million more were displaced from their homes. Katrina caused damages estimated at more than $100 billion. There have been many other well-documented disasters in the annals of American tragedies—the Blizzard of 1888; the 1900 devastation of Galveston, Texas, due to a huge tidal surge; The Great 1906 San Francisco Earthquake; and the great Dust Bowl, covering 50 million acres in the south-central plains during the winter of 1935–1936, to name just a few.

Katrina actually began to form at 5 P.M. on August 23, 2005. The National Hurricane Center in Miami, Florida, issued its advisory about a tropical storm system off the coast of the Bahamas that would become

Hurricane Katrina. As millions of Americans watched in fear, the storm evolved into a mammoth hurricane in the next seven days, triggering Governors Kathleen Bianco of Louisiana and Haley Barbour of Mississippi to declare states of emergency in their respective states.

It made landfall in Florida and then along the Gulf Coast in Mississippi, Louisiana, and Alabama with its winds blowing at about 175 miles an hour leaving in its wake a shocking trail of destruction and human misery. Katrina destroyed just about everything in its way, including massively flooding the proud, historic city of New Orleans, ultimately killing more than 1,800 people, inflicting pain and suffering on thousands of others, and leaving millions homeless and property damages in the billions of dollars.

Katrina laid to waste hundreds of years of American tradition in a beloved city known for its great music, its unmatched hospitality, and its annual, world-renowned Mardi Gras. In short, it was a severe blow to America's pride and prowess—the second disaster in an already wounded land still recovering from the unprecedented terrorist attacks on New York City nearly four years earlier. Our nation's invulnerability was being tested by massive destruction—by man and by nature.

When Katrina's full impact was measurable on August 29, 2005, inhabitants of the states hit by the storm were not only stunned by its unstoppable force, but they were dismayed and frustrated by the apparent inability of our government on all levels—local, state, and federal—to respond effectively to the awesome crisis.

As the government's own report to President Bush would later state: "Hurricane Katrina and the subsequent sustained flooding of New Orleans exposed significant flaws in Federal, State, and local preparedness for catastrophic events and our capacity to respond to them." Emergency plans at all levels of government, from small town plans to the 600-page National Response Plan—the federal government's plan to coordinate all its departments and agencies and integrate them with state, local, and private sector partners—were put to the ultimate test, and came up short. Millions of Americans were reminded of the need to protect themselves and their families. There was little doubt at the time that Hurricane Katrina would go down in history as the most destructive natural catastrophe in American history.

It has, indeed. But the unfolding story of how the response to the catastrophe was so badly bungled by first responders at all levels of government remains on the minds of the American public as much as the disaster itself. It is instructive to recall exactly what the president and his press secretary were telling the public about the storm, clearly showing how both were, no doubt, trying their best to calm the victims and the nation as a whole by putting the best spin possible on the actions taken by the administration, even as the disaster unfolded on the ground and an uncoordinated response led to the loss of life and property. Following is a chronological, excerpted record of how the press secretary kept the press informed about what the president was doing during this build-up to the unprecedented crisis.

On August 25, 2005, only two days after the dire warnings from the National Hurricane Center had been broadcast nationwide, Deputy White House Press Secretary Trent Duffy, accompanying the press on a visit to the Crawford Middle School in Crawford, Texas, at noon, quickly set the scene to burnish the president's credentials as an involved, active participant in the plan that would be put into place for what was sure to be an unmitigated disaster. Speaking to reporters, he said:

> Let me say a quick note about Tropical Storm Katrina. The President has been informed regularly about the tropical storm, and federal authorities are coordinating with Governor [Jeb] Bush and Florida officials on preparations. The government is ready, we're watching, and we're taking steps to make sure that people get to safe areas or take the proper precautions from the storm. We're also moving to ensure that all relief and recovery resources are in place so that these efforts can take place real time following any storm event. [There were no questions from the press.]

On August 29, Press Secretary Scott McClellan at a morning "gaggle" with the press on Air Force One en route to Glendale, Arizona, went to work carefully laying out the details of what the president was doing to prepare for Katrina. "I would like to begin by updating you a little bit on Hurricane Katrina, from our standpoint," he said calmly and matter-of-factly, thus reducing the palpable anxiety that could be seen among the news people present. Said McClellan: "Shortly, some White House officials on board will be participating in a videoconference call with federal and state officials from aboard Air Force One. This is something the White House has been doing both from D.C. as well as from Crawford over the last few days . . . calls with the federal authorities and with state emergency management operation centers."

In an assuring tone, McClellan informed the press that all was functioning as anticipated.

> *The President, this morning, spoke with our FEMA head, Mike Brown. Mike gave the President an update* (italics added). Katrina remains a dangerous storm.

We are coordinating closely with state and local authorities. We continue to urge citizens in those areas to listen to local authorities. Medical assistance teams and rescue teams have been deployed, and we're continuing to coordinate all activities very closely to make sure that the focus is on saving lives. That's where the top priority is right now, and that's where it will remain. The President also, just a short time ago, approved major disaster declarations for the states of Louisiana and Mississippi. This will allow federal funds to start being used to deploy resources to help in those two states. This is something that was done verbally, and the governors of those states have been notified of that approval.

Asked if the president had any plans to go to Florida, where his brother, Governor Jeb Bush, had his hands full, McClellan responded:

Right now, our focus continues to be on making sure that we're saving lives and focused on getting help to those who are in harm's way. Quick update. The President spoke with FEMA head Mike Brown again on the plane, and the staff participated in a videoconference call. One of the main things that Brown emphasized was that it remains a serious situation, and there's still a lot of concern about storm surge, flooding, the damage and destruction on the ground, power outages, and things of that nature. And on the conference call, there were updates from all the different states that were being received, as well. And federal and state and local authorities continue to work round the clock. The storm is still over these impacted areas, and it remains a very serious situation. And the President continued to ask questions of Mike Brown to make sure that we were doing everything in our power to save lives and to help those in need.

McClellan had touched all bases.

What the White House press secretary could not report to the press—presumably because he was unaware of everything that went on during that videoconference—on that day, Sunday, August 29, 2005, was the full contents of the meeting of the major players managing the crisis, who had briefed Bush, during that videoconference. According to the Associated Press, the videotaped briefing Bush received of the storm before Hurricane Katrina made its full impact contradicted statements the president later made in defense of his administration's failed response. Max Mayfield, National Hurricane Director, had told the president during the videoconference that the integrity of the levees was *"a very very grave concern"* (italics added). Just days later, the president claimed: "I don't think anybody anticipated the breach of the levees. They did anticipate a serious storm, but these levees got breached.

And as a result, much of New Orleans is flooded, and now we're having to deal with it and will," he said.

The fact was that Bush was warned of a possible breach of the levees during the videoconference. According to The Associated Press, the transcripts showed that Bush was warned by the head of the National Hurricane Center about the potential for breached levees. The transcripts also show that FEMA Director Michael Brown warned the participants that the Louisiana Superdome was under water and could become a *"catastrophe within a catastrophe"* (italics added).[6]

The entire fiasco was put into perspective by a report requested by Bush and submitted to him a year later on June 23, 2006, by Frances F. Townsend, assistant to the president of the United States for Homeland Security and Counterterrorism, in which she stated that some lessons were learned in the handling of Katrina and that it would require "a sustained commitment over time by the federal government as well as by the State and local governments that have essential duties in responding to disaster."[7]

On August 31, 2005, McClellan kept up the drumbeat by relaying a sense of action. During his press gaggle aboard Air Force One en route to Andrews Air Force Base, McClellan recited another list of government officials who had participated in another videoconference with Bush who had left Crawford for D.C. Among the participants McClellan named were Deputy Chief of Staff Karl Rove; Deputy National Security Advisor J.D. Crouch; Andrew Card, who was on the videoconference from Maine; and Vice President Cheney on from Wyoming. In Washington, at the White House, there were Homeland Security Secretary Michael Chertoff and Deputy Secretary Michael Jackson; Homeland Security Advisor Fran Townsend; Claude Allen, head of the Domestic Policy Council, who was overseeing the White House Task Force; Dan Bartlett, White House communications director; and other staff members. This was geared to give the distinct image that the president had rallied all of his top aides around him and was fully engaged. McClellan reported that among the issues discussed were the options for an evacuation of the Superdome in New Orleans, the flooding going on in New Orleans and Mississippi, and work going on to fix the breaches in the levees.

There was also a good bit of discussion about what they were looking at doing to fix the levees with the Corps of Engineers. McClellan also mentioned the security situation. [Martial law, he told the press, had been declared in Mississippi and Louisiana.] McCllellan said they talked about the National Guard response and that the president wanted to make sure that Mike Brown "was getting all the cooperation he needed from all the different agencies within the federal government on the ground. Mike expressed that he was getting good cooperation within the federal government."

The press secretary added that other topics discussed were "continuing to develop a long-term strategy for addressing the issues involved here, particularly the displacement of people." And they also talked about the Strategic Petroleum Reserve and the loans or the exchanges of oil to address the disruption in the supply. McClellan went out of his way to emphasize that Chertoff had declared Katrina

> an incident of national significance, which means that the national response plan that we have developed has been activated. This is the first time it's ever been activated. It's really there for major disasters or emergencies that really overwhelm state and local resources, and require coordination across the federal government to help the state and local efforts that are going on. And it enables us to really fully mobilize all agencies within the federal government under the Department of Homeland Security, under his oversight.

The reporters dutifully took down Chertoff's views, but wondered among themselves what did it all mean? And how does it translate to action on the ground? One reporter asked: "There really are some pretty grave concerns about the future of New Orleans, and as you know, it's one of the country's great cities. What can the President say to provide some sort of comfort or reassurance about the future of New Orleans and the rest of the region, of course, too?" McClellan sidestepped the question: "Our thoughts and prayers are with all those in the affected communities, those who have been displaced. The President is focused, first and foremost on saving lives, and a close second to that is sustaining life."

However, the press secretary, when asked about federal funding to help pay for the effort, gained back some ground with this spin: "I would expect a supplemental is going to be needed in a situation like this. There's money available for the urgent needs right now, and [other] resources available. We are certainly going to do everything from the standpoint of the federal government to make sure that the needs are met." Asked whether the president intended to personally visit the region, McClellan, at first, tactfully replied: "We don't want to do anything that would be disruptive of the immediate needs that people are trying to meet." But then, asked how important it would be for the president to make a personal appearance, the press secretary stepped up to the plate and spun a solid base hit, making his boss look like the "compassionate conservative" that he calls himself. McClellan responded, unambiguously: "The President will visit the region on behalf of the American people to get a first-hand look at the ongoing response and recovery efforts, as well as to hear from people on the ground who are involved in the response efforts, as well as those who have been impacted by it." In the meantime, he added, the president's plane would do a "flyover" to get a close look at the flooding and the damage firsthand.

On cue, the next day September 1, McClellan announced that the president would visit and tour the Gulf Coast region and get a closer look at the enormous devastation from Katrina. At this point, McClellan earned his pay by alluding to the president's responsibility to be on the ground with the people most affected. "The hearts and prayers of the American people continue to go out to all the citizens in the affected areas of the Gulf Coast," the press secretary said.

McClellan then spun the story to make Bush look as if he was responding. He told them that Bush's scheduled visit on September 1, 2005, was another way for the president

> to show the nation's support and compassion for the victims and our appreciation for those who are helping with the ongoing response and recovery efforts. It is an opportunity for the President to get a first-hand, up-close look at the response and recovery efforts, and to hear from those on the ground. It is also a time, simply, to offer some encouragement and comfort to boost the spirits of the people, those who are helping in the response, and those who have been displaced by the hurricane.

McClellan found another opportunity to spin the story by putting an individual face on the event—and he did: "The President continues to spend much of the day focused on the federal government's response efforts," reported McClellan. "This morning the President called Petty Officer Josh Mitcheltree of the United States Coast Guard. He is a swimmer who has been involved in the search and rescue efforts. The President expressed his appreciation for his efforts and the round-the-clock efforts of his colleagues. Hopefully, it helped to boost their spirits during this trying time."

And then McClellan—always on his toes—handed out two more newsworthy items for the media to pick up, making Bush continue to look good: "Right now, the President is having lunch with [Federal

Reserve] Chairman Alan Greenspan," he said. "The purpose of the meeting is to focus on the economic impact [of Katrina]." This was followed by a kernel of news that got the full attention of the press: "This afternoon, the President will meet with former Presidents Bush and Clinton to announce an effort that they will lead to raise private funds for victims of Katrina. This is similar to the effort they led with the tsunami relief, where they helped to raise more than $1 billion in an unprecedented effort to help people in that region."

In sharp contrast to the action-oriented scenario of videoconferences, briefings, and government measures constantly cited by McClellan, giving the impression that federal officials were on top of the situation, the press over the next few days was monitoring the scene just as closely and getting an entirely different—and far worse—picture of the panic, chaos, and lack of order where Katrina had just about blown everything away. One reporter asked bluntly:

> People on the ground, Scott, are questioning why it's taken three days or more for federal help to arrive, notwithstanding all of the preparations. There's considerable bitterness in some places. We had one woman ask on camera last night, where's the cavalry? And then there's been editorial criticism across the country of the President for not acting sooner, or not coming back sooner. What do you say to all that?

McClellan went into his spin routine again. Up to that time, it had served him well. He read a long a long list of actions the government was taking. But even so, when he finished, a reporter asked, bluntly:

*Q: But none of that means anything to somebody who has been living on an interstate overpass for the last three days, without food or water, or any kind of assistance, local or federal.*

McCLELLAN: As we were passing over the region yesterday, we saw people that were standing on those highways, those highways that just disappeared into the water. We saw people that were on rooftops. We saw helicopters in the distance engaged in search and rescue operations as we were passing through the region. Our concern, first and foremost, is with the people who have been displaced or affected otherwise by this major catastrophe. . . . But we certainly understand the frustration coming from people on the ground who are in need of help and we will continue working to get them the assistance that they need. We appreciate the efforts of all those in the region who are working round-the-clock to make sure that they are getting help.

The Q&A continued: Responding to a question from another reporter about reports of shootings at helicopters and in hospitals, McClellan used this occasion to make the president look strong and determined: "The President made it very clear earlier today that we will not tolerate law breakers, we will not tolerate price gouging, we will not tolerate insurance fraud, and we won't tolerate looting. And there is a zero tolerance approach when it comes to these issues."

One member of the press corps finally popped the 64,000-dollar question: "Based on what you have said today, and what the President said this morning on television, is it fair to say that the President feels that all the help has been provided as quickly and in sufficient quantity as possible?" This became a major issue during Katrina as it became clear to millions of people across the country that help was *not* (italics added) provided either "quickly" or "efficiently." But to his credit, McClellan added, frankly: "For those on the ground who are still in need of assistance, I think they would tell you that it hasn't. They need that help yesterday." This may not have been spin but, like all candid answers to questions, it certainly added to the press secretary's credibility.

On the other hand, the salient issue of whether funds that might have been available for Katrina had been diverted to fight the war in Iraq came up—a reasonable conclusion that any well-informed observer could conclude. "Do you find any of this criticism legitimate? Do you think there is any second-guessing to be done now about priorities, given that the New Orleans situation was sort of obvious to a lot of the experts?" a reporter queried.

The press secretary quickly spun his reply with the well-worn political cliche: "This is not a time for finger-pointing or playing politics. I think the last thing that the people who have been displaced or the people who have been affected need are people seeking partisan gain in Washington. This is a time for the nation to come together and help those in the Gulf Coast region. And that's where our focus is."

Then one on-the-ball reporter commented, surprisingly:

> Scott, since the briefing started, I've gotten a number of emails from people saying that correspondents who've been in Baghdad and New Orleans say Baghdad feels safer to operate in; people saying that it's absolute chaos in the streets here; message boards on the Internet are going crazy. They're frustrated that you're deflecting this to FEMA. Is the White House properly, adequately concerned?

McClellan, perhaps for the first time since he began his Katrina press briefings, seemed almost at a loss for words. "Deflecting what to FEMA?" he asked, somewhat defensively. "You're deflecting all specifics to the FEMA briefings," the reporter replied. McClellan: "No, I'm not. I've given you some updates, but they [FEMA] are the ones who are in charge of operational aspects on the ground. And the Department of Homeland Security is in charge of the operational aspects from Washington, D.C. And they're pulling together officials that will have the most updated information for you. So your characterization is just wrong."

Nine long days after Katrina first hit, the president made his first visit to the hard-hit area, landing in Mobile, Alabama, on September 2, 2005, where he was briefed on Hurricane Katrina at Mobile Regional Airport by FEMA officials. As columnist Frank Rich observed in *The New York Times* on April 22, 2007: "He [Bush] took his sweet time to get to Katrina-devastated New Orleans." FEMA Director Michael Brown, who was to come under severe criticism and then lose his job because of the federal government's inadequate response to the emergency, was greeted by the president. He received a friendly slap on the back from Bush who then made his now-infamous comment, *"Brownie, you're doing a heck of a job"* [italics added], *The Times* story reported. It was a phrase that would acquire a life of its own for years to come.

It was at once ironic—and very telling—of course, that Bush, who came under heavy fire to dismiss Brown, did just that only eight days later. According to an account in *The Washington Post* on September 10, 2005, "Brown was stripped of duties overseeing the relief efforts, ordered back to Washington and replaced by Coast Guard Vice Adm. Thad W. Allen. Officials said the president's aides wanted a more effective, hands-on manager at the scene."

Finally, on the night of September 15, 2005, Bush stood in shirtsleeves with the lights of the photographers and TV cameras trained upon him, standing in Jackson Square in New Orleans as he addressed the people of that crippled city and the entire nation:

> Tonight so many victims of the hurricane and the flood are far from home and friends and familiar things. You need to know that our whole nation cares about you, and in the journey ahead you're not alone. To all who carry a burden of loss, I extend the deepest sympathy of our country. To every person who has served and sacrificed in this emergency, I offer the gratitude of our country. And tonight I also offer this pledge to the American people: Throughout

the area hit by the hurricane, *we will do what it takes, we will stay as long as it takes, to help citizens rebuild their communities and their lives*" (Italics added).

The president also addressed the issue of race—which had been bubbling up among the discontent expressed by residents of New Orleans—head-on:

> As all of us saw on television, there's also some deep, persistent poverty in this region, as well. *That poverty has roots in a history of racial discrimination, which cut off generations from the opportunity of America* (Italics added). We have a duty to confront this poverty with bold action. So let us restore all that we have cherished from yesterday, and let us rise above the legacy of inequality. When the streets are rebuilt, there should be many new businesses, including minority-owned businesses, along those streets. When the houses are rebuilt, more families should own, not rent, those houses. When the regional economy revives, local people should be prepared for the jobs being created. (*Author's Note*: Unfortunately, his pledge has yet to be fulfilled.)

On September 27, after Congress had launched an inquiry about the mishandling of Katrina, a reporter asked McClellan at his press briefing: "Has he [the President] been watching or been briefed on Michael Brown's testimony before Congress today, and does he have any reaction to it?" McClellan responded with a textbook use of spin, letting the question go by and stating: "No, he hasn't really caught any. . . . Washington tends to focus on finger pointing. The President is focused on problem solving. He wants to make sure things are getting done that need to get done. We're focused on working together with state and local officials to get people who have been affected what they need."

McClellan put some distance between the White House and the congressional hearings by adding:

> And it's important that Congress move forward and do a thorough investigation of what went wrong and what went right, and look at lessons learned. We want to fix what went wrong, so that we can make sure we've done our part to prevent some of what happened in the aftermath of Hurricane Katrina from happening again. And so Congress is having hearings to gather the facts. It's important to be able to step back and gather those facts, so that we can apply the lessons learned from this catastrophe.

As the year drew to a close, McClellan had compiled enough information for an impressive briefing intended to convey the positive story of what the Bush administration had done to cope with Katrina. On December 15, 2005, McClellan called upon Homeland Secretary Chertoff to speak, and he tried to wow the press with a barrage of facts and statistics and dollars spent on the recovery. Then McClellan called on New Orleans Mayor Ray Nagin, who thanked the president for honoring his commitment to help to rebuild New Orleans and to rebuild the Gulf Coast better than it was. But Nagin also sent a clear message that not enough had been done: "We need levees; we need protection; we need housing support; and we need tax incentives to encourage businesses and residents back into the area," said Nagin. He also played politics for his constituency: "The President has heard that call. Congress has moved from the state of having a little bit of Katrina fatigue to now moving very quickly to address [our] priorities."

President Bush's first mention of Katrina in the new year of 2007 was a passing reference in his January 23, 2006, State of the Union speech, in context with a number of developments that he saw as "hopeful" in the nation. Bush said all the right things about how the government had committed $85 billion to the people of the Gulf Coast and New Orleans and the nation should pitch in to help. On January 29, 2006, McClellan was once again asked about Katrina: "Is the President satisfied with the pace of the rebuilding?" McClellan handled this one smoothly: "The President, I think is—look, we want all of the areas struck by Katrina to be rebuilt as quickly and effectively as possible, and we continue to do what we can to assist local officials as they pursue that goal."

The press's hard-hitting questions continued, nonetheless, at the outset of McClellan's February 13, 2006, briefing: "Scott. Turning back to [the] blame game, when former Director Michael Brown testified before Congress, nothing was mentioned about the fact that he's had contact with the administration and meetings with White House officials since leaving his position. Are you going to provide any names of people that former Director Brown has met with since he left the government?" McClellan finessed this question, too: "I don't know about any specific ones you're referring to since he left the government. I know that he helped provide important information for our comprehensive lessons learned review."

There was more bad news for the Bush team on February 15, 2006, when several U.S. senators blasted Homeland Security Secretary Chertoff for his part in mishandling the response to Katrina. According to an Associated Press story filed on that day, the beleaguered Chertoff admitted that the federal response to Hurricane Katrina "fell far short of providing immediate help to the Gulf Coast that could have saved lives." Chertoff's Senate testimony came the same day a House panel released a scathing report concluding that deaths, damage, and suffering could have been decreased if the White House and federal, state, and local officials had responded more urgently to Katrina.

"There are many lapses that occurred, and I've certainly spent a lot of time personally, probably since last fall, thinking about things that might have been done differently," Chertoff told the Senate Homeland Security and Governmental Affairs Committee about the August 29 storm. He called the hurricane "one of the most difficult and traumatic experiences of my life."

The House report—called "A Failure of Initiative"—found ample fault with state and local officials, including delays in ordering early evacuations in New Orleans. But it also criticized President Bush for failing to get more deeply involved as the crisis unfolded. Chertoff, who oversees the Federal Emergency Management Agency, which coordinated the federal response, promised the senators he would repair many of the shortfalls by the start of the 2006 hurricane season on June 1. The 520-page report added, "Government failed because it did not learn from past experiences, or because lessons thought to be learned were somehow not implemented." In one memo that reached the White House shortly after midnight August 30, 2006, a FEMA official reported levee breaches, submerged houses, hundreds of people on rooftops and bodies floating in the water. Others, two days later, described a shooting of a National Guardsman at the Superdome and a hostage situation at Tulane Hospital that turned out to be false.

The sharp criticism of Brown and his staff was validated a few months later when Frances Fragos Townsend, assistant to the president for Homeland Security and Counterterrorism, stated in her report to Bush on February 23, 2006, that she found significant flaws in the Homeland Security department's national response plan for dealing with emergencies, making 125 recommendations. Under Bush, FEMA—which had been an independent agency reporting directly to the president during the Clinton years—was placed under the Homeland Security Department in the massive reorganization of government departments and agencies to consolidate the nation's resources in the aftermath of 9/11.

In a meeting soon after the report was submitted, Bush met with his Cabinet and issued a statement, which read in part: "We will learn from the lessons of the past to better protect the American people," Bush said after the meeting. "I wasn't satisfied with the federal response." According to the Associated Press story, the report looked at the handling of Katrina and the aftermath as a "systemic failure rather than pointing fingers at individuals." It concluded that "inexperienced disaster-response managers and a lack of planning, discipline and leadership contributed to vast federal failures during Hurricane Katrina."

One year after Katrina had hit, Bush returned to New Orleans on August 29, 2006, and expressed optimism about the future of that city. According to one story reported by Tabassum Zakaria of the Reuters news agency, "Bush stood in the city of jazz and pledged that the federal government would do better if another disaster hit. He said New Orleans had survived fire, war and epidemics, and always came back 'louder, brasher and better,' and that he saw the same resolve this time. 'It's always been a city of second chance.'" He again said he assumed full responsibility for the federal government's slow response to the disaster, which pushed his popularity to new lows and raised questions about his leadership.

In another effort to restore some credibility to the Bush team, on that same day, McClellan arranged for a press briefing with Don Powell, federal coordinator for Gulf Coast rebuilding, and Admiral Thad Allen, commandant of the Coast Guard, both of whom did their job: report on all the good things they could think of to help the administration. The site of the press conference was in New Orleans. Both men tossed a ton of statistics at the reporters about how the government was working to restore the city. At the end of the briefing, the reporters asked questions about the status of the levees and what category hurricane they would withstand. Allen responded by saying he thought levees were being rebuilt "to pre-Katrina authorized levels." Powell said that should there be overtopping, there very well could be some flooding, but "it would not be catastrophic type flooding."

With the dawning of a New Year, 2007, the beat went on. On January 16, 2007, Press Secretary Tony Snow was asked: "Tony, a year-and-a-half after Hurricane Katrina and still slowness in rebuilding and finding (inaudible). Why is Hurricane Katrina not going to be a major part of the State of the Union next week? And where does the fault lie now?" Snow, who had an informal style of dealing with the reporters, replied: "Well, I'm not going to give—there's been enough blame. I think it's important—there are tens of billions of dollars available for reconstruction in Louisiana, Mississippi, and elsewhere, and it's important to make sure that people not only take the steps so that they can make that money available to people, but that you get to the business of rebuilding New Orleans."

Snow continued: "I'm not going to—I know you're going to want me to say, we're at fault, they're at fault. Not going to do it. There clearly are different paces of reconstruction going on in different states and jurisdictions, and we will do everything we can to encourage and support local officials. The federal government has made a sizeable commitment in terms of funds, and there is still a lot of that available for local use."

Snow was asked: "Okay, on the issue of funds, only a little less than a hundred people have received a stipend a year-and-a-half later." The press secretary conceded: "It is slow. It's absolutely slow. And as you know, that's been a matter of some concern politically down there." The questioner followed up: "So where does the fault lie? Could you put the finger on the head?" Here Snow invoked a little humor to change the mood: "No, darlin', I can't. (Laughter)"

In point of fact, neither Katrina nor New Orleans nor the Gulf Coast was mentioned by the president in his 2007 State of the Union speech— undoubtedly on the advice of his close political advisors who probably saw nothing to gain. But the White house press corps continued to bring up Katrina as a main topic—and Tony Snow managed to keep it under control. Some examples: At the press briefing on January 29, 2007, Snow was asked why Bush did not mention Katrina in his State of the Union message. Snow lightheartedly offered a non-answer and said, "I'm just not going to play the 'hindsight' game."

Pressed by the newsmen that by not mentioning Katrina, Bush was "downgrading" the issue, Snow said it was hard to argue that some-body who has put on a push to spend $110 billion on a problem as ever downgrading it, and added the president was committed, stating that "$110 billion speaks for itself." Asked why the officials in New Orleans were not moving very quickly, Snow offered the standard reply: "Look, I'm not going to point fingers, but this is something that's now in the hands of local jurisdictions, and they have the opportunity. They're the ones who now—the ball is in their court."

On February 28, 2007, Snow was questioned about the pace of the recovery, with one reporter suggesting that it had "stalled out." Snow spun his answer by repeating Bush's goal: "The President wants to see progress on all fronts—reconstruction, and also dealing with social ser-vices." In another briefing the same day (February 28, 2007), Snow was in the driver's seat—taking the opportunity to spin the question toward all the things the president had been doing about Katrina. He even managed to allude to "No Child Left Behind," telling reporters that edu-cation would be on the top of the restoration agenda in New Orleans.

And so it went. By the summer of 2007, even though New Orleans had begun to show signs of life and the Mardi Gras had returned, conditions in most of the area were miserable—especially administering to those who were ill. According to one PBS reporter,[8] the Trauma Center was just getting back on its feet. One of the problems the hospitals had was pervasive mold, but the overall system has been left in a full-blown state of crisis. These are Americans who lost a safety net. And six out of eleven acute care hospitals in the city were still closed, and fewer than one-third of the health care professionals had returned. Getting more providers back had been a tough sell because of the lack of housing and the rising crime rate. Meanwhile among New Orleans residents who returned, thousands are jobless and without health insurance and in need of medical care.

In addition, an article in *The Nation*[9] reported:

> In New Orleans East, one can still drive past block after block after block of empty, wrecked buildings. The same is true in the Lower Ninth Ward and other parts of the city. While Katrina has also devastated mainly white areas . . . it is the city's former black majority, and its poor, who are having the hardest time returning home. They either did not want to come back or they cannot afford to. Many don't have jobs waiting from them or a place to live. According to a study by the Brookings Institution, only two percent of those eligible for federal resettlement programs had received checks.

The article continued: "The real proof of Washington's indifference is on the ground in New Orleans. Rhetorically, both the White House and Congress support Category 5 hurricane protection for New Orleans. But not a dime has actually been authorized, much less spent, to implement that goal, says Mark Davis, a professor of environmental law at Tulane University."[10]

Making things even worse is the fact that FEMA wasted $3.6 billion tax dollars[11] awarding Hurricane Katrina contracts to companies with poor credit histories and sloppy paperwork. All in all, despite the administration's attempt to look as if it were handling the biggest natural disaster in the nation's history, it has been judged a major failure. On top of all this, the Army Corps of Engineers revealed that after nearly two years of work and an expenditure of $7 billion on repairing the city's 350-mile levee system, large swaths of the city—including the most vulnerable neighborhoods—are still likely to be flooded in a major storm; even worse, some areas in the northern part of New Orleans could be overrun by eight feet of water. Progress was made on the levees, the report stated, but the findings—more than a year behind schedule—gave insurance companies and homeowners alike cause for great concern.[12]

In mid-summer 2007, the news was still depressing. According to *The New York Times*:

> All over the city, a giant slow-motion reconstruction project is taking place. It is unplanned, fragmentary and for the isolated individuals carrying it out, often overwhelming. Those with the fortitude to persevere—and only the hardiest even try—must battle the hopelessness brought on by a continuing sense of abandonment At the same time, whole blocks in the Central Business District remain lifeless. The poorest districts, with tens of thousands of their inhabitants still stuck outside New Orleans, seem abandoned. The downtown complex of hospitals is moribund, as officials squabble over how to bring it back and as upstate legislators have plotted its relocation to another city.[13]

Moreover, one newspaper reported that the five major private hospitals were going to lose $400 million by the end of 2009, hospital executives told a congressional subcommittee in August 2007. The executives attributed the losses to increased costs from the effects of Katrina—increases in insurance and utility rates, bad debt and uninsured patients, and paying higher salaries to attract and keep doctors and nurses.[14] Indeed, by mid-summer 2007, for those residents still there, there remained little hope that New Orleans would ever return to the city it once was.

The cover of *Time* Magazine said it all in August 2007: "Two years after Katrina, the flood wall is all that stands between New Orleans and the next hurricane. It's pathetic. How a perfect storm of big-money politics, shoddy engineering and environmental ignorance is setting up the city for another catastrophe." The story itself began: "The most important thing to remember about the drowning of New Orleans is that it wasn't a natural disaster. It was a man-made disaster, created by lousy engineering, misplaced priorities, and pork-barrel politics."[15]

Not even the most creative press secretary in the world could spin Katrina's aftermath in any way that could make it appear that any substantial progress had been made. Most political pundits refer to Katrina as one of the most badly handled press relations incidents in recent history due, in large part, to the lack of follow-through by government. The media will continue to monitor the progress well into 2008 and thereafter. One presidential candidate even pledged in 2007 to appoint one person who would stay in New Orleans and report what was going on to the president on a daily basis. Those kinds of political promises are rarely kept, but the pledge reflects how important the devastated area is in the national political process.

Finally, perhaps the worst indictment of all—more important than the physical damage done to the community of New Orleans—is the psychological pain inflicted on the citizens, especially the children. Writes Dr. Marc Siegel in a weekly magazine after a visit to the city last fall:

> According to researchers at Louisiana State University, there has been a dramatic increase in depression anxiety, and post-traumatic stress. The Society for Research in Child Development found that 40 percent of the children who have returned to school suffer such psychological problems as sadness, clinginess, difficulty concentrating, irritability, and risk-taking behavior. . . . Two years after Hurricane Katrina, a state of psychiatric emergency persists. New Orleans psyche has been badly damaged. Rebuilding it is one of the city's most important reconstruction projects.[16]

The damage is almost irreparable. Only a miracle—or many years of work by government together with private enterprise—can help New Orleans recover from Katrina. No amount of spin can turn the image of this beleagued city around.

## Notes

1. Frankel, Max. *The New York Times,* May 8, 1970.

2. Editorial, *The New York Times,* May 7, 1970.

3. Speakes, Larry, with Robert Pack. *Speaking Out: The Reagan Presidency From Inside the White House* (New York: Avon Books, 1988), p. 105.

4. Author's interview with Larry Speakes, April 30, 2007.

5. Author's interview with Larry Speakes, April 30, 2007.

6. When the videotape was released on March 2, 2006, it drew criticism from Democratic National Committee Chairman Howard Dean. On August 30, 2006, McClellan held a press gaggle at the Naval Air Station North Island, San Diego, California, in the morning in which he told reporters that the president had decided to return to Washington, D.C., the next day in time to chair a late afternoon White House interagency task force meeting on the response efforts to Hurricane Katrina. "It continues to supplement and strengthen our response efforts," said the

press secretary. Commenting on the contents of the videotape, Dean issued a statement on what he called the Bush administration's

> disturbing pattern of not telling the American people the truth. These latest revelations make two things perfectly clear: this President can't tell the truth to the American people, and this Republican Congress has failed to uphold its constitutional duty to hold him accountable. Republicans in Congress have consistently stonewalled Democrats' efforts to hold a thorough investigation of what happened in the run up to Hurricane Katrina, and during the disastrous federal response. No wonder there's a collapse in confidence in the Bush Administration and the Republicans in Washington. The American people know the President disregarded vital warnings, and later misled them about it. The message this video sends to the Republican leadership in Washington is that the facts will get out. Democrats will continue to fight to make sure that continues to happen, and to restore leadership in Washington that tells the American people the truth.

7. Based on a White House Report dated June 23, 2006, from Frances Fragos Townsend, assistant to the president of the United States for Homeland Security and Counterterrorism to President Bush. An excerpt of the text follows:

> Though there will be tragedies we cannot prevent, we can improve our preparedness and response to reduce future loss and preserve life. And while we will work diligently to implement immediate improvements, it is important to recognize that the true transformation envisioned in this Report will require a sustained commitment over time by the Federal government as well as by State and local governments that have essential duties in responding to disasters. The Report and recommendations are submitted in the hope of ensuring that the harsh lessons of Hurricane Katrina need never be learned again.

8. Susan Dentzer, health correspondent, PBS "The News Hour with Jim Lehrer," April 24, 2007.

9. *The Nation*, May 7, 2007, p. 24.

10. Ibid., p. 25.

11. *Time* Magazine, May 7, 2007, p. 22.

12. *The New York Times*, June 21, 2007, p. 1.

13. *The New York Times*, July 2, 2007, p. 1.

14. *The New York Times*, August 3, 2007, p.14.

15. *Time* Magazine, August 13, 2007, cover and p. 10.

16. Siegel, M.D. *The Nation*, September 10–17, 2007, pp. 4–5.

# CHAPTER 5

## DOMESTIC CONTROVERSIES

*The Clarence Thomas Nomination: 1991*
George H. W. Bush
MARLIN FITZWATER

When President George H.W. Bush nominated Judge Clarence Thomas for a seat in the U.S. Supreme Court on July 2, 1991, few observers had a clue about the huge controversy that Bush's choice would touch off. Thomas, an African American, had been selected to replace Justice Thurgood Marshall, the first African American to be appointed to the Supreme Court in 1967 by President Lyndon B. Johnson. Marshall was a devout liberal dedicated to the cause of equal justice and a powerful force on the Supreme Court to bring equality to all minorities. Thomas was viewed as the polar opposite of Marshall politically.

A known conservative, he opposed quotas and racial preferences and had long been known to oppose government-imposed affirmative action programs. As a result, his nomination was opposed by civil rights organizations, women's groups, and the National Bar Association. In his year as a federal appeals court judge, he did not have an occasion to rule on affirmative action, but he has long been outspoken in taking the legal position that government affirmative action programs are unconstitutional.

Even though the atmosphere in the country was far more conservative than it had been for many years—part of President Ronald Reagan's legacy—Thomas was seen as too far to the right. Moreover, he had only served two years as a federal judge. Nonetheless, the Senate Judiciary Committee took up Thomas's nomination at its hearings. The initial questions and answers were relatively routine. Thomas claimed that he had not formulated an opinion on legal abortion and the issue was not pursued any further. More testimony followed and, even though the Committee was split on its decision seven to seven, it was sent to the full Senate without any recommendation. That was only the beginning of what was to become one of the most contentious hearings in Supreme Court history.

When the nomination came up on the floor of the Senate, near chaos broke loose when Anita Hill, a law professor at the University of Oklahoma, openly accused Thomas of having sexually harassed her when she had worked for him during the time he served as director of the federal Equal Employment Opportunities Commission. Her accusations included inappropriate remarks he made about sex after she had rejected an invitation from him to date her. However, seemingly contradictory statements by Hill and other testimony for Thomas by former female associates weakened the case against him. In the end, the Committee did not find sufficient evidence to corroborate Anita Hill's claim.

The press had a field day, and the story became front-page news across the nation with Thomas and Hill trading charges and counter-charges. Thomas became so agitated that he labeled the entire procedure "a high-tech lynching for uppity Blacks." Many of the senators conducting the hearings were especially rough on Hill, who could not produce any evidence of her accusations. Accordingly, the battle became his word against hers.

During all of this time, Press Secretary Marlin Fitzwater told reporters at his briefings that the president remained confident that Thomas would be appointed. On October 15, 1991—the day that the Senate was scheduled to vote—Fitzwater remained positive and confident throughout the briefing. As is clear from the transcript of that session, Fitzwater rose to the challenge of skeptical questions during the grilling by reporters and was able to spin the entire affair in the president's favor.

*Q: Where will the President be during the debate and vote?*
FITZWATER: I would expect he'll be here; probably watch the vote from his study off the Oval Office. I'm sure that he'll be watching at least portions of the debate as it proceeds through the Senate today.

*Q: Has he talked to Thomas in the last three or four days?*
FITZWATER: I don't believe so, not since we last reported the discussion. No recent discussions.

*Q: How do you think the votes are going to come down?*
FITZWATER: We believe that Judge Thomas will be confirmed. I'll leave it at that.

*Q: Why do you think so, Marlin?*
FITZWATER: Because he's an outstanding candidate and he'll make a great addition to the Supreme Court.

*Q: What's your headcount?*
FITZWATER: Don't have a head count.

*Q: On what are you basing that outstanding candidate?*
FITZWATER: On his record of experience in the Circuit Court—

*Q: He's been on it one year.*
FITZWATER: His experience—well, I am not going to argue with you.

*Q: Do you think that the fact that the President nominated Clarence Thomas and stood by him through all this controversy is going to improve the President's standing among black voters?*
FITZWATER: I think it will improve the President's standing among all voters. Judge Thomas is a good man, and he'll be a good addition to the Supreme Court. And we expect the American people will appreciate that.

*Q: How many phone calls has the President made already to senators who might still be undecided?*
FITZWATER: He has made several phone calls. We won't discuss any of them. The recipients are free to talk about their phone calls, but we won't talk about who the President is calling.

*Q: Can you describe what role Bush played in formulating the "attack her" strategy? Did he discuss it with his aides? Did he propose it? Did he know about it?*
FITZWATER: There wasn't any such strategy from the White House; it's just not true.

*Q: How do you explain the Justice Department, White House Counsel's role—*
FITZWATER: There were people who helped with the hearings, but everything that occurred was on national television and watched by jillions and jillions of people. So you saw it all.

*Q: That's a non sequitur.*
FITZWATER: What do you mean?

*Q: She's asking you how—she's not actually happened, she's asking you about the behind-the-scenes strategy that led to attacks on her, and was the White House involved.*

FITZWATER: As [Senator] Joe Biden [D-DE] said at the—Senator Biden said at the beginning of the hearings, they were designed to find out the truth of the situation as best they could, and the members of the committee questioned along those lines, and that's the way it developed.

*Q: You said that you expect this battle to help the President with all voters, black and white. Some analysts have said that this may give you—there may be a perception that the President hasn't taken seriously the entire issue of sexual harassment. Do you think this could cause any problems for the President among women voters? And do you think that after his is over that the President will do anything to demonstrate his concern on that issue?*

FITZWATER: First of all, we take sexual harassment very serious. Everyone knows our position, that there's no room for that in the workplace or anyplace else, as I said last week. But the opinion polls show that people have watched these hearings, they've made clear their own judgments about it, and they understand the issues involved. And that's all very helpful.

*Q: But will the White House do anything—you said last week that you were reluctant to get into any kind of debate on specifics of this controversy. Once this controversy is over are you going to do anything—is the President going to make a speech or modify your position on the civil rights bill, or whatever, or try to demonstrate—*

FITZWATER: We think all of our positions have been good ones and all of our future positions will be good ones. And we'll speak out on the issues of the day as they arise.

*Q: Has the President expressed any surprise at the volume and strength of public sentiment on this? With the Congressional switchboard registering more than 600,000 calls in a day—those are just the ones that have got through—the volume you've got here—has the President expressed any surprise that this touched such a nerve nationally?*

FITZWATER: No, I don't think so, although I haven't heard him say anything on that point. I would say that we're very gratified by the public attention that has been focused on this and the outcome in terms of their expression of support for Judge Thomas, understanding of the issues. With this kind of television coverage, I think it is expected that we'd have a large kind of attention by the population, and that's good. We ought to have more government and public affairs events that are covered live by the television networks.

*Q: Is the President worried at all by some of the people who have been quoted, for example, in The New York Times yesterday, saying they believed Anita Hill's story, which, in effect, means they believe Clarence Thomas has perjured himself, but that they didn't think it was important enough to block his confirmation?*
FITZWATER: This is a matter for the Senate to decide and we'll let them do it.

*Q: Marlin, what procedures does the White House have for employees who work either here or in the old EOB to investigate complaints of discrimination based on sex, race, religion or age?*
FITZWATER: I'll have to get that for you, but I'm sure there are processes similar to those throughout the government, but I don't have them with me.

*Q: The President expressed appreciation for the support Clarence Thomas was getting from all Americans. But in his last public comment, he made special notice—took special notice of the support he's getting among African Americans, black Americans. Now, what was the reason for him taking special note of that? Was that to send a message to those Democrats who are wavering? Who have black constituents; take a look at your poll results here before you make up your mind?*
FITZWATER: That was essentially media-driven, because the polls all out that morning, that was the major category. ABC, USA Today and CBS all had polls out essentially on two issues: all Americans and their views, and blacks and their views.

*Q: Will the President call Thomas before or after the vote, and if so, might there be some kind of photo opportunity?*
FITZWATER: I'm sure he'll talk to Judge Thomas at some point, but right now it hasn't been established. I don't think he knows exactly where he wants to be at that point and so forth, but we'll let you know.

*Q: Does the President agree with the Judge that the hearings amounted to a "high-tech lynching of an uppity black man?"*
FITZWATER: Well, I'm not going to get involved in this debate. The vote's tonight; we'll wait and see.

*Q: Are you willing to say that the White House had no involvement in the hearings that we've just witnessed over the last three days?*
FITZWATER: We worked with the committee members from the very beginning, sure.

*Q: No, in terms of going against Professor Hill?*
FITZWATER: We did not orchestrate anything like that.

*Q: Did White House officials though, Marlin, or officials at the Justice Department play a role in gathering the evidence that was used in questioning Anita Hill?*
FITZWATER: I don't know all the discussions. They worked with the committee from the very beginning. But you saw me struggle here at the podium for three days with every question that I got, 21 pages of transcript for two days in a row, to never say anything negative about Anita Hill. And our strategy and our purpose and our intent from the beginning were never to do that. And that was providentially directed.

*Q: So did the President call anyone there and say, gee, I hate what they're doing to her, please stop?*
FITZWATER: I don't know.

*Q: Why did the President direct you not to say anything negative about Anita Hill?*
FITZWATER: Because we thought it was appropriate for the committee to look into this. They were holding the hearing, they would be asking the questions. And it's a matter that would be resolved by the Senate.

*Q: Did the White House know that Thomas was gong to bring race into it or was that something totally on his own?*
FITZWATER: He said under oath that the statement was seen only by himself, his wife and Senator John Danforth (R-KY).

*Q: Marlin, do you have any explanation for Judge Thomas' testimony during his initial statement even when he said that he was brought to Kennebunkport to be nominated, he was discussing with the President, that apparently the President told him, according to the Judge, "Clarence, you've made it this far on merit; from here on out it's politics?"*
FITZWATER: That we knew what the confirmation process had become, and it's exactly right. He faced a political process from that day on.

*Q: That would seem to suggest that the White House had planned a political campaign for Judge Thomas from the beginning.*

FITZWATER: No, we recognized what the process had become. Ever since Judge [Robert] Bork, they've made it a political process.

*Q: Are you confirming the quote?*

FITZWATER: I don't know whether he made the quote or not, but I don't think it matters whether it's confirmed. The fact is it's true, that ever since the Bork nomination the Senate has made it a political process.

*Q: You talk about dissatisfaction with the process and that it will be done differently. Are there things that the White House could do differently that would affect the way this goes or is this totally an issue that involved the Senate?*

FITZWATER: Well, the Senate controls the process.

*Q: So there's nothing you could do differently that would have affected the course of this nomination?*

FITZWATER: I haven't had a chance to make a review of the whole matter, but the Senate controls the process.

In the end, the Senate approved the Thomas nomination as associate justice of the Supreme Court by a narrow fifty-two to forty-eight margin. They had won the battle—with quite a bit of help from Fitzwater, who managed to fend off the ever-hungry press looking for controversy and White House culpability. It was a tribute to Marlin Fitzwater's ability to remain cool under fire and to spin the story to the White House press corps in a civil, mannerly way—a technique for which Fitzwater would win wide support among the media itself. They knew how to try to stir things up—and they knew that Fitzwater knew how to keep things as calm as possible.

The next morning, *The New York Times* read:

> Judge Clarence Thomas, who was born to unlettered parents living in abject poverty in rural Georgia, won confirmation as an Associate Justice of the Supreme Court tonight by one of the narrowest margins in history, barely surviving an accusation by one of his former assistants that he had sexually harassed her. After an all-day debate, during which President Bush brought heavy pressure on wavering Senators and the public flooded Capitol Hill with telephone calls and telegrams, the Senate voted 52 to 48 in favor of the 43-year-old judge. Eleven Democrats joined 41 of the 43 Republicans in

supporting him. Interviewed after the vote, Judge Thomas diplomatically stated: "This is more a time for healing, not a time for anger or animus or animosity," Judge Thomas said later tonight, standing under an umbrella outside his house in Alexandria, Va. Referring to the fierceness of the 107-day fight over his nomination, he added, "We have to put these things behind us and go forward.[1]

The vote constituted a victory for the president.

It is fair to say that Marlin Fitzwater—by virtue of his steady-as-you-go, hands-on policy of remaining calm in the midst of what appeared to be chaos—helped persuade the press that Clarence Thomas was the right choice by the president when he repeated again and again that President Bush stood squarely behind his nominee and was not deterred by the heated exchanges going on in the Senate hearings. This is an outstanding example of how, with the aid of a skilled press secretary like Fitzwater, a president can overcome tough opposition and obtain a confirmation from the Senate for his Supreme Court nominee.

---

## The "No Child Left Behind Act": 2001
### George W. Bush
### ARI FLEISCHER/SCOTT MCCLELLAN/TONY SNOW

---

President George H.W. Bush said he wanted to be known as "the education president" but, ironically, it would be his son George W. who made a bold move to wear the education mantle. On January 8, 2002, the younger Bush signed into federal law a piece of bipartisan legislation known popularly as The No Child Left Behind Act. While singularly admirable in its concept, reportedly the legislation was the brainchild of Bush's political Svengali Karl Rove, who wanted an education program pitched particularly to urban black and Hispanic minorities who are voters.

The bipartisan legislation—the Bush administration's most publicized achievement—called for an expenditure of $26.4 billion and was passed by the Congress on December 18, 2001. The thrust of the No Child Left Behind Act of 2001 (Public Law 107-110), known as NCLB, was to coordinate a myriad of federal programs with the goal of dramatically improving the performance of U.S. primary and secondary schools through increasing new standards of accountability for states, school districts, and local schools—all of which would be monitored and evaluated by Secretary of Education Margaret Spellings in Washington. To her credit, Spellings conceded that in order to measure its full impact, more time was needed before its results could be fairly judged. She said the administration had written the best bill it could, but a lot has been learned since it went into effect.

Since it was signed into law, a number of questions have arisen about how effective it is. Indeed, many states have objected—first to the fact that it came without mandated funding, thereby putting all the financial responsibility on the states and town school districts. And second, the Act required that all teachers by the end of the 2006–2007 school year be "highly qualified" as defined in the law—an extra expense and burden for which states are not reimbursed. The law set certain nationwide standards that teachers must meet, requiring that all students be tested annually. Supporters of NCLB claim the legislation finally brought accountability in public schools for the first time on a national basis, and it aimed at closing the gap between minority students in school districts with less money and those in more affluent districts which can afford a much higher per pupil expenditure.

Despite the high praise it has received from the White House and other high government officials, many initial backers have become critical of the way it has been carried out. The heart of the matter is the administration's failure to adequately fund it. Senator Edward M. Kennedy (D-MA), one of the legislation's initial sponsors, has claimed that the "tragedy" is that these long overdue reforms are finally in place, but the funds are not. This complaint is echoed by educational and public interest groups. Opponents argue that the funding shortfalls mean that schools are faced with the system of escalating penalties for failing to meet testing targets and they are denied the resources necessary to remedy problems detected by testing.

In addition, there have been allegations of classroom corruption by the administrators of the programs on the local level. The system of incentives and penalties allows a strong motivation for schools, districts, and states to manipulate test results. For example, schools have excluded minorities or other groups to doctor the records of school performance to reduce unfavorable statistics. Evidence has accumulated that these and other strategies have created an inflated perception of NCLB's successes, especially in states with high minority populations. Furthermore, the incentives for improvement have caused schools to lower their standards, critics charge.

Critics have argued that the overwhelming focus on standardized testing as the means of assessment encourages too much classroom emphasis on preparing students for their tests, to the detriment of other creative methods that individual teachers could be teaching. Standardized tests have also been accused of cultural bias, and the practice of determining educational quality by testing students has been called into question. NCLB's focus on just math and reading scores is challenged by critics as likely to be ineffective for a generation of students in poorly performing schools, as schools may strip away much of the broader education in order to elevate scores on just two indicators, leaving open—say some critics—too many ways for a school's educational staff to fail.

Opposition comes from all parts of the political spectrum—including tens of thousands of online protestors who have signed a petition demanding the repeal of the 1,100-page bill. Some conservative critics have argued that NCLB violates conservative principles by federalizing education and setting a precedent for further erosion of state and local control. Libertarians and some conservatives further argue that the federal government has no constitutional authority in education. Yet another objection is that as a result of receiving federal funds, all secondary schools are required to provide military recruiters the same access to facilities as the schools provide to higher education institution recruiters. Schools are also required to provide contact information for every student to the military if requested, and schools are not required to tell the students or parents. Ignoring these complaints, the White House has steadfastly stood by its initial position that No Child Left Behind is the best solution to America's education problems. The campaign to bolster its image was launched by the White House press office from the very beginning and has not let up.

Press Secretary Ari Fleischer told reporters upon its signing in 2002 that it was a landmark bill. He hailed it as a "major breakthrough" in the history of educational reform—a badly needed shot in the arm to a lagging educational system, which was not serving the vast majority of borderline students. Fleischer said at a press briefing that the education bill President Bush signed into law included an ambitious federal commitment to teaching reading, which is expected to emphasize phonics over other methods of early reading instruction. The press secretary added the administration was requiring schools to adopt "scientifically based" ways to teach reading, a phrase that education officials interpret as referring to systematic phonics in contrast to other approaches.

Meanwhile, the media was reporting that debate was expected to heat up between educators who emphasized teaching children to read through immersion in good books and those who believed in phonics, which emphasized drilling children in sounding out letter combinations and words. Media reports said that most teachers tried to balance the two approaches, but the Bush administration contended that the balance has shifted too much away from phonics.

NCLB also gave parents more flexibility in choosing schools their children would attend. It was also the latest in a series of educational reforms initiated over the years by a half dozen presidents before Bush. Nonetheless NCLB was, by all reports, the most all-encompassing bill in recent decades, and at the time was hailed as a major breakthrough in bringing standards in American education up to the levels enjoyed by other leading democracies. There was little reason to believe that it would, in a very short time, become the subject of controversy in the Congress.

Bush's White House press secretaries—happier on the offense than defense—have played a major role in spinning the importance and success of this Act, despite growing criticism from states, school districts, and individual schools themselves. Beginning with the latest endorsement, here's what some of the press secretaries had to say: In his press briefing six months after it had been signed into law, Fleischer heaped praise on the significance of the Act by spinning its importance and trying to explain away the fact that Congress had failed to allocate funds to support the Act. In doing this, he went out of his way to talk about how much the Bush administration was spending on education. Excerpts of his June 10, 2002, briefing follow:

*Q: Ari, the Democrats are saying that the President has not lived up to his commitment in terms of funding this act. Is that the case?*

FLEISCHER: Well, you know, Washington is a town where spending is very easy for people to do. After all, they're taking the taxpayers' money and spending it. *And the fact of the matter is our nation today is spending the historically highest amount of money on a federal level of education ever* [italics added]. And for some people, the highest level isn't ever high enough. But under the President's budget, the federal commitment to education in dollar terms is higher than ever. And it represents a boost in education to $53.1 billion, an increase of nearly $11 billion since the President took office. So, yes, this President is committed to funding for education, to full funding for education, to proper funding for education. But, again, for some people the highest ever isn't high enough.

*Q: Are there some unintended consequences of this plan that the President might want to address, such as children from failing schools are unable to be placed in more desirable schools for lack of openings, just as an example?*

FLEISCHER: Well, as you know, one of the reforms that the President has sought, but did not get, was to help children who were in failing schools so they could be able to move to the school of the parents' choice, including private schools. There were some modest reforms that were put in there that allowed them to move to more limited options, in terms of other schools that were successful. But what the President is going to talk about this afternoon is how this bill helps to improve education for children, because it really focuses on lifting up standards and not teaching down, but building and lifting up by having standards set at a level that are achievable, but also mean that children actually learn. They're not set at levels so low that parents have kids who graduate from class unable to read, even though they were able to advance. That's what this does. It creates a new standard, a standard of higher expectations, which the President is confident our schools can achieve. And he's given them the resources and working with the teachers and provided the training to make that happen.

The following January, just prior to the president's meeting with school principals and administrators and members of Congress at the White House, Fleischer once again brought up the importance of the Act. He told reporters on January 8, 2003, "The President will shortly have an event in the East Room, to make remarks on the one year anniversary of the No Child Left Behind Act. The President is very much looking forward to gathering with school principals, school administrators and members of Congress and members of the Education Department to commemorate this important anniversary—a top priority in this administration."

On January 15, 2004, Press Secretary Scott McClellan once again emphasized how important NCLB was to the president in his briefing with the press:

> The President has pursued a bold agenda that increases opportunity for all Americans. One of the most important reforms he has worked to implement is the No Child Left Behind Act. This is the most sweeping reform to education in years. And it will help ensure that every child has the opportunity to learn and succeed. The President believes in every child, and believes that every child can learn and succeed, but what we need to insist on is high standards and accountability from our public schools. And the President—the

President's plan insists on results. And, as you often hear him say, this is an approach that rejects the soft bigotry of low expectations.

In 2005, the White House press office brought up the subject of education again at the start of the year. On January 18, McClellan stated, in answer to a question about whether NCLB was expanding: "There certainly is an aspect to that in which government is more involved." A year later, on January 6, 2006, McClellan told the press: "As you all know, the most important factor in determining one's compensation is your education. And that's why the President from the beginning has talked about the importance of education; that's why he supported No Child Left Behind. No Child Left Behind is working."

On January 31, 2006, McClellan once again talked to reporters about the Act: "The President will build on the success of No Child Left Behind and propose 70,000 high school teachers to lead advance placement courses in math and science. We'll bring in 30,000 math and science professionals to teach in classrooms and give early help to students who struggle in math so they have a better chance at good high-wage paying jobs."

Nonetheless, 2007 was a year in which there was mounting criticism of the Act for failing to show sufficient results nationwide. Press Secretary Tony Snow was very eager to put some spin on his answers to questions. On January 3, 2007, Snow—talking generally about some of the accomplishments the Bush administration had made in conjunction with the Democrats in Congress—stated at a press briefing: "No Child Left Behind was the product of bipartisan work." Here are a few Q&As.

*Q: What does the administration feel the prospects are for [the president's] conservative social agenda now that there are big changes taking place on the Hill?*

SNOW: I think the way to look at it is now you're going to have a Democratic Congress and they will have to go through the process of drafting bills, marking them up, debating them—well, maybe in the Senate anyway—and then having a process where people have to engage in proper compromise and debate, and when we start seeing the product of those legislative deliberations then we'll be in the position to tell you where the President will stand on certain things.

Three weeks later, on January 23, 2007, Snow staunchly defended NCLB at a press briefing: "The No Child Left Behind Act is working.

It's closing the achievement gap. We've raised standards for students across the country and improved accountability. The President will insist that Congress, in reauthorizing it, strengthen the law, but also make sure that Congress does not water down the law or backslide and call it reform."

At a briefing on February 2, 2007, Snow commented:

> We need to understand how students learn math and science. And so we have called for a national panel to do just like we do with No Child Left Behind, to look at how students learn, to study and analyze the curriculum, and then to make recommendations so that the nation's schools will be able to use that curricula to get students interested in math and science and help them, as well. . . . *The President will build on the success of No Child Left Behind* [italics added].

This was quickly followed up on February 12, 2007, when a reporter asked: "No Child Left Behind is up for reauthorization, and there's a somewhat controversial provision in there right now, requiring standardized tests for immigrant children after they've been here a year, regardless of their proficiency in English. Why is the administration opposed to alternative assessments for children who aren't proficient in the English language?" Snow, who prides himself in admitting when he cannot answer a question, responded: "I cannot answer that question. I will find out."

Two weeks later, NCLB was still a hot topic: On February 28, 2007, a reporter said that the president and his Cabinet met with the nation's governors to talk about certain issues. Further, the reporter said the governors expressed concern over No Child Left Behind, referring to the issue of flexibility—and complained that not enough money had been available. "Has the administration heard anything from these concerns that it is willing—that it can take into account?" the newsman asked. Snow disagreed with the wording of the question. "Well, I think what's interesting is, first, on No Child Left Behind, the governors expressed support, I believe, unanimous support for No Child Left Behind in terms of supporting its reauthorization. We believe in flexibility, too."

The next month, on March 15, another reporter asked Snow at a briefing: "Is the President worried about eroding support for No Child Left Behind?" Snow, who rarely shows any signs of anger, bristled a little, and replied with a frown on his face:

> No. The President is deeply committed to No Child Left Behind. And it's important to make sure not only that we have standards for schools, but that

we extend to every child—from kindergarten straight through 12th grade—the opportunity and the promise of good education, so that they are equipped to intellectually—they have the intellectual tools and capabilities to deal with a workforce in which they're going to change careers any number of times; that they're going to have the intellectual abilities. And the President is committed to making sure richer, poorer, wherever you live, you're going to have those opportunities. And he is strongly committed to it and he's working with Democrats and Republicans.

The reporters pressed on:

*Q: We know he's committed to it, but what about Republicans who signed on it before, but have now expressed interest in other legislation?*
SNOW: Well, I think, again, there are plenty of conversations that are ongoing. But the President feels confident that we're going to get reauthorization of No Child Left Behind, and, furthermore, that it's vital to American students.

At the press briefing the following week, March 22, 2007, a reporter asked a question about how effective the Act had been to date. Once again Snow repeated the White House mantra: "The President made it clear every time he advocates for No Child Left Behind that education is vital. Is it the cure-all? No. But it is certainly an important element in separating those who succeed from those who do not—not only economically, but also in terms of their personal lives." The answers underline a tendency for press secretaries—when pressed—to repeat the same answer they had given previously. This was particularly the case with Scott McClellan, but others did the same thing. Snow was pressed at his March 22 briefing about the "bad blood that's developing" between Democrats and Republicans and how that would affect his domestic agenda, including No Child Left Behind.

Ignoring the bad blood reference, the press secretary rejected the questioner's assumption of partisanship and turned the question around—as he often did—replying:

Look at No Child Left Behind. You had Ted Kennedy and George W. Bush working together. There are a number of issues on which the President has made common cause with Democrats and Republicans, and frankly, what we're offering is a good deal for both parties on really serious issues. Now, if the American public sees that all Congress can do—all that's going to happen in Washington is squabbling over things while the funding runs out for troops—while we don't get things done on energy independence, while we don't reauthorize No Child Left Behind, while we don't move on immigration—they're going to say, why did we bring you here? There's a powerful incentive for members of Congress to work with us, and a powerful incentive for us to work with them so we get important stuff done. And again, I've been in a lot of these meetings, and they have, for the most part, been very respectful and constructive, and I do think things are going to get done. A friend of mine once said, "Washington is a town where the urgent overwhelms the important." And quite often we get a sense of urgency about the news of the day, and we forget that ultimately the people brought members of Congress and the President here to do work, and not to squabble.

Positive and negative reports on No Child Left Behind have come from all sectors of the nation. Some opponents have argued that local government has failed students, necessitating federal intervention to remedy issues like teachers teaching outside their areas of expertise, and complacency in the face of continually failing schools. Some local governments say that local standards have failed to provide adequate oversight over special education, and that NCLB would allow longitudinal data to be more effectively used to monitor adequate yearly progress.

Why has NCLB not lived up to expectations—at least in the eyes of its critics? Many say the Congress should scrap NCLB and introduce a plan that is more in sync with the needs of the twenty-first century. "When Congress passed George W. Bush's signature education initiative [NCLB], it was widely hailed as a bipartisan breakthrough—a victory for American children. Now, five years later, the debate over the law's reauthorization has a decidedly different tone," wrote Linda Darling-Hammond, in the May 7, 2007, issue of *The Nation*. "As the [Congress] considers whether the law should be preserved—and if so, how it should be changed—high-profile Republicans are expressing their disenchantment with NCLB, while many newly-elected Democrats are seeking a major overhaul as well." Most critics say that NCLB has stalled because of lack of federal funds, which has caused many states and a teacher's association to file lawsuits against the federal government.

The topic of NCLB came up at a press conference on September 19, 2007, with Press Secretary Dana Perino, who managed to spin her reply so that it appeared Congress—not the President—was holding up progress. The colloquy follows:

*May I ask a question related to No Child Left Behind? Secretary Spellings yesterday indicated that even if that law is not reauthorized that it could still*

*continue on the books without reauthorization. But if that were the case,*
*wouldn't that mean there would be no federal funding for it? And then if*
*there's no federal funding for it—*

MS. PERINO: No, we have our budget request up, [and] the Congress hasn't worked on any of their budget priorities for this year yet.
They haven't sent us appropriations bills. I take that back, obviously,
they may be working a little bit, because they have some things in
committee. They just haven't passed anything yet. The No Child Left
Behind reauthorization—what Secretary [Margaret] Spellings is saying, is that if you can get to a reauthorization, you can then hopefully
infuse some additional resources into it, of which the President has
asked for.

On October 11, 2007, Perino continued to spin progress on the No
Child Left Behind when she told reporters: "The President, under No
Child Left Behind, one of the things that he wants to do is close the
achievement gap between minority and white students so that we can
make sure that everyone is getting the education that they deserve.
Those are the types of things that can set the country up to be com-
petitive from now well into the future."

Nonetheless, it seemed clear to critics of the NCLB program last fall
that it was not in need of repair, but rather in need of replacement. For
example, the highly-respected educator, Diane Ravitch, professor of
education at New York University and former assistant secretary of
the Department of Education for Research in the Clinton administration from 1991–1993, commented in an Op Ed article in *The New York*
*Times* on October 7, 2003:

> Despite the rosy claims of the Bush administration, the No Child Left Be-
> hind Act of 2002 is fundmentally flawed. The latest national tests show that
> academic gains since 2003 have been modest, less than posted in the years
> before the law was put into place. In eighth-grader reading, there have been
> no gains at all since 1998. The main goal of the law—that all children in the
> United States will be proficient in reading and mathematics by 2014—is sim-
> ply unattainable. The primary strategy—to test all children in those subjects
> in grades three through eight every year—has unleashed an unhealthy
> obsession with standardized testing that has reduced the time available for
> teaching other important subjects. Furthermore, the law completely frac-
> tures the traditional limits on federal interference in the operation of local
> schools.

> Unfortunately, the Congressional leaders in both parties seem determined to renew the law . . . with only minor changes. But No Child Left Behind should be radically overhauled, not just tweaked. . . . Unless we set realistic goals for our schools and adopt realistic means of achieving them, we run the risk of seriously damaging public education and leaving almost all children behind.

Finally, the influential spokesperson for the United Federation of Teachers, Randi Weingarten, put her finger on the heart of the matter when, in an Op Ed column in *The New York Times* on October 14, 2007, she stated:

> We consistently shine a light on the importance of high quality teachers in every classroom. So we initially had high hopes when Congress passed President Bush's No Child Left Behind Act with bipartisan support in 2002. Unfortunately, it has become clear that serious flaws in NCLB are preventing it from helping all children succeed. In fact, it guarantees its own failure by requirements that all children are to be proficient in math and reading by 2014, a laudable but increasingly unrealistic goal. If NCLB is to be more than a slogan, Congress must fix the law to create an accountability system that measures what is and what is not working, rather than relying solely on high stakes testing.

As this book went to press, the question of funding had not yet been taken up in the Congress in 2007.

---

## Faith-Based Community Initiatives: 2002
### George W. Bush
### ARI FLEISCHER

---

When President George W. Bush, a self-described man of God and a born-again Christian, completed his second year in the White House, he and his close advisors believed that it was time to propose the president's long-awaited Faith-Based Community Initiatives program. It had been the topic of some controversy during the 2000 campaign when Bush first proposed it. The key issue involved determining how the government could allocate taxpayers' money to private churches and other religious organizations without violating the nation's generations-old policy of separation of church and state. The phrase "separation of church and state" is nowhere to be found in any of the original documents authored by the founders. It is, rather, drawn from the First Amendment, which states: "Congress shall make no law respecting an establishment of religion, or prohibiting the free exercise thereof."

The founders who drafted the Constitution in 1787 were largely men of deep religious conviction who believed in God, and who were deliberately omitting any reference to God. This was, nonetheless, ironic inasmuch as in the beginning of the Republic it was the churches that ran local governments and it was the churches that provided education, levied taxes, and instilled a sense of morality. Thomas Jefferson is credited with coining the phrase "wall of separation" between church and state, but it followed a decade after the approval of the First Amendment in 1791. The First Amendment is often cited as the cornerstone for the constitutional prohibition against merging the activities of church and state.

The generations-old tension between the separation of the powers of the church and the state was never starker than when George W. Bush entered the White House in 2001. Carrying out his campaign promise, he announced his Faith-Based Initiative on January 30, 2001, which was designed to assist and encourage faith-based groups to use federal monies to combat chronic problems among the poor such as drug addiction, homelessness, and alcoholism. In fact, Bush made this topic his first Executive Order, creating the White House Office of Faith-Based and Community Initiatives.

At a press briefing on January 29, 2001, the day before the president's announcement of the initiative, Fleischer skillfully laid the groundwork for the president's speech, spinning the topic in advance by answering any potentially controversial questions. He cited the initiative as a substantive example of Bush's "compassionate conservatism" philosophy, emphasizing that it was entirely legal, badly needed, and would help millions of Americans. This kind of briefing was intended to disarm the press and alleviate in advance any concerns reporters might have had. It is instructive to see just how the press secretary repeatedly emphasized that the line between church and state was not being crossed:

FLEISCHER: You will be shortly getting the copies of the executive order the President signed earlier today, creating the Office of Faith-Based Initiatives. I'm happy to take any questions.

*Q: Ari, why should this faith-based initiative not be interpreted as an unconstitutional funding of religious institutions in America?*
FLEISCHER: Because as the President made clear in his statements just a little while ago this will not be funding religion, but this will be

funding faith-based organizations of a wide variety of views that bring social help to people in need. It's not the religious aspect of what they do that's getting funded, it's the community service aspect and there are other parts of this, too, that increase—focus on increasing peoples' ability to give to charity and to nonprofits.

*Q: How do you make the distinction, when it's all going on under the same roof?*

FLEISCHER: Because the programs that they will provide are not going to be programs that preach religion. They're going to be faith-based programs—

*Q: How do you know that?*

FLEISCHER: —that help people to improve their lives, which has been the experience that we have seen already with some of the faith-based programs that are privately funded, that are big successes.

*Q: What about the idea that religious organizations don't have to adhere to civil rights laws, and they may not be held to the same standards as private organizations who provide these social outreach functions—*

FLEISCHER: The President's focus will be on helping programs that work. He takes a look at the poor in our society, the people who have the most difficult needs, and he sees a need to help those people to improve their lives. And he recognizes that there are limits to what government programs can do. But that doesn't mean that our country and our society should give up on those who are in need—addicts, alcoholics, and the homeless. And we have seen throughout our society that these faith-based programs, which often are strapped for cash, do work. They improve people's lives. And that's why he is determined to push ahead.

*Q: A lot of these organizations work when people see the light, when they accept a faith. And so isn't this, in effect, government funding conversions?*

FLEISCHER: No, this is a voluntary program where those who seek to participate should have other options. Faith-based groups can often be the answer that helps people get off the street and back into life.

*Q: A lot of these groups hire only people of their religion and work only for people of their religion. Isn't that discrimination?*

FLEISCHER: Well, I think as we just saw from the variety of people who participated in a very powerful meeting with the President, we have people from all walks of life, all religious faiths and backgrounds joined together in saying that the power of faith can lift up peoples' lives.

*Q: Some churches are concerned that there will be strings attached to the federal money, and this can be a way to influence the churches.*

FLEISCHER: Well, as you'll see in the proposals he sends up tomorrow, as the bill works its way through the Congress, all concerns will be addressed.

*Q: Do you expect the issue to wind up in the courts?*

FLEISCHER: I think we can draft something that is fully in accordance with the Constitution and, frankly, I think you're also going to see a large outpouring of bipartisan support for this.

*Q: Ari, do you have to deal with legislation [to resolve] questions about possible discrimination?*

FLEISCHER: Clearly, anything that goes beyond the power of an executive order will have to be dealt with legislatively.

*Q: As you deal with the social service component, how do you make sure that everyone is honest? There is a firewall that organizations are going to have to establish to make sure that they're not supporting their religious activities?*

FLEISCHER: This is not going to fund religion, but this is going to fund faith-based groups that provide social services.

The following day, January 30—when Bush actually announced the program—Fleischer's press briefing brought more questions from reporters, including the interpretation of Bush's personal appearances at churches and whether or not they had any political value:

*Q: The President attended a church Sunday that is a predominantly black and inner-city church. Is it very common that presidents go to churches that are great, no doubt about it, but by appearing there, they also can improve their political standing and push for their political agenda?*

FLEISCHER: No, I think that anybody who knows President Bush knows the importance of faith in his life. When he goes to church, he goes to church for reasons that have to do with faith, and nothing else.

*Q: Is the President joining that congregation?*

FLEISCHER: No, I think he is going to follow a tradition that has been done in Washington, that he's going to go to a couple different churches. He may ultimately settle on one church, I'm not sure, but that's going to be a private matter and a private decision.

Meanwhile, the Bush team went ahead full steam, implementing the initiative. On December 12, 2002, Press Secretary Ari Flesicher, on Air Force One en route to Philadelphia, held a "gaggle" [off-camera] for the press about the importance of the Faith-Based Initiative. The president was headed to a church in Philadelphia, Fleischer explained, where the Office of Faith-Based Community Initiatives had identified at-risk youth as one of the target populations where we need to help Americans at risk. Fleischer explained that the program was designed for children of jail inmates, describing them as "one of the most endangered groups in America today."

He cited the fact that there are 1.5 million children across the country who have parents incarcerated in state and federal prisons. "These children," he explained, "are six times more likely than their peers to suffer from problems such as juvenile delinquency, alcohol and substance abuse, and poor academic performance. Without effective intervention, 70 percent of these children will likely follow their parent's path into prison or jail." The program the president was visiting, Fleischer told them, was called the Amachi Mentoring Program—one of the nation's leading programs for mentoring children of prisoners. He said the president would visit, at which time he would sign an executive order that would make it easier for faith-based groups to work with the federal government to compete for and receive federal funds while retaining their religious character.

Then, with a spin that defined the president as "a caring, compassionate man," Fleischer stated: "The actions the President is taking today will help ensure that groups like this, that very often are the best groups in society to help those who have been left behind, will no longer be denied funds simply because they have a religious nature. The President looks at people in America who have been left behind, they deserve every shot at making it in America, and believes that these barriers serve as an impediment to helping people make it in America."

The Bush administration went all-out in its effort to encourage churches to apply for funds that would help the poor and those in need. The president's executive order—although not directly addressing hiring rights on federal grants, made clear that organizations were not to be barred from participating in federal grants just because they have a religious name or religious board of directors, or governing articles and mission statements that are faith-based. Bush's spokesmen made it clear that while the president respected the separation of church and state, the wall he wanted to tear down was the wall that separates the poor from effective programs. This initiative, simply put, was about better care for the poor.

Despite the highly publicized launching of the initiative, it did not take long before serious reservations about donating federal monies became a barrier. For example, a government report released on August 17, 2001—less than a year after it was announced—charged there was bias against religious groups. Some federal agencies refused to give money to religious groups for their charitable work despite laws that allowed the organizations to compete for federal grants, a White House survey reported.

Blaming government officials for demonstrating a strong bias against religious groups, the survey of five government departments found recurring examples of officials who imposed restrictions far beyond anything required by law or regulations. Officials reported that "the system" had been hostile to community-based and faith-based groups. The survey, titled "Unleveled Playing Field," cited the Department of Housing and Urban Development, the Departments of Justice, Health and Human Services, Education, and Labor as showing reluctance to give out grants.[2]

Despite this criticism, Bush made it crystal clear during a trip to New Orleans at the outset of 2004 that he was personally committed from a religious point of view to helping every single victim of Katrina. Said Bush: *"We want to fund programs that save Americans one soul at a time"* [italics added]. Since then, the Bush administration has pointed to its record: Billions of dollars have been awarded to faith-based organizations on an increasing basis every year since it was launched.

Nonetheless, with the war in Iraq in the forefront of the news and all of his other domestic political troubles, by early 2007 critics were claiming that the faith-based program had almost become an afterthought to Bush and had been reduced in stature since it was announced. After six years, it seemed unusual to many observers in the media that Bush did not even mention it in his 2007 State of the Union message—usually a platform for a president to boast about his accomplishments from the "bully pulpit." Formerly viewed as one of the fundamental building blocks of Bush's domestic agenda, many observers believe that the initiative—which was envisioned to be a major part of his legacy—had all but disappeared from the news, although it was still giving out millions of dollars in grants. On the other hand, it was facing several tough court battles all the way up to the U.S. Supreme Court.

Bush's religious convictions are no secret to the American people. He frequently has referred to his faith in press conferences and in his speeches. And he has been quoted in a number of newspapers and books referring to his faith in God when it came to the war in Iraq. E. J. Dionne Jr., a *Washington Post* columnist and co-chair of the Pew Forum on Religion and Public Life, shed some light on Bush's faith in a television interview.[3]

Asked about Bush's adherence to his faith, Dionne replied:

> I know Bush, in his own presentation of himself early on [when he was governor of Texas], was very open about his personal religious experiences and how they helped transform his life. So in the first instance, Bush chose to do this himself. To that, he grafted on his interest in faith-based programs which grew organically from that . . . those faith-based programs in turn became an important part of his presidential campaign and what he cared about when he came to power. So the interest in this is not made up, and it predates 9/11.

---

### Evolution vs. "Intelligent Design": 2002
### George W. Bush
### SCOTT MCCLELLAN

---

The longstanding acceptance in American public education of Darwin's treatise "On the Origin of the Species" as the mainstream theory of evolution hardly seemed like a controversy that would be revived in the modern era. Ever since the famous "Monkey Trial"—known better as the Scopes Trial in 1925 [*Scopes v. State*, 152 Tenn. 424, 278 S.W. 57 (Tenn. 1925)]—it did not seem possible that it would be challenged again eight decades later. That well-known trial tested the legality of a law passed in 1925 barring the teaching in any state-funded educational establishment in Tennessee of "any theory that denies the story of the Divine Creation of man as taught in the Bible, and to teach instead that man has descended from a lower order of animals." Instead it upheld the argument that all of the world and its species derived from the word of God—or the Bible. The landmark trial was made famous by the fictionalized accounts written for the 1955 play *Inherit the Wind* and the 1960 Hollywood film of the same name.

Nonetheless, although that historic decision appeared to be locked in history as a permanent part of the fabric of American jurisprudence, the issue was revived in the twenty-first century by the religious Right—or the "Born Again" Christian wing of the Republican Party.

It took hold during the early years of the Bush administration and, when challenged in court in Pennsylvania, it became front-page news across the nation—again.

In that decision, the court decided that a new name (but an old concept) called Intelligent Design—in other words, God and the Bible—should *not* [italics added] be included in the school's curriculum.[4] The main reason it became big news again was because Bush—while alleging generally that he did not want to meddle in state matters—let it be known that he clearly favored the Bible as the source of all knowledge about the creation of man, once known as "Creationism." But Press Secretary Scott McClellan spun it deftly, so as not to make it appear that the president was speaking out against a judicial decision. On December 20, 2005, Federal Judge John E. Jones III decided the case in favor of the plaintiffs, disallowing the intelligent design materials from the biology class.

Nonetheless, on that same day, McClellan held a press briefing in which the $64,000 question came up, and—despite the ruling—put a clever spin on his answer, offering up an image of the president as an open-minded man who had a worldly outlook on the issue. One reporter asked: "On the ruling about intelligent design in Pennsylvania, does the President think that ruling should be challenged? Does he have any thoughts on it?" McClellan took the tack that, since the Bush administration was not a party to the case, he was not going to comment about the specific legal decision. But then he added a little spin: "The President has said that such decisions should be made by local school districts. He's long held that belief and he's long stated that belief. [But] The President has also said that he believes students ought to be exposed to different theories and ideas so that they can fully understand what the debate is about." In other words, Intelligent Design should be taught in the schools along with evolution—although McClellan did not say this in so many words.

## Notes

1. *The New York Times*, October 16, 1991.
2. Becker, Elizabeth. *The New York Times*, August 17, 2001.
3. "Frontline" on April 29, 2004.
4. Wikipedia:

> The use of the term "intelligent design" began in response to a 1987 United States Supreme Court ruling involving Constitutional separation of church

and state. Its first significant published use was in a 1989 textbook intended for high-school biology classes. The following year a small group of proponents formed the Discovery Institute and began advocating the inclusion of intelligent design in public school curricula. The "intelligent design movement" grew increasingly visible in the 1990s and early 2000s, culminating in a 2005 trial challenging its intended use in public school science classes—the "Dover trial." In *Kitzmiller v. Dover Area School District*, a group of parents of high-school students challenged a public school district requirement for teachers to present intelligent design in biology classes as an alternative "explanation of the origin of life." U.S. District Judge John E. Jones III ruled that intelligent design is not science, that it "cannot uncouple itself from its creationist, and thus religious, antecedents," and concluded that the school district's promotion of it therefore violated the Establishment Clause of the First Amendment to the Constitution.

# CHAPTER 6

## GLOBAL ISSUES

*The Energy "Malaise" Speech: 1979*
Jimmy Carter
JODY POWELL

Long before Jimmy Carter became president of the United States in 1976, the issue of nuclear energy was etched in the American psyche—and it remains that way today. Not only was the harsh memory of Hiroshima and Nagasaki seared in the minds of millions of adult Americans—even though the dropping of two atomic bombs were generally seen as the only way to end World War II quickly—but the public had taken a wait-and-see attitude about building and using nuclear power plants for peaceful purposes.

Everyone knew it would be a costly but worthwhile endeavor—if for no other reason than it would be an excellent way to create a new source of energy and help America shed its generations-old dependence on foreign oil—but it also held out the hope of our nation becoming energy self-dependent, while also improving the environment. Nonetheless even as nuclear plants were being built and made functional, there was an underlying fear among a majority of Americans that nuclear power plants constituted an accident waiting to happen.

It did. At 4 A.M. on March 28, 1979, at the Three Mile Island nuclear power plant near Harrisburg, Pennsylvania, the failure of several systems combined to bring about by far the most serious accident in U.S. commercial nuclear power plant operation in history. Although no one was killed or injured at the time, it scared the life out of plant workers and members of the nearby community. The accident was attributed to a core meltdown—a melting of the reactor's stainless steel fuel rods or the enriched uranium pellets within them. But, fortunately, there was no explosion. The crisis ended when experts determined on Sunday, April 1, that because of the absence of oxygen the likelihood of an explosion was considerably reduced.

It was a defining moment that the cool-headed White House Press Secretary Jody Powell used to launch what would soon be a major energy program with—of all things—an increase in the use of nuclear power as its centerpiece. It was a brilliant way of spinning what could have turned out to be a major political setback. Putting this accident in historical perspective, at that time White House officials said, there were seventy existing nuclear plants in operation in the country and ninety-two more reactors for which permits had been granted.

Ordinarily, an accident like this would set off all kinds of alarms and the press would be aching to find some way to blame the administration in office. In this case, Press Secretary Powell, in response to a question about the president's reaction in light of Carter's upcoming speech on how to meet the nation's energy needs, played down the importance of the accident: "The questions that we are dealing with [in the energy plan] don't relate directly to this [Three Mile Island]." Among the items that the president was considering at that time were actually speeding up the process by which nuclear plants were licensed and resolving the politically and technically difficult questions of disposing of nuclear waste—an issue that has continued to plague every administration in Washington to this day.

At his press briefing on August 29, 1979, Powell spun the story as a low-key concern, attempting to keep the press corps calm. In fact, Powell used the occasion in his Q&A to press for speeding up legislation for the approval of additional nuclear power plants—one of the president's important priorities. His Q&A shows how he did this:

*Q: Does the President have any further involvement in the nuclear accident in terms of investing and getting any reports?*
POWELL: That specific matter is not something that is direct Presidential responsibility. However, he is, of course, concerned about that incident, or any such incident. He did yesterday direct that he receive a full report on the matter. He has already begun to receive information on it.

*Q. From whom?*
POWELL: Through the National Security Council, and I would assume they could get it from the Nuclear Regulatory Commission, Energy, and other agencies, perhaps. I don't have anything to add to it, and I don't intend to try to brief on it.

*Q: For example, is that mishap in any way going to alter what the President might say about dependence on future nuclear energy in his [upcoming] energy message?*

POWELL: I don't think so, no.

*Q: Does the fact that there was absolutely no danger whatsoever to the public, does that—is that seen by the President as something that could actually be used in trying to calm public fears and hysteria?*

POWELL: It does appear from the information that we have that none of the workers received more than a portion of the permissible levels of exposure, and that does provide some reassurance regarding safety procedures. And our understanding is that there is no off-site hazard.

*Q: Is the president still considering sending a bill up to speed the licensing?*

POWELL: He has had one up there for a year. We would like very much to see some action on it. The president met with people to talk about his problem a couple of days ago, and I think there came from the meeting some feeling that given the more palatable nature of the energy problem now, that some consensus might be forming to move that legislation. One of the problems we faced in the energy area that has come up repeatedly in every meeting that I have attended—both with members of Congress and with people in the Administration—is our overall institutional problem of acting and implementing decisions once they are made. The whole licensing problem with nuclear power is an example, problems relating to the Alaska pipeline, and there are others relating to transportation and so forth. Those problems will have to be dealt with in any long-term solution to our energy problem.

Powell was carefully laying the groundwork for Carter's speech on energy, which, his administration hoped, would rekindle a sense of urgency and optimism among the voters. A few months later—on July 16, 1979—Carter delivered his long-awaited $140 billion plan to insure energy autonomy for the nation, and in it he emphasized that the use of nuclear power was vital if this was to be accomplished. The entire $140 billion, Carter said, could be covered by the proposed "windfall" profits tax on oil companies, "so that never again will our nation's independence be hostage to foreign oil." Sound familiar? Although this speech by Carter describing what he called "a crisis of confidence" in America was initially well received, many objected to the tone of what was soon dubbed as Carter's "malaise" speech. First, he invited people from all walks of life to meet with him at Camp David, and admitted that he had been out of touch with ordinary people, and then he launched what he hoped would be his legacy: a comprehensive energy plan for America for decades to come.

In his press briefing on the morning of July 16, 1979—the day the president gave his long-awaited energy speech in Detroit before the annual convention of the Communications Workers of America— Powell announced first that, "This briefing will be on background for attribution to Administration officials." The reason? The backgrounder would have more credibility if it came from an unnamed White House source rather than his press secretary. He steered the reporters to several passages in Carter's speech, pointing out that nuclear energy would be brought to the fore as a mainstay of the president's energy plan.

The president's speech touched all bases: energy conservation, compliance with government controls and quotas on oil distribution, gasoline prices, lower temperatures of all nonresidential buildings, and greater dependence on mass transit, among them. In addition he prescribed action plans at all levels of government, local, state, and national. Powell's objective was to ratchet up the impact of Carter's speech by spinning it as one of the most important policies of his administration. Said Powell: "The energy crisis is so severe that there simply comes a point for critical energy projects when we can't allow delay at the local levels that what is critical to the nation."

Prior to the nuclear accident, after his first year in office with an oil shortage rapidly increasing, the president decided to take some proactive steps to improve his image on energy. Americans who watched Carter during his years are not likely to forget the image of him on the TV screen in the Oval Office on February 2, 1977, wearing a cardigan sweater and turning down the temperature while delivering his first national television address on energy policy. Not long afterward—on August 4—Carter demonstrated his sincerity in saving energy by creating a new, cabinet-level Department of Energy, headed by James Schlesinger. On October 13, 1977, in a press conference Carter attacked oil companies for perpetrating what he called "the biggest rip-off in history." Obviously, all of these events in one year helped Powell spin a good story in terms of what the President was doing to save energy.

---

*"Reduce Our Dependence on Foreign Oil": 2006*
George W. Bush
TONY SNOW

---

Twenty-seven years after Jimmy Carter called on the nation to adopt an energy program that would sharply curtail America's dependence on foreign oil, President George W. Bush addressed the same issue with a similar plea. But Bush's plea was even more compelling because he linked it to the national security of our nation. Accordingly, Bush's press aides, Press Secretary Tony Snow and Deputy Press Secretary Dana Perino, brought the White House press corps together for full briefings in advance of the annual speech.

Spinning the news has reached the sophisticated point where the finely tuned White House communications apparatus offers press secretaries an opportunity to preview the importance—and thus the positive aspects—of a the State of the Union message. Here are excerpts of the lengthy press briefing conducted by Tony Snow on January 23, 2007, at 2:01 P.M. before Bush gave his address that night. In this instance, as is often the case, the press secretary invited to the briefing some of the administration's top experts to emphasize the administration's point of view on topics in the message. Participants in this briefing included Counselor to the President Dan Bartlett, National Security Advisor Steve Hadley, and Deputy Chief of Staff for Policy Joel Kaplan, who gave an overview of Bush's energy policy. Snow opened the briefing by announcing that two officials would give them a preview of the president's forthcoming proposals.

Joel Kaplan started by saying the president was going to lay out "a bold and ambitious proposal on energy." He reminded the press of the president's last State-of-the-Union speech the previous year in which he had stated that America "has an addiction to foreign oil," and that he would talk that night about how that creates a national security risk for the United States because "it leaves us vulnerable to hostile regimes and to terrorists." He whetted the appetite of the newshounds by disclosing that Bush would announce a bold new initiative to reduce gasoline usage by 20 percent in ten years—by 2017. He also said that on the supply side, the president would propose a new alternative fuel standard of 35 billion gallons—a mandatory fuel standard by 2017. "So it's a very ambitious goal, but it's one we think is achievable," Kaplan said.

On the demand side, he said, the president would propose that Congress authorize a reformed and modernized CAFÉ (Corporate Average Fuel Economy) system for passenger cars, that would allow the Secretary of Transportation to increase fuel economy in the same way we've done for light trucks, and by doing so, save up to 8.5 billion gallons of fuel. That will allow the United States to save 20 percent of our gasoline usage in 2017. "Obviously," he added, "that's a very ambitious, but achievable goal. Although it will help reduce our dependency on foreign oil, it won't eliminate it." Kaplan said Bush would call on Congress to double the current capacity of the Strategic Petroleum Reserve to 1.5 billion gallons. A reporter asked Snow if doubling of the Strategic Petroleum Reserve tied to foreign oil would interrupt oil flow from the Middle East.

Snow, leaning heavily on the national security rationale, spun his answer to demonstrate how Bush was showing vision and bold leadership at the outset of 2007:

> It's merely a matter of providing for energy security. As U.S. consumption has gone up, the capacity of the Strategic Petroleum Reserve to provide a cushion has, in fact, decreased over the years, and what we're doing is we're rebuilding the cushion. It certainly does fit into the overall picture of energy security, but it is not specifically designed for that. As President, he has the ability to articulate issues and he's got a responsibility for dealing with them. And he's doing so, I think, in a refreshing and innovative way. These are bold proposals. As the debate proceeds and as people begin to grasp precisely what he's talking about, I think they're going to get a sense of a President here who really is being bold and visionary when it comes to dealing with these issues.

Kaplan emphasized that Bush would talk about the importance of continuing the research and development. But to reach the goal of 35 billion gallons equivalent in 2017, he added, the United States is going to need to see some technological breakthroughs.

> And that's why the President is setting this goal so that investors, venture capitalists, researchers, scientists are all focused on that goal and can expedite and accelerate that technology. And we're optimistic that it can happen. And when it does, we'll be able to meet that goal. And the President will continue and will mention in his speech his support of safe, clean nuclear power, which if you're serious about climate change, you have to be—you have to support clean, safe nuclear power, because that's the only source we've got today in ready supply that provides power with net zero emissions. So the President will continue to support those initiatives that have actually had a tremendous amount of success so far. It's also important to note that under this President's climate change policy, we're making significantly more progress than any of our friends and allies.

The press secretary stepped in again to put a positive spin on the President's accomplishments in energy: Between 2000 and 2004, while our economy was growing 10 percent, our carbon emissions grew by 1.7 percent, as compared to the European Union, which had economic growth of 7 percent and carbon emissions growth of 5 percent.

"So we've been making good progress under this President, and we'll continue to make progress with the types of energy policies the President is talking about tonight. Look, this is a bold, new proposal. I think ultimately we will see the wisdom of it and understand why it's a proposal that is in the best interests of all Americans," added Snow.

---

### Action on Global Warming: 2007
#### George W. Bush
#### Tony Snow

---

President George W. Bush gave lip service to the environment for five years, but in his first term—even after he appointed Christine Todd Whitman, the former governor of New Jersey and an environmentalist, to be head of the Department of Environmental Protection (EPA)—his administration tied her hands and little was accomplished. In fact, the president expressed serious doubts about the veracity of "global warming" and tossed it aside as nothing but a lot of hot air.

Bush finally acted in May 2007 after the U.S. Supreme Court on April 2, 2007 announced a five-to-four decision that the Clean Air Act provides the Environmental Protection Agency with the authority to regulate global warming pollution. This was the first global warming case to reach the Court. Greenpeace was one of the original petitioners in *Massachusetts v. the Environmental Protection Agency*. It called on the EPA to regulate carbon dioxide as a pollutant and sought to reduce emissions from new vehicles. Some Democratic observers said former vice president Al Gore's enlightened crusade helped to ignite the Bush administration's newfound interest in the environment, as well.

Prior to the Court's decision, environmentalists claimed there had been a pattern of the Bush administration paying lip service to the issue, but not taking action until, finally, it was legally compelled to. Even then, critics still maintained, nothing would actually be done by the time the executive order he issued took effect.

A reading of some of the White House press office's comments offer plentiful evidence of the effective spin that the White House delivered on the topic of environment. After coming under heavy fire from the environmental movement as well as a number of politicians from states whose environment is being threatened, Bush finally made a commitment in his State of the Union speech on January 23, 2007, in which he stated:

> Extending hope and opportunity depends on a stable supply of energy that keeps America's economy running and America's environment clean. For too long our nation has been dependent on foreign oil. . . . so as we continue to diversify our fuel supply, we must step up domestic oil production in environmentally sensitive ways. (Applause.) America is on the verge of technological breakthroughs that will enable us to live our lives less dependent on oil. And these technologies will help *us be better stewards of the environment, and they will help us to confront the serious challenge of global climate change* [italics added]

Following are comments from White House Press Secretary Tony Snow in response to reporters' questions making the case that the issue is not a new one for this administration—in fact, Bush had it on his list of issues when he took office in 2001. Snow's spin on this issue can best be illustrated in his press briefings in 2007, as follows:

- February 1, 2007:

> You have an administration where not only on regulation but also environmental issues, we've spent more money on environmental research than all the other governments of the world. It is an administration where the President in the summer of 2001 was talking about man-made global warming and the need to address it through innovation, and created a panel that involves key Cabinet members in going after the sources of pollution and emissions. So the fact is, we do have an aggressive set of regulations in place. The largest source of scientific data on climate change comes from the United States. I understand that there will be people who say their voices are not heard, but we will be happy to provide you in great detail because I now have a stack that is about this thick that goes through the processes and the data that have been gathered. *No administration in American history, and none on the face of the Earth, has been more aggressive in trying to do sound science on this than this administration* [italics added].

- February 7, 2007:

> What has this administration done? Well, we have spent more money on technology and research than anybody else—$9 billion on basic scientific research strictly into global warming, which very likely is more than the rest of the world combined. In addition, $29 billion total on technology. What happened, for instance, in the previous administration is that there was talk of Kyoto, which would have been economically ruinous and would have

thrown a lot of people out of work. The President, instead, has aggressively pursued ways of trying to clean the environment that don't have to make people lose their jobs, and in effect—and, at the same time, proceed on all the major areas where pollution is concerned. I have talked before about industrial pollution. We've got clean coal technology programs.

We have alternative fuel programs for auto emissions. We're talking about nuclear development, which is now championed by, among others, Greenpeace. *The fact is no administration has been more aggressive, no administration has put more money into research, and none has been more committed to basic peer review research on climate change than this one* [italics added]. And furthermore, on the negotiation side, not only are we talking about follow-on negotiations when it comes to climate change with our allies, we've also been dealing with the developing world, which was not at all included within Kyoto, offering them technology, and really taking the kinds of steps that demonstrate real seriousness, not simply giving the speeches, but walking the walk. The President really does believe that it is important to address climate change, and, incidentally, to address issues of pollution, as well, on the industrial side, on the transportation side. And that is why he laid out a whole series of initiatives in the State of the Union address.

• March 2, 2007:

*The President has made it clear that he believes in cleaning the environment. He thinks that global warming exists. He thinks that we need to mitigate it* [italics added]. He has put together a proposal that will lead to very significant reductions in vehicular $CO_2$ emissions. He also believes that you can have your clean air without having to put a crimp on the economy. And, as a matter of fact, a cleaner environment can be and should be consistent with robust economic growth. And that's the way we've been approaching it. If people think that they have innovative new ways to do it, it's going to create some opportunities out there for folks to perform services that a lot of people want to see. We're at a point in our economy and we've been here for quite a while, where cleaner water and cleaner air are, in fact, things that people desire. And there are any number of industries right now that are profiting handsomely from that desire. And what you want to do to the best extent possible is to unleash people's creative abilities, so that they can train their energies on a problem like that, and try to deal with it.

• March 20, 2007:

*This administration has pursued sound science and pumped more money into environmental research than any administration in American history* [italics added], and taken more aggressive action not only in acknowledging the reality of climate change, but also trying to deal with it in a constructive way.

• March 22, 2007:

The President has put a lot of money into clean coal technology. We think that it is absolutely important because, you're right, coal-fired plants right now are polluters. China is building one a week. *We think it's important, for the sake of the United States and the rest of the world, to help clean up the environment by having a clean-coal technology that has the capability, effectively, of reducing greenhouse emissions to zero* [italics added]. And take a look—it's been a priority item for the President for a long time. The President has also talked about nuclear power as also a non-polluting form of energy that we think holds a great deal of promise for allowing people to keep their jobs and have their clean air, too. We think that you can keep the economy going at full-speed and, at the same time, continue to clean the air—which is why, incidentally, *the United States has a better record in cleaning the air than any other major industrialized country* [italics added]. It's something that everybody wants. And there are profits aplenty to be made by folks who figure out how to generate energy and do important economic activity without pollution.

These are but a few examples of how the White House press secretary, realizing that the news is moving faster than the president on a key issue, saw questions from the press as an opportunity to gear up the administration's posture on the environment and global warming. Some cynics believe that the White House's campaign on the environment is a case of "too little, too late." Yet, Tony Snow's repeated efforts to persuade the press corps represent, at the very least, a full-blown public relations campaign to regain much of the ground that the Bush administration had ceded prior to the Court's decision. Only the passage of time will tell.

In May 2007, Bush issued an executive order, which appeared to indicate that he was finally recognizing the dangers of global warming. This turnaround was due to two major outside developments: First, on February 2, 2007, the United Nations scientific panel studying climate change declared that the evidence of a warming trend is "unequivocal," and that human activity has "very likely" been the driving force in that change over the last fifty years. (The last report by the group, the Intergovernmental Panel on Climate Change, in 2001, had found that humanity had "likely" played a role.) Second, the U.S. Supreme

Court's April 2, 2007 decision, in which it ruled five to four that the EPA had the power to set auto emissions standards if it concludes that those emissions contribute to global warming and thus harm human health. Experts have testified that roughly 70 percent of greenhouse gas emissions in the United States are from vehicles and industrial sources, and called for alternative fuels and more fuel-efficient cars—an echo that has been heard since the days of Jimmy Carter in the 1970s when there was a severe gasoline shortage.

Tony Snow hailed this executive order as major progress against climate change, but some environmentalists criticized the president for failing to set a specific goal and timely deadline for reducing carbon dioxide emissions and for failing to ask the federal departments of energy, transportation, and agriculture to help write the EPA's new rules. Skeptics said the energy and transportation departments have become too close to the energy industry and U.S. automakers and may try to water down the proposed regulations.

What those regulations would look like was anything but clear. Press Secretary Tony Snow said the president's position opposing mandatory emissions caps had not changed and that the president wanted to implement new regulations "on a voluntary, an innovation-based basis."

At a press briefing on May 14, 2007, Snow said:

> The President's position has been pretty clear on this, and what he's really looking at is effective ways of trying to cut emissions. The market-based approach seems to work. Again, if you take a look at what the United States has done in terms of reducing carbon intensity, we've done a better job than anybody else in the world. What the President has said all along is, let's figure out ways to engage and invest in technology, because ultimately what you're really talking about is a change in technology not only in terms of what is effective as an energy source, but also how you utilize it. And that goes everywhere from clean coal to nuclear power to biofuels to hydrogen cells, the whole bit. So I think rather than trying again to jump into what is an ongoing set of conversations, I'm not going to advance the ball other than to remind you of the aggressive stance the President has taken, and doing it in terms of outreach. He has discussed it with each of our key allies. And really the question is, do you try to set up a mandatory system, or do you try to set up an innovation-based system? The President prefers innovation.

Environmentalists said Bush's directive was tantamount to taking a used car and fixing it up to be a shiny new "pre-owned" car. *The New York Times* was quick to take the president to task with a sharply critical editorial on May 18, 2007, in which it stated, in part:

> Confronted with soaring gasoline prices, a Congress growing more restless by the day about oil dependency and a Supreme Court demanding executive action on global warming emissions, President Bush stepped before the cameras in the Rose Garden the other day and said, essentially, nothing. He announced that he had ordered four federal agencies to "work together" to devise regulations reducing greenhouse gases." He also renewed his call for greater investments in alternative fuels. But neither he nor the cadre of designated briefers who followed him provided any detail, so nobody knows whether he will in fact end up asking for more efficient cars or what sort of alternative fuels he has in mind or, more broadly, what sort of reduction in greenhouse gas emissions he hopes to achieve.

At this point, Bush's spin machine went to work. On May 18, 2007, Snow was asked about global warming at his briefing. Snow—much to his credit as a spokesman who tried his best to give factual rather than contrived answers—candidly told reporters why Bush had acted on the environment. Said Snow:

> A couple of things on global warming. Number one, let's make it clear about the U.S. commitment to climate change, which is unparalleled in the world in terms of financial resources, in terms of support for science, in terms of advocacy, in support for new technologies. And the President has made it clear that his view on this is, global warming exists; it has human contributions. And what we need to do is to figure a way forward that is going to enable economies around the world to grow, and at the same time, to pursue the laudable and necessary goals of cleaner air and a cleaner environment. . . The President is going to ask people to look for ways on a regulatory basis to move forward with the goals of both programs, and at the same time continue to encourage Congress to go ahead and act. After all, this is a proposal that seems to give both parties what they say they want in terms of pursuing energy independence and at the same time pursuing a cleaner environment. So there ought to be a pretty good bipartisan basis for passing such legislation. We'll continue to work it.

On October 24, 2007, Press Secretary Dana Perino continued to spin the administration's forward-looking views on climate change. In a press briefing, she stated:

> This administration's policy on climate change is an open book. There is robust information about where we stand on policy, on the science, on the initiatives, and on the international cooperation that we have initiated under this president. Anybody who wants to look at what the president thinks about climate change needs only to look back three weeks ago to when he gave a major address on climate change when he invited all 15 of the major economies of this world to come together to work on a solution—work on a path to get to a solution to help the growth of greenhouse gas emissions. And we have an open book on the subject.

And Perino continued in a briefing on November 20, 2007: "We recognize the dangers of climate change; we recognize that we need to reduce greenhouse emissions; we recognize we have a role in that. And that's what we're working on."

Nonetheless, in November 2007 a federal appeals court in California invalidated the Bush administration's year-old fuel economy standards for light trucks and sports utility vehicles because they failed to take into account the economic risks of climate change—just as Congress was preparing legislation on global warming and the EPA was weighing its response to the high court decisions. Despite the administration's reassurances, it is doubtful at this writing, say the experts, that anything will change in the near future. Some environmentalists, nonetheless, took some solace in Bush's eleventh hour recognition of the issue.

# Selected Bibliography

Aikman, David. *The Spiritual Journey of George W. Bush: An Inside Look at the Faith of the President and Its Impact on the World* (Nashville, TN: W Publishing Group, 2004).

Allen, Charles F., and Jonathan Portis. *The Life and Career of Bill Clinton, The Comeback Kid*, A Birch Lane Press Book (New York: Carol Publishing Group, 1992).

Ambrose, Stephen E. *Nixon, The Education of a Politician, 1913–1962* (New York: Simon and Schuster, 1987).

Ambrose, Stephen. *Eisenhower, The President* (New York: Simon & Schuster, 1984).

Bernays, Edward. *Propaganda* (New York: Ig Publishing, 1928).

Bernstein, Carl, and Bob Woodward. *All The President's Men* (New York: Simon & Schuster, 1974).

Bimber, Bruce, and Richard Davis. *Campaigning Online: The Internet in U.S. Elections* (New York: Oxford University Press, 2003).

Blumenthal, Sidney. *The Clinton Wars* (New York: Farar, Strauss and Giroux, 2003).

Bourne, Peter G. *Jimmy Carter, A Comprehensive Biography From Plains to Postpresidency* (New York: Scribner, 1997).

Bruni, Frank. *Ambling into History: The Unlikely Odyssey of George W. Bush* (New York: HarperCollins Publishers, 2002).

Burkholder, Donald. *The Caretakers of the Presidential Image, 1973* (Detroit, MI: Wayne State University, 1973).

Campbell, Colin, and Bert A. Rockman (eds). *The Clinton Presidency* (Chatham, NJ: Chatham House Publishers, 1996).

Cannon, James. *Time and Chance: Gerald Ford's Appointment With History* (New York: HarperCollins Publishers, 1994).

Clinton, Bill. *My Life* (New York: Alfred A. Knopf, 2004).

Dallek, Robert. *An Unfinished Life: John F. Kennedy, 1917–1963* (Boston, MA: Little, Brown and Company, 2003).

Dallek, Robert. *Flawed Giant: Lyndon Johnson and His Times, 1961–1973* (New York: Oxford University Press, 1998).

Dallek, Robert. *Lone Star Rising: Lyndon Johnson and His Times, 1908–1960* (New York: Oxford University Press, 1991).

Daniels, Jonathan. *White House Witness, 1942–1945: An Intimate Diary of the Years with F.D.R.* (Garden City, New York: Doubleday & Company, 1975).

Dawley, Alan. *Changing the World* (Princeton, NJ: Princeton University Press, 2003).

Derschowitz, Alan M. *Taking Liberties* (Chicago: Contemporary Books, 1988).

Derschowitz, Alan M. *Liberalism* (Tuscaloosa, AL: University of Alabama Press, 1994).

Dickenson, Mollie. *Thumbs Up: The Life and Courageous Comeback of White House Press Secretary Jim Brady* (New York: William Morrow and Company, 1987).

Donaldson, Sam. *Hold On, Mr. President!* (New York: Random House, 1987).

Donkin, Richard. *Blood, Sweat and Tears* (New York: Texere, 2001).

Downie Jr., Leonard. *The New Muckrakers* (Washington, D.C.: New Republic Book Co. , 1976).

Fitzwater, Marlin. *Call the Briefing! Reagan and Bush, Sam and Helen: A Decade with Presidents and the Press* (New York: Time Books, 1995).

Fleischer, Ari. *Taking Heat: The President, the Press, and My Years in the White House* (New York: HarperCollins, 2005).

Fritz, Ben, and Brendan Nyhan. *All the President's Spin, George W. Bush, The Media and The Truth* (New York: Simon and Schuster, 2004).

Gallagher, Hugh Gregory. *FDR's Splendid Deception: The Moving Story of Roosevelt's Massive Disability—and the Intense Efforts To Conceal It From the Public* (New York: Dodd, Mead & Company, 1985).

Genovese, Michael A. *The Watergate Crisis* (Westport, CT: Greenwood Press, 1999).

Gergen, David. *Eyewitness to Power: The Essence of Leadership, Nixon to Clinton* (New York: Simon & Schuster, 2000).

Goodwin, Doris Kearns. *Lyndon Johnson and the American Dream* (New York: Harper & Row, 1976).

Goodwin, Doris Kearns. *No Ordinary Time: Franklin and Eleanor Roosevelt: The Home Front in World War II* (New York: Simon & Schuster, 1994).

Grossman, Michael Baruch, and Martha Joynt Kumar. *Portraying the President: The White House and the News Media* (Baltimore, MD: Johns Hopkins University Press, 1981).

Hagerty, James C. *The Diary of James C. Hagerty* (Bloomington: Indiana University Press, 1983).

Halberstam, David. *War In A Time of Peace: Bush, Clinton, and the Generals* (New York: Scribner, 2001).

Hamilton, Nigel. *Bill Clinton: An American Journey, Great Expectations* (New York: Random House, 2003).

Harris, John F. *The Survivor: Bill Clinton in The White House* (New York: Random House, 2005).

Hayden, Joseph. *Covering Clinton: The President and the Press*, Praeger Series in Presidential Studies (Westport, CT: Praeger, 2002).

Hillsman, Roger. *The Cuban Missile Crisis: The Struggle Over Policy* (Westport, CT: Praeger, 1996).

Hyland, William G. *Clinton's World. Remaking American Foreign Policy* (Westport, CT: Praeger, 1999).

Isikoff, Michael. Uncovering *Clinton: A Reporter's Story* (New York: Three Rivers Press, 1999).

Jackson, Brooks, and Kathleen Hall Jamieson. *Un-Spun, Finding Facts in a World of [Disinformation]* (New York: Random House 2007).

Jamieson, Kathleen Hall. *Dirty Politics: Deception, Distraction, and Democracy* (New York: Oxford University Press, 1992).

Jamieson, Kathleen Hall, and Paul Waldman. *The Press Effect* (New York: Oxford University Press, 2003).

Kern, Montague, Patricia W. Levering, and Ralph B. Levering. *The Kennedy Crises: The Press, the Presidency, and Foreign Policy* (Chapel Hill: University of North Carolina Press, 1983).

Klein, Joe. *The Natural: The Misunderstood Presidency of Bill Clinton* (New York: Doubleday, 2002).

Klein, Woody. *Lindsay's Promise: The Dream That Failed* (New York: MacMillan, 1970).

Kurtz, Howard. *Spin Cycle: Inside the Clinton Propaganda Machine* (New York: Free Press, 1998).

Kuypers, Jim A. *Press Bias and Politics: How the Media Frame Controversial Issues*, Westport, CT: Praeger, 2002).

Lakkoff, George. *Don't Think of An Elephant: Know Your Values and Frame the Debate*, The Essential Guide for Progressives (White River Junction, VT: Chelsea Green Publishing, 2004).

Lawson, Don. *Presidential Scandals* (Washington, D.C.: CQ Press, 1990).

Leacacos, John P. *Fires in the In-Basket: The ABC's of the State Department* (New York: World Publishing Company, 1968).

Liebovich, Louis V. *The Press and the Modern Presidency: Myths and Mindsets From Kennedy to Clinton* (Westport, CT: Praeger, 1998)

Liebovich, Louis V. *Richard Nixon, Watergate, and the Press: A Historical Perspective* (Westport, CT: Praeger, 2003).

Maltese, John Anthony. *Spin Control: The White House Office of Communications and The Management of Presidential News* (Chapel Hill: University of North Carolina Press, 1992).

Manchester, William. *The Death of a President, November 1963* (New York: Harper & Row, 1967).

McCullough, David. *Truman* (New York: Simon and Schuster, 1992).

McFarland, Gerald W. *Mugwumps, Morals, and Politics, 1884–1920* (Amherst, MA: University of Massachusetts Press, 1975).

Miller, Nathan. *F.D.R., An Intimate History* (New York: Doubleday & Company, 1983).

Morgan, Ted. *FDR, A Biography* (New York: Simon and Schuster, 1985).

Moyers, Bill. *Moyers on America: A Journalist And His Times* (New York: New Press, 2004).

Nelson, W. Dale. *Who Speaks for the President? The White House Press Secretary from Cleveland to Clinton* (New York: Syracuse University Press, 1998).

Nimmo, Dan D. *Newsgathering in Washington* (New York: Atherton Press, 1964).

Parmet, Herbert S. *George Bush, The Life of a Lone Star Yankee* (New York: Scribner, 1997).

Patterson Jr., Bradley H. *The White House Staff, Inside the White House and Beyond* (Washington, D.C.: Brookings Institution Press, 2000).

Patterson, Thomas E. *Out of Order* (New York: Random House, 1994).

Pease, Otis. *The Progressive Years* (New York: George Braziller, 1962).

Pemberton, William E. *Exit with Honor: The Life and Presidency of Ronald Reagan* Armonk, NY: M.E. Sharpe, 1997).

Pollard, James E. *The Presidents and The Press* (New York: MacMillan, 1947).

Powell, Jody. *The Other Side of the Story* (New York: William Morrow & Company, 1984).

Reinsch, J. Leonard. *Getting Elected: From Radio and Roosevelt to Television and Reagan* (New York: Hippocrene Books, 1988).

Rozell, Mark J. *The Press and the Ford Presidency* (Ann Arbor, MI: University of Michigan Press, 1992).

Salinger, Pierre. *P.S.: A Memoir* (New York: St. Martin's Griffin, 1995).

Salinger, Pierre. *With Kennedy* (Garden City, NY: Doubleday & Company, 1966).

Schlesinger Jr., Arthur M. *A Thousand Days* (Boston, MA: Houghton Mifflin, 2002).

Schlesinger Jr., Arthur M. (ed). *The Coming To Power: Critical Presidential Elections in American History* (New York: Chelsea House Publishers, 1971).

Sorenson, Theodore C. *Kennedy* (New York: Harper & Row, 1965).

Speakes, Larry, with Robert Pack. *Speaking Out: The Presidency From Inside the White House* (New York: Charles Scribner's Sons, 1988).

Spragens, William C. *The Presidency and The Mass Media* (Washington, D.C.: University Press of America, 1979).

Spragens, William C., with Carole Ann Terwood. *From Spokesman to Press Secretary: White House Media Operations* (Washington, D.C.: University Press of America, 1980).

Stephanopoulos, George. *All Too Human: A Political Education* (Boston, MA: Little, Brown and Company, 1999).

Strober, Deborah Hart, and Gerald S. Scrober. *Reagan, The Man and His Presidency: The Oral History of An Era* (New York: Houghton Mifflin, 1998).

Thomas, Helen. *Front Row at The White House: My Life and Times* (New York: Simon & Schuster, 1999).

Thomas, Helen. *Thanks For The Memories, Mr. President* (New York: Scribner, 2002).

Thomas, Helen. *Watchdogs of Democracy? The Waning Washington Press Corps and How It Has Failed the Public* (New York: Scribner, 2006).

Thompson, Kenneth W. *Three Press Secretaries on the Presidency and The Press: Jody Powell, George Reedy, and Jerry terHorst* (Lanham, NY: University Press of America, 1983).

Thompson, Kenneth W. *Ten Presidents and The Press* (New York: University Press of America, 1983).

Turell, David J., M.D. *Government by Political Spin* (Lafayette, LA: Huntington House Publishers, 2000).

Tye, Larry. *The Father of Spin: Edward L. Bernays and The Birth of Public Relations* (New York: Henry Holt and Company, 1998).

Vestal, Bud. *Jerry Ford Up Close: An Investigative Biography* (New York: Coward, McCann & Goghegan, 1974).

Walker, Martin. *The President We Deserve, Bill Clinton: His Rise, Falls, and Comebacks* (New York: Crown Publishers, 1996).

Weinberg, Arthur and Lila. *The Muckrakers* (New York: Simon & Schuster, 1961).

White, Theodore. *The Making of the President, 1972* (Atheneum, NY: Atheneum Publishers, 1973).

Woodward, Bob. *The Agenda: Inside the Clinton White House* (New York: Simon & Schuster, 1994).

# Index

# ABOUT THE AUTHOR

Woody Klein is a former press secretary to New York Mayor John V. Lindsay. He is an award-winning political and investigative reporter for *The Washington Post* and *The New York World-Telegram & Sun*; an adjunct professor of journalism; and an award-winning historian. He is the author of *Westport, Connecticut: The Story of a New England Town's Rise to Prominence* (2000), winner of the Connecticut League of History Organizations' Book Award; *Toward Humanity and Justice: The Writings of Dr. Kenneth B. Clark, Scholar of the* Brown v. Board of Education *Decision in 1954* (2004), winner of "Best Book of the Year" award from the Connecticut Press Club in 2006; *Liberties Lost: The Endangered Legacy of the ACLU* (2006); *Lindsay's Promise* (1970); and *Let in the Sun* (1962). He has taught at New York University, The New School, the University of Bridgeport, Fairfield University, and Iona College. Klein is a graduate of Dartmouth College and the Graduate School of Journalism, Columbia University. He lives with his wife, Audrey, in Westport, Connecticut.